The Most Important Book Ever Written

Uncovering mankind's hidden twin path future – will we accept the great future on offer?

Richard C. Pearson

ISBN-13: 9781492951377
ISBN-10: 1492951374

Read this important personal message from the author to the reader before entering the book

You have to be asking yourself why is this the most important book ever written, or thinking to yourself this is a grossly over-inflated claim or a sales pitch. Well, as you are about to find out, mankind is on the brink of potentially the greatest positive shift in life in our long history and this book is the "ticket to ride" to make that happen. So, now you are faced with two enormous claims for one book, aren't you just a little curious to know more? Turn off your phone and your PC, raise the "do not disturb sign", you are in for some shocks and a journey with no holds barred (and potentially a great future at the end of it).

First and very important! – and please be truthful with both me and yourself, do you REALLY want a better life and will you do whatever it takes to achieve this? Are you prepared to dis-engage from all the life-time programming that has stolen your true life away so that you can see through all the deceit, fraud and cheating you have suffered (which at this moment you do not know about)? Are you willing to at least try and believe that which you at first will probably disbelieve? Are you willing to accept that our lives have been hijacked and replaced with a second rate substitute? AND! are you open to discover the five star much improved life that is on offer to you IF you can do the above? If not, return this book to wherever you bought or borrowed it and ask for a refund as this book will only work if you are open to change, open to accepting a great new life, open to the absolute truth that we have been robbed of the great life we should be living right now. It is your choice.

Question: what stands in the way of you and a great new life?

Answer: **YOU** and that is all.

This is the plain and simple truth, a great new future awaits you, it awaits us all and the only thing standing in the way of all of us and a greatly improved life is that we just won't believe it. In fact we are more likely to fight against the idea of the possibility of a better life as we have all become so lost in the many problems of daily life and we find it impossible to accept good news. We are more inclined to laugh at the potential of a greatly improved life than accept it. Good news in this day and age is rejected as we have lost so much hope, belief and faith in life.

Here then is not just good news, it's great news: your astounding new life is real, your greatly improved future is yours to have and it's not a fairy tale, so get ready to kiss goodbye to austerity – debt – social unrest – war & fighting – miserable news stories and welcome true abundance into your life. **Do NOT doubt any of this**.

Little by little, piece by piece I am going to chip away at you to try and break down your resistance to truth (which as yet you do not know you have). Frequent repetition of my messages, the open exposure of fraud that has robbed you of a great life, the reasons you have been defrauded of your true life will be revealed in plain simple language. We all have to stop fooling ourselves when we hide from the truth, yes truth can be painful if it goes against our personal beliefs, do we really want to accept deceit as a better alternative to truth when a great life is on offer? Life for most people at the moment can be described as feeling like being "up a creek without a paddle", worse still, our boat is full of holes and sinking. We just cannot carry on fooling ourselves any longer that there is no problem to sort out. It is only ourselves we are trying to fool, trying to make ourselves feel better when deep down we know we have been misled. **The positive way forward is to accept we have been fooled and do something about it.** Will you stay were you are stuck in a mundane life that hits problems and stumbling blocks often? Or will you accept change and truth and the chance to go forward to a vastly improved life?

When sitting down to prepare this book I was faced with an enormous dilemma, I know the only way to sort out the major failures of the world is to first clearly identify what the problems are, as only then can they be fully corrected. It is the uncovering of the full details of our problems that presents the dilemma mentioned above as I know one of the best ways to resolve problems is to do so with a positive approach, positivity is key to creating a great future. By digging up and exposing all the problems this can depress and frighten those who have the truth of our predicament finally laid bare, which goes against a positive approach. However, I also know that we just cannot proceed forward until we effectively deal with the full scale of our problems, leaving unfinished business behind is a drag on forward momentum. Knowing all this I felt that there is no other option other than to make it clear to people that we do have some very major problems and to uncover them, but! to make it very clear **a great future awaits once we have gone through the pain of accepting our problems and then sorting them out.** We have no other choice, we have to accept then deal with our problems and not ignore them or pretend they do not exist – then the doors of a magnificent future can begin to open. So please do not take fright or force the knowledge we have major problems to the back of your mind, know that by accepting our troubles we can sort them out once and for all. Be brave, be strong, be positive – you are on the brink of a new much improved future.

You do not know this! **Before us all is the greatest period of positive growth in human history**, a time that should witness what will seem like the rebirth of mankind into a future of unlimited potential and expansion. How hard is this for you to believe, that a great future awaits? How hard is your mind working to have you reject the statement? As unbelievable as it may seem, the future holds great advances in human life, a life you would choose for yourself. Before this can take place, we have no choice other than to make the most important decision in the whole history of mankind by choosing which life path we follow from a twin path option. At the same time we must discover many hidden truths that we must learn.

Today the futures of all human life on our planet rests firmly within the hands of the ordinary people of the planet who must take it upon themselves to grab back control of their lives from those who have subtly stolen our present and futures from us (to be explained later). Never in world history have we faced such a momentous moment where our whole future and that of the world depends so much on the decisions and actions we all take next. Naturally this you can only do once you learn the full details of the vital decision needed to be made, which is one of the goals of this book. Are you confused and asking why you do not know that this massive life changing decision has to be made and what it is? You will soon find this out as you read on, let me forewarn you that it will be something of a shock to your reality and understanding of life when you discover that this required life changing decision is being hidden from you.

Please understand that I have "watered down" some of the information that the book contains as it is very provocative and I have also chosen to leave out completely a number of extremely controversial items for the same reason. Can you believe all of this? Or will you bury your head in the sand by dismissing it as nonsense? Disbelieve all of this and you could lose out like you have never lost out before. Today we can choose to change all present and future life patterns for the people of the Earth by deciding which direction we take from two distinct pathways before us, *two very different futures*:

1. **Pathway One** is the pathway I am sure you would choose as it leads to a life we would normally only dream of, a pathway that few believe is possible and one that nobody would expect to be achievable. Pathway one is the life we would choose for ourselves as it delivers freedom, joy, abundance in many areas of life such as health – wealth – happiness. Pathway one will remove the shackles of a miserable life so many are experiencing across our world and deliver huge potential for a life of unlimited positive expansion. This future is being purposely hidden from us by people we wrongly trust.

2. **Pathway Two** is the path we are already travelling, the life we are experiencing now and as most people would agree it's not a pathway we would willingly choose to travel for ourselves. There is so much that is wrong and not working on this pathway, the people of the world tread this painful journey with many heavy burdens to carry. It is this pathway we can choose to leave and switch to the path we would want and it will not be as difficult to do as you may think. This is the pathway that we have been forced to take by people we wrongly trust.

The way to reject the failing and negative pathway two is to replace it with the positive freedom of pathway one. This can happen when first, you are fully aware that there exists an alternative pathway to our present route and second, to take action to switch to this much more fulfilling pathway. While you are unaware of an alternative improved life pathway you are prevented from attempting to switch to it, which is exactly why it is hidden from us all. We all have a part to play to make the changes we need to switch pathways, it is a relatively minor part but it carries with it major positive change to greatly benefit everyone. We all must make a contribution to create the momentum that carries us forward to a great new future and not leave it to a small band of willing workers to do all the grafting. One reason our world finds itself in such a mess today is that too many people sit back and let others take the lead and do all the work. Remember, anything worth having needs effort to achieve it. This next comment is one of the many vital comments contained in this book and it would be a good idea to note it down or mark this page, **"there is only one way to change the world and our lives for the better and that is to do it ourselves"**. Nobody else is going to do this for us, certainly not our leaders, we have to take the responsibility to act to make the changes we all wish for.

This book will uncover all you need to know to decide to switch pathways from the grossly under achieving pathway two to the life we rightly deserve on pathway one. This is not fantasy or the flimsy thoughts of an "airhead daydreamer", it's all based solidly on facts. Your important part in all this is to disengage the lifelong programming you have received, which you have yet to learn about and to see things for what they can be should you choose to grab the life you richly deserve. The only thing that stands between you and pathway one are your own doubts and disbelief that have been programmed into you from too many years of travelling along pathway two.

"people cannot face truth as truth is reality and reality may be too hard to handle when we learn that our beliefs are wrong and always have been".

If I could have the message above flashing in bright neon lights across the page, I would as it is so true – we cannot handle our deep held beliefs being exposed as incorrect. We feel foolish when faced with the reality that we have been led astray by people we placed trust in, people we believe in and we cover up our embarrassment of being fooled so badly by rejecting truth and accepting deceit as this does not hurt our pride as much. No matter how hard you fight against this principle, when it comes down to the truth you will find it is 100% accurate. A red mist of rage will come across people when confronted with truth that goes against their own personal beliefs. This is another reason our world is going so badly wrong, we accept deceit to save ourselves from looking and feeling foolish.

This book could be the biggest challenge of your life as it openly challenges your life as you believe it, will you run and hide from the challenge or rise to the challenge and accept the great alternative life being offered?

* * *

You could be asking yourself how can we choose to forge a new life of freedom and escape the present failing life, the answer is very simple as by the act of deciding to control our own futures, we set the process rolling into action. It is a proven fact that we anticipate our futures based on our past experiences, therefore we expect more of the same and do not believe the future can hold a better life. Predicting our future based on the past is a recipe for disaster as **the past does not represent the future** and we have to realise this. The only way the past can partly represent the future is if we fail to change from failing actions learned in the past, which does allow the past to affect our future as we stay stuck in the rut grooved in the past, this is why change is so vital.

If you do not change, neither will your future

With our past life having been taken over and controlled by outside interests and we have been thoroughly brainwashed and act out our lives based on the brainwashing – we cannot foresee a better future, which is why we must act to change our impression of life. If you do nothing to change your life and how you visualise it, then your life will not change and you will receive more of the same failures and stumbling blocks. In truth we are far more powerful than we understand, our thoughts and intentions are the building blocks to a new improved future as thoughts and intentions show us the actions and route we need to take. We have sat back and let our lives unroll without taking a "hands on" approach to life and this is how our lives and futures were so easily removed from us, we allowed our lives to be shaped for us (mis-shaped is a better description). It is not knowing that we are capable of taking charge of our futures that holds us back, therefore the discovery that we are more than capable of taking charge of our own destinies will begin the process of positive change. Now is the time to move forward and the way to do this is to decide we will go forward and then to take action to physically proceed forward.

There is great wisdom in the saying "follow your dreams", we have to act to make our dreams come true and move towards our dreams or our dreams remain unfulfilled within our heads and nowhere else. Our abilities to control our own futures have been taken from us by our lack of interest in ruling our own lives and from careful outside programming throughout our lives, this programming initiated by the very people we trust – our leaders. They knew exactly what they were doing and how to achieve their plans by gradually taking more and more control of all aspects of our lives, fully knowing we would not suspect what was happening as we were too lazy, too disinterested and too comfortable "sitting back" and inactive. This malicious planning IS pathway two as described earlier and I will set out to prove this to you. At this moment we would find it hard to run our own lives as for such a long time we have been made to respond to the orders, rules and regulations of our leaders, we find it difficult to think outside of our enforced comfort zones. That is all about to change as by accepting to switch to path one, this will deliver back our lives to ourselves and the abilities to choose our own futures. What have we got to lose by changing?

Without any doubt whatsoever, we have before us the greatest time of human expansion in history, our potential future is truly awesome and our lives can climb to new highs we never would believe possible at this moment. Be sure, very sure, this is not a dream, not a half-baked theory, it is based on established facts and completely cemented in reality. To experience this time of unending potential we have to accept and see that the potential is real by raising our heads up and above the mediocre life we are presently suffering. Suffering is the appropriate word to use as life for the majority is a long way off of the life we would choose for ourselves, somewhere along the way our lives have become seriously lost in direction, purpose and joy. Most of us are treading water and standing still or going backwards as our lives hit one stumbling block after another which drags down our spirits and we feel very low in morale and have little or no belief or hope in the future. Our teenagers and young adults must be very dis-spirited when searching for decent employment as even a college degree does not guarantee a job higher than a checkout operator in a supermarket. At this moment in time we probably have the highest educated unemployed sector in history, this is such a terrible waste of these young futures. The prospects for jobless "over forties" is not much better, losing a career at this age can be a nightmare and means a complete change in career, living standards and lifestyle. At this moment in time the future only holds the reality of growing numbers of unemployed who cannot make a worthwhile contribution to their lives and society. This is not the way that life is meant to be and we know it. What is happening and why it's happening is mostly a mystery to us all and that is why this book has been written – to uncover and explain why we are at this depressing and stagnant stage in our history. You want answers and you are about to receive them, you want a better life and you are about to learn how to easily achieve this, it is time to learn "what the hell is going on with life". Be assured, life can change for the better, it will become great and it will live up to our expectations as we leave behind todays negative times when we stimulate life to present to us the true life we deserve.

At a time we should rightly be living the greatest most phenomenally successful period in human history we find ourselves being defrauded of an exceptional life by the very people we place our trust in. Our lives should have blossomed several years ago into times of total freedom, immense joy and contentment and not times of austerity, global unrest with no end in sight of the social misery hurting us all. Yet a great life does still await us should we choose to open our eyes to the truth of our present situation, by accepting the truth of our world we can throw open many doors leading to a vastly improved new way of life that we should already be living. To arrive at this new destination in life we must first understand what is happening in our world, why we have descended into such a dire mess and who is responsible. Do you seek a better life, a great future for yourself and your family, more joy and contentment? Then please read on with an open mind, that's all that is asked of you.

Free your mind to see the great future that is rightly yours

Its "crunch time", time to face up to what is really going on in our world and I guarantee that at first you will not be happy and will feel very let down when you discover the true world we live in. You are about to find out why our lives are back tracking with no forward motion, why we are sinking fast while a great life we should be enjoying is being lost to us. The life you believe in does not exist, it is all fraud, we the people of the world have been "sold down the river" and our lives we should be experiencing have been hijacked and replaced with a second rate fake. **A very large part of the massive fraud that has been imposed on us is designed specifically to make us totally unable to accept the truth of the above statement, daily brainwashing of us all is a major factor in the fraud.**

You may laugh in derision or reject completely the statements above without investigating the truth held within all of the words, to reject that we have all been seriously lead astray all our lives would be one of the biggest mistakes of your life, because as I will try to establish, it is all 100% true. Why should you learn and accept this now, today? Because we still have in front of us the greatest era in the history of mankind, a time that will fulfill our deepest dreams as the world changes up to new levels of what can only be described as magnificence. Is this a daydream of a New Age believer lost in his own mind talk? Absolutely not as you will find out inside the book that follows – I only work with hard facts and not dreams or conspiracies. Your task as you read through this book is to keep an open mind and do not prejudge anything until you have read everything contained in this book, then make up your own mind on what you want to believe and the actions you choose to take.

This will come as a surprise to you - **you are one among the most fortunate people in the long history of the world as you have the rare chance to choose your own future and reject the present negative times.** Waiting before you and the whole of humanity are two distinct pathways for all our immediate futures, one leads to an unparalleled dynamic and joyous future we would all choose to experience. The other path we would definitely reject as it is the one we are all following at the moment and leads on to what can only be described as hell, which naturally none of us would select. The people of the world would undoubtedly choose the pathway to what would be a passage leading us as near to paradise as we are ever likely to get and our leaders would definitely choose to stay on the nightmare path we find ourselves travelling at this moment. Shockingly, these two scenarios are based on fact and not my personal opinion, as this book will easily prove.

The only problem with this twin path theme is that the people of the world do not have a clue it exists as it is being concealed from them by our leaders who fear a loss of power and control over the people should the people choose to lead more of their own lives and make their own decisions. You could sit and read these words all day and still find them difficult to believe while they sink in, the saddest thing about this is that this idea is 100% reality and not hype, not a story line, not a conspiracy theory. In truth you will probably need to pinch yourself many times to see if your dreaming while reading this book as there are many similar big shocks waiting for you inside its pages. Never before in the whole of human history have we approached a more monumental moment in time with such life changing implications as we do now and unfortunately - we do so without knowing it, which means ultimately that the opportunity will be lost (unless of course we act to make it happen) We are on the verge of a spectacular new considerably improved way of life, which can only happen if we take action and will not happen while our leaders purposely hide the truth from us. It would be no stretch of the truth to say that we have before us the decision to experience heaven and avoid hell, which is why we *must* wake up to this crucial decision our leaders are hiding from us before it's too late.

Important although this book does give many opinions and details about the fraud and "mis" leadership that has stolen our rightful lives from us, the book is not written as an expose of the fraud etc. The fraud etc. is the proof of my subject and not the subject itself, the subject matter of this book is the explanation that **we do have a great future waiting on another pathway and that we need to realise this – before it's too late.** We do have to recognise the fraud first, as this will help us to move away from it, reject it and encourage us to change to the greatly improved pathway that awaits.

My sanity, my purpose and intent will be questioned by many for writing this very exciting life transforming book that reveals many deeply hidden secrets of the world. The subject matter of my book is both interestingly shocking and very absorbing, nobody could be blamed for being surprised and shaken by the text if they had no prior knowledge of the subject matter. To dismiss the text would be a huge mistake as the text of the book is all about our lives and the frightening reasons why they do not live up to our hopes - and more importantly, what to do about this. Some of my friends and family will reject the book contents just as many people will as their understanding of life is called into question. This I expect and could guess which of my family and friends will reject the suggestions. There is nothing wrong with that, I know many people will be unable to absorb what is written due to our lifetime of outside programming. There will be no "browbeating" from me on people to accept my message, we all have personal choice and this must be respected. For those who do accept the messages the potential rewards are never ending, their lives should flourish as their understanding of the world opens up. If I am philosophical about the book it would be that I expect rejection from many who I believe will remain stuck where they are now, but I hope they change their views in the future when they see the progress being achieved by those who do grasp the books message. Something else I fully expect is criticism and howls of protest and my reaction will be "so what!", freedom of choice is something I deeply respect and would never try to silence anyone for having personal opinions, just as I hope I am not condemned for having my own personal opinions.

- Some people will try to cover up the topics of my book from fear of exposure of their dark actions
- Others are so skeptical of new information they would find it hard to accept if it came from their own mother
- Many would find the information uncomfortable because they are not used to seeing the truth and find truth unrecognisable
- Sadly many will resist the truth because they have lost so much faith and belief in life they disbelieve that a better life is possible
- Finally some people will reject hearing truth as they are in fear of anything that challenges them and which does not fit into their confined comfort zone

The people of the world have to make sure that this time of transformation is firmly under their control and benefits them and not allow our leaders to take command to benefit themselves alone. Everyone has to prepare for the changes as to many people change is feared because it brings the unknown and uncertainty, which understandably can be frightening. What we should be doing is to look forward to the time of transformation as it will be a greatly improved era on the one that we are experiencing now and the one planned for us all. We must welcome change with open arms, not fear it.

We have passed through The Dark Ages, two World Wars, The Black Plague, The Cold War, The Gulf War, The Great Depression and so many other disastrous times, these were threats that people knew all about, our present worse case scenarios are hidden from us by the people we mistakenly trust. This next comment is another of the most important in the book and must not be underestimated, "there are few people in the world who are aware of the **true** depth of our problems that we need to escape from". We are on the edge, the very brink of two completely different scenarios for our future and this is being hidden from us – deliberately!

- Today we can achieve the greatest advancement in human life to a level far beyond our greatest hopes and dreams that is as close to paradise as we ever will achieve
- or we could see mankind snuffed out in a milli-second, this is the reality we all face.

Throughout my positive book, which is not an "end of the world", "doom and gloom" prediction, I aim to present a balanced argument for the subjects covered, my strong desire is for the reader to make up their own mind on the subject matter. The principle of delivering a balanced presentation does though run into a brick wall as on one side of my argument there is a mountain of detailed conclusive evidence who did what – when – who to – how much – where, and lists what the end result was/is. While on the other side of the argument is a painfully small (microscopic) ant hill in comparison of denial of the points offered (and from some of the people named as the perpetrators of the acts). It is so very frustrating for information and denials to be stifled as I always seek balance in any discussion, the book that follows will highlight why so much is hidden (hint – it is not for our benefit or our good).

We need those on the ant hill side, our politicians, economists, bankers, leaders to stand up and publicly state categorically that the worrying points raised in this book are groundless and that they support the principle of freedom of choice and true democracy. Until our leaders willingly do the above, there will remain a deep and growing distrust of them and the people will reach a point that they must surely rebel, that moment in time has got to be approaching rapidly as tempers become more frayed while the people suffer so often. The people of the world are getting more and more angry, their patience is wearing thin and it's all coming to the boil with protests, demonstrations and riots spreading around the globe. These demonstrations could be the catalyst that sparks the end of all the deceit in our world as for the first time the truth of why our world is suffering can surface for all to see.

As I will explain later in the book, following our politicians, bankers, economists is like Alice chasing the white rabbit down the rabbit hole into Wonderland, she found herself in an unreal world where nothing is as it at first seems. Our world is a mirror image of Alice's Wonderland, very little that we believe of life and how it operates is true. Our leaders have led us astray and created a very false world which they achieved by brainwashing us all each and every day. While that last statement may confuse you now, by the time you reach the end of the book you will understand it and know for yourself how true it is.

More and more "whistle blowers" are appearing and spreading the word on secretive government moves against the people, which make the whistle blowers unpopular with governments for exposing the truth, but heroes to the people. The whistle blowers are getting braver and more open with their exposes and it is an area I expect to grow as more "dirty" government secrets are aired in public. Some of these exposes are destined to really lift the lid off of so much "skullduggery" from our leaders and finally show them in their true light. Dark hidden secrets will bring down governments and leaders and the best advice for them would be to go now while they are ahead, this I am sure of. The people of the world are re-discovering their power, driven on by failing decisions and secretive actions of our leaders that hurts the people so much and it would be true to say that our leaders have seriously underestimated the people and what they can achieve. Politicians, leaders, bankers should beware and be afraid as their dark secrets are surely about to come back to haunt them. The growing protests around the world are being driven on by modern technology which propels the impact of the actions to greater levels, protests are being organised via the Internet, smart phones and social networks, "it's all very organised" and that is also why it will spread worldwide fast. The most likely outcome of this "organised" modern day peoples revolution is that we shall see linked worldwide protests and demonstrations closely planned to coincide with each other on chosen days. In my opinion, from looking at the escalation in public protests along with the use of modern day technology, we can expect to witness the largest organised demonstrations against politicians and leaders in world history. Our leaders talk of transparency, let them be the first to prove their own transparency by clearing up the considerable doubts and fears surrounding them. Our leaders must regain trust and show they do have our futures uppermost in their minds and not secret personal agendas. They have to re-balance the evidence which at the moment casts them as deceitfully rogue and power obsessed, they must do this or step down before mobs remove them forcefully.

If I am accused of being negative or pessimistic then I would argue that the accusers have not read the book properly. If anyone accuses me of verbally attacking The UK or The USA they are complete fools as these countries along with the country I live now are top of my list for the perfect places to live. It is only the wicked people who are endangering our world that I pour scorn on, nobody else and I do not believe that these people have a scrap of affinity or affection to any country, they only follow personal agendas. We all have a great future waiting for us, first we have to change the actions of our leaders.

**"today we have the real chance to peacefully
rescue our world from our mis – leaders"**

Whether you believe all, much or little of what the book that follows presents you, please keep in mind that the majority of the people of the world are clueless of the truth about their lives and are very much in the dark of most of the actions our leaders take. Bearing this in mind, why shouldn't the text that follows be true, absolutely "on the button" and as close to the truth as you will ever get? By believing that which follows, you can gain, by disbelieving that which follows - you have much to lose.

* * *

Throughout the book I will add a "what if" paragraph to try and prompt the reader to consider "what if" the text just read is true when the reader may me doubting its truth.

* * *

Please note that I have personally edited the book and I may not have found every misspelt word, every piece of bad grammar, please excuse me for that. Also I have not written the book to be a literary gem, my sole aim is to get the message out to as many people as possible, other people can pick up the literary prizes. You will be recommended to use Internet search engines to look up information often in the book, I personally never use Wikipedia as I feel they lean heavily in bias towards governments and the secret organisations you will learn about later (that should earn me a "cutting" review from them and will be interesting) and twist the readers thoughts away from what may be the truth. But do not let my personal thoughts stop you using Wikipedia.

Contents

Dedication

This book is dedicated to the people of the world, the incredible "long suffering" people who I call "everyday members of the population", factory workers – shop workers – office workers – farm workers – builders – public service workers – military – police - the housewives – the retired – the children – the unemployed and many more. These people are the backbone of any and every society, they should command far more respect than they are offered, which is why I dedicate my book to them and salute them. For too long "The People" have been overlooked, used and ignored, this book is for them to help them advance into a new age, a new way of life they richly deserve.

About the Author

Richard C. Pearson is a lifelong student of life, a pacifist who has dedicated much of his own life to helping others find and achieve an improved life for themselves through thousands of hours of voluntary work. An experienced and qualified Life Coach and runs his own coaching service, Magic Wand Life Coaching. He is also a qualified Spiritual Coach and Psychic Development Coach and a Law of Attraction Practitioner. He is an experienced psychic awareness and development coach, teacher of positive thinking and personal self-improvement and has coached thousands of people through regular lectures, group coaching evenings, one to one appointments and on-line working. Richard has made full use of the Internet to help thousands of people with frequent messages and blogging going out to a large audience. Working on a one to one basis with people who are suffering desperate situations in their lives has been a common practice in recent years. Peoples problems may be different, we all go through pain, grief and suffering, alleviating as much of the suffering as possible is Richards aim.

Richard discovered late in life that a "gift" he thought was a normal practice for everyone was in fact "special", when he discovered this gift to be that he is a natural clairvoyant. After discovering this detail he trained with some of the best tutors in The UK to enhance the use of this ability. This stood him in good stead when he himself hit a part of his life that he experienced severe change and trauma and his training allowed him to come out of this period undamaged and a much improved person. Clairvoyance is classified as "clear seeing", which does not necessarily and only mean seeing a vision of the future, sensing the future first and forming a picture in the mind after sensing is Richards way. Richard does have a very strong clairvoyant "sight" as well and is able to "see" and describe places he has never visited. This side of his clairvoyance, which is known as "remote viewing", has remained unused for a few years now as the other areas became used more widely.

When Richard lost most of his hearing in his right ear and this was replaced with loud tinnitus (noise in the ear), his ability to hold down a normal job diminished along with his hearing. He moved to The Netherlands with his Dutch wife Simone and young daughter so that Simone could be the family "bread winner". This gave Richard something few people have the chance of experiencing – time! This time was used to its fullest as Richard jumped at the opportunity to further his knowledge and study for up to twelve hours a day and seven days a week. This study was not to be a study of past discoveries, it was a study of all the many new ideas and data that is spewing out from fresh books, the Internet, lectures and something new – webinars. A webinar is an on-line event broadcast to all who sign up for the webinar, this is received via a PC and beamed to the PC's audio system. Wonderful new and innovative details flowed out through the webinar broadcast, much of which challenged established thinking, information that was readily passed on to Richards various groups of students and friends. The lifelong student was in his element with the fresh ideas opening his eyes to the real world that few others get to learn.

For over ten years Richard kept experiencing a strong message to write the book that follows, an urge he refused to acknowledge as in his words "who is he to write such a deep and important book about the deceit of life?". Wherever that strong message came from, it eventually won and the many years of learning from this "lifelong student" is what follows.

Today, even after completing the book, Richards obsession with learning about life and to pass on his learning continues unabated, though he readily accepts conspiracy theories have a truthful base, he much prefers factual hard evidence.

Richard is a seeker of truth and not a conspiracy theorist, revolutionary or a trouble maker, he believes solidly that "the truth will set us free" and that "only the truth will suffice". He does not consider himself to be an expert in the subject matter of this book, more someone with the knack of discovering the important information that matters the most to people and to relay this to people in such a way that they can fully understand the information easily. Much of the information in this book is still secretive to the masses, it is the aim of this book to remove that secrecy and ensure everyone learns of this highly important data. Please do question the information and do not accept anything without first checking back up information, this way you will find out for yourself the dark secrets our world conceals from us all AND the great future that awaits.

Acknowledgements

Without the many true experts who have taught me so much and in so many different ways, this book would not have been possible, they are the true pioneers of opening up the hidden facts of what is happening in our world. If we were to total up all the research that has gone into producing this book I am sure it would amount to thousands of years if you take into account the many researchers and their personal research work time.

The task I set myself was to bring together the learned works of these pioneering experts into one collection of shortened easy to follow script, I cannot take any credit for their tireless work and their dedication to show their findings. These researchers are brave souls who worked under threat of death in many cases as their work led them into dangerous waters while challenging the secret plotters working undercover and we must all salute them for this fact alone.

Within this book you will find links to millions of pages of data logged on the Internet, tens of thousands of book titles, millions of videos loaded for all to witness and we must all thank and acknowledge the researchers, authors and investigators who made that possible.

Can I personally thank the many people who sent me detailed information over the years, new fresh details that helped me form the changed impression of life I have now and to be able to pass on their news so that others may benefit. May I also thank the large number of people I have worked with in my group evenings and lectures for "opening up and sharing their pain, their experiences" you taught me so much. To my old groups in Cambridge and Worthing who displayed so much willingness to learn, I acknowledge your contributions to this book as you improved my experiences and knowledge, allowing me to experiment, learn and grow.

Without the great words and teachings from the many webinars I sat and listened to, I do not believe I would have expanded my knowledge so far, thank you, especially to Darius Barazandeh for his great series of webinars I would never want to miss. Lynne Klippels book publishing webinars inspired me so much, Jeffrey Howard for his wonderful webinars at the Visionary Business University. Great coaches all.

Last but not least I acknowledge some of the "Old Masters" who published classic magnificent books: Dale Carnegie – Napolean Hill – Wallace D Wattles. Onto the newer classic writers Tony Robbins – John Assaraf – Eckhart Tolle – Esther and Jerry Hicks – Lynne McTaggart – Gregg Braden – Dr. Wayne Dyer – Dr. Joe Dispenza – Deepak Chopra – Esther and Jerry Hicks and so many more. Special praise goes to Rhonda Byrne for producing The Secret which introduced so many new people to positive thinking. Extra special thanks to all at the Silva Method and to Jose Silva, you have led and others have followed, you changed the self-improvement movement and made it what it is today, true pioneers of change.

THE MOST IMPORTANT BOOK EVER WRITTEN

WRITTEN

Part One

You do not know the real world!

one

Could This Be The Turning Point In Life You Have Been Looking For?

* * *

If you have not read the opening pages of this book "an important personal message from the author to the reader" please go back and read it now as it sets the scene of the whole book.

* * *

Can you imagine this? There are no austerity measures, we are abundant in many ways, health – wealth – happiness – contentment. Our nation's economies are not only in the black, they are thriving and stable. Green energy is the energy source we all use and our world environment goes from strength to strength, free from pollution. There are no wars, no fighting, no rebellions, no demonstrations or revolutions. Famine and water shortages are a thing of the past.

Is the above too much to ask of your imagination? Should we stop and take a breather while you take all this in? Here is the welcome news for you – all of this is waiting for us all to accept and the only thing that stands in our way of this almost dreamlike state is – ourselves! That's right, us, we, you and me. You see, if we can all just sit down and take some time to understand what a great future we have and to take the relatively small steps required to make this future happen, all of the above mentioned is ours to have. It is only (and that is ONLY) ourselves that will stop this great future happening and that is why I am going to work very hard on you to convince you that it is all ours to have. I have got to force my way past the lifelong programmed barriers you have received to show you we are leading lives that are not the lives we should be living, much more is on offer. Are you ready? ready to enter into something different, a new greatly improved life, one you would choose for yourself. Ditch your skepticism, bury your doubts, there is too much on offer to lose out to by being a doubting skeptic.

The world stands at the threshold of a totally transformed new way of life – thank goodness for that!

Without realising it the people of the world are "in the throws" of the biggest change to how we live life in the history of mankind, life will never be the same again for all of us **(one way or another)**. Before us all are two distinct separate pathways opening up, one leads to a magnificent new world of unlimited human expansion, great joy and positive change, the other can only be described as a pathway to somewhere we would not want to be (sadly this IS the path we are treading right now and you do not know the full truth of this pathway) The year 2015 is looming large as the year that the massive changes mentioned will begin to really take a grip, leading up to then we are sure to be faced with very unnerving times as the pace of change accelerates. I fully expect national economies to show serious cracks opening up from late 2013 to late 2014 and stock markets – bond markets – currencies will take some severe hits and I foresee social unrest and rioting escalating to mass levels never witnessed before. There is also a growing possibility of serious conflict between major powers, do not dismiss this possibility. Obviously this will lead to even more misery for the people of the world and yet I feel this time of financial and social collapse should be welcomed with open arms.

Most people will fail to see when all the financial and social collapse happens that it is a very welcome development as it clearly and

finally demonstrates to us all that our systems are hopelessly flawed and need a good shakeout (dumping would be a better word!).

When things go so badly wrong, this is always an indicator that our systems and beliefs are either obsolete or just plain unworkable. The people of the world should welcome the financial fallout as it will openly expose the severe fraud that is taking place with economies and much more. When the dust settles from the various crumbling economies the world will be in a much improved stronger position to tackle head on the many problems that exist. While serious problems are hidden and we do not learn of the full extent of the problems, they cannot be tackled and therefore they do something that they do best – **multiply and grow**. Here then is the perfect chance to learn from past mistakes to shape a new improved future for all, you must not fear what is going to take place, welcome it. As you read through my book I ask you to do something similar to the above, learn from past mistakes, do not be frightened of what takes place as we move towards the positive pathway we would happily choose for ourselves.

> **" As difficult, improbable and controversial as it is may seem, there has never been a better time to be on the Earth than right now as our world transforms, fast"**

Of course this idea above is controversial and near impossible to believe when you consider that world economies are crumbling before our eyes, wars – mass protests - fighting are everywhere and accelerating, we stagger from one major crisis to another and our environment is breaking down before our eyes. What should worry us more than anything though is the fact that we never fully discover the true depth of the troubles we face as they are hidden. Today discover in plain language for yourself what is going on under the cover of secrecy, learn about the world you do not know about and – discover the great new life that is being offered to us all - I am not at all sure which will shock you the most.

* * *

**"The way we believe our lives work in the world
and the reality of how they actually work are light
years apart. <u>We do not know the real world.</u>"**

* * *

The greatest period of expansion, freedom and human advancement is knocking at our door begging to enter into our lives, standing firmly in the way of these truly magnificent times are a number of obstacles from our past and present, which must be removed. For while we do indeed have a long period of potential sustained growth and unending joy ahead, we are faced with a desperate situation at this present moment in time which is much worse than people realise. Without knowing it, the people of the world have two potential futures waiting to be accepted, these are very much in the form of "good news – bad news" scenarios. The good news is that life for us all can shift sharply upwards to a new level of total joy, freedom and wonderment in the very near future, the bad news is the very widely reported details that there are advanced plans in place of many hideous secret plots to among other things - slaughter 90% of the world's population (read about this later). Now you could never find a more diverse scenario for anything anywhere than the good news – bad news stated above and the majority of people will just not be able to take all this in and believe it, which is why this book *is* **the most important book ever written**.

Few of us normally have the opportunity to find out what is going on under the surface of life, we are kept in the dark, that is until now. This is the most important book ever written as it lifts the cover off of the deceit and lies that have been forced on us all and exposes the true world we do not know about. We are hovering at the threshold of two possible futures, you must find out as much as you can about both as they are so different and one has got to be avoided at all cost. Yes there are thousands of books which touch on the subjects inside this book, I have yet to find a single one that is aimed only at the ordinary people of the world which will help open their eyes to the truth, these are the people with the most to lose, so why bypass them? Two diverse futures await, the only way we can accept the great future is to reject the unwelcome future and you will never do that until you learn about both in **plain understandable every day simple language**.

The world is tentatively hovering on the brink of entering into the greatest and most prolonged abundant period in its history, a time of great change, exceptional human expansion, freedom and real "all round abundance". This statement must come as something of a surprise to all who are suffering so desperately in so many ways throughout the world at present and to many this must appear very improbable with all the harsh problems our world faces. There is only one minor proviso and sticking point to the statement above, we will have to make this new life happen, it will not take place on its own without our effort, the ride is great - but it is not a free ride - we have to earn it. Nobody is going to come along and drop into your hands a great new future, YOU have to achieve this yourself by taking some form of action, there are no free rides.

With distrust and feelings of hopelessness rising across the world when we realise that we rarely discover the truth of what is really going on in our world, people are becoming heavily disillusioned with life. This naturally leads to the rejection of those we believe are responsible for what is going wrong - our leaders, which is an easily proven point when were faced with the widespread protests and demonstrations against governments and banks around the whole world. Protest is a normal human reaction that grows ever stronger day by day as we continue to lose further belief and patience with our leaders as social misery drags on and on. Nevertheless, a great unlimited future does beckon for the seven billion inhabitants of the Earth who could see the most positive changes to life ever witnessed. You may be thinking to yourself that this is another New Age "live in hope rebirth of humanity story" or a pipedream from some "peace on Earth disciple", it is not! I only deal in facts and not fantasies, not conspiracies.

It should be glaringly obvious to everyone that the world cannot carry on as it is with a growing threat of World War Three, world population exploding, famine & drought rife and worsening around the world, national economies are collapsing and wreaking havoc with so many diverse problems and our world is considered by very many people to be run by undercover secret organisations. Sensible people know that we will not emerge out of these modern day problems until we admit to the true depth of our predicaments and put them right. It must be obvious to everyone that our present policies do not work and only massive change on a scale never seen before will turn things around. We do have a great future once we accept the true seriousness of our present situation and take the appropriate actions needed to change for the better.

Today we face making the most important decision in all of history – do we carry on as we are to an almost certain collapse of humanity, or completely change direction to a positive life of growth and equality. If world leaders (political – religious – financial – business etc.) cannot change their ways and "see the light", they should step aside to allow in sensible people that will. The people of the world make up approximately 99.9% of the population and our leaders 0.01%, the 0.01% are ruining the world with their failing actions and decisions for the 99.9% majority. This cannot continue. Don't you think that it's time to find out what is really going on in our world, to discover the truth and remove the covers from the hidden plans and plots aimed against us? We are being fooled and misled and to a depth you will find unbelievable when you discover the truth. When you do finally see the truth your eyes will probably light up in realisation of what has been going on as "the penny drops".

All of the above and more is waiting for us to wake up to and grab right now if we were to rouse from our slumber and see the real world for what it is. This book will carefully explain exactly how to open your eyes to this wondrous future by first explaining what we all need to change prior to welcoming in this new way of life. Nobody can say with any honesty that our present world is not in an enormous mess, very little in our world is working as well as we would choose it to and as everyone knows "if something is not working it is a clear indication that were on the wrong pathway and that it is time to grasp change". The most suitable description for our world at this moment has to be that it is "on a path of self - destruction" and only the people of the world can change this as our leaders are those who have initiated the moves causing the problems. Only the insane keep following a pathway that obviously leads to ruin, which is where our world finds itself at this moment – on a fast track to ruin led their by our leaders decisions. To step off this ruinous pathway is the commonsense action the people must take and take it now while they are still able to. To welcome the changes we need into our lives we first have to thoroughly understand what we must change and why, a process that may appear to some to be a painful passage, let me assure these people "the pain is well worth the gain". We have to understand what is going on before it is possible to move ahead, we cannot leave behind unfinished business and we have to learn the truth of our situation. People who refuse to learn the truth and to discover what is really going on in life remain stuck to the past, they cannot move on and go forward while held back by fear and ignorance of the truth. The brave and the sensible go forward, realists go forward, the fearful and the disbelievers are left behind, do you want to be left behind with the fearful and disbelievers? Put aside your fears and read this book in its entirety, do not be disturbed by the truths that are exposed, these will be issues that are left far behind in history as the great new future unravels.

The "way of life" that we presently believe in, the very way we think that all life runs in our world is a total fraud and our idea of life which we trust and follow throughout our time on earth is the biggest confidence trick the world has ever witnessed. Virtually everything we are taught about life is a false impression deliberately designed to mislead and cheat us, the true life we should all be living has been stolen from us and replaced with what amounts to a life of slavery and obedience to the people who have defrauded us. You could read the statements above a hundred times and for the majority the truth in the message will not sink in and be accepted. In truth, the truth of the message is far more likely to be rejected for a number of reasons which are discussed in this book. Our falsely imposed impression of life is the biggest fraud ever conceived in history, the worst possible trick played on mankind in human existence and few would be willing or able to recognise and accept this is so, such is the depth and absolute brilliance of the deception. The people of the world deserve to know the truth as they have been robbed of the true life they were meant to have. The people have done nothing wrong and do not merit such shoddy treatment from our leaders who are playing out their personal power games.

Change is the greatest deception "chain cutter" available to man. When change is geared to delivering a great life for everyone on the planet, do you have any other choice than to accept change and allow a great future to open up for you and everyone? Should you choose to unchain and release your unlimited life there is a very simple way to achieve this – which you must discover for yourself today.

You are about to read one of the most positive life changing books in print, though at first it may not seem so. Keep reading to the end, do not give up on the book as it is designed as a journey taking the reader step by step to a very positive conclusion. The text has purposely been kept as brief as possible to allow the reader to concentrate only on its crucial messages, there is no "filler" to thicken out the book and I have tried to write the book as if the reader and I the author are sitting face to face in conversation. The book is a basic level introduction to the life of deceit we are all subjected to every minute of every day which chains us to a false impression of life. At no time did I attempt to write a "masterpiece of literature", my only aim is to get the details out to as many people as possible and in a way that is easily understandable for all who read it. Technical details, complicated theories, sophisticated text will not be found anywhere between the covers of this book, it's all been carefully designed to deliver its major messages in as short a space of time and in a clear concise format – short and sharp! There are numerous books in print about life and its challenges, they are generally far too complicated, which I learned from personal experience. The text of this book is written in simple, sensible "people talk" with no bull, no lies, no deceit, no "beating about the bush", if you want to finally discover "what the hell is going on" and why the world is in the mess it is – this is the book for you. This book is for the people of the world who have had their eyes forcedly closed for them – their minds shut down for them – their freedom taken away from them, all without having the faintest clue this was happening.

Have you ever sat down and tried to figure out why so much is failing within life and what has gone wrong? Where did it all start to go so badly astray? Do you ask yourself why life is passing you by and you do not seem able to make any progress? Well fasten your seat belts because you are about to find out!

There are certain negative actions that if we continue to follow will make the negative scenarios suggested by this book become an absolute reality:

1. Ignore the messages even though we believe them because we do not think there is an alternative and that we have no option other than to accept what is served up to us
2. Disbelieve the messages as they challenge personal beliefs
3. Be too frightened to listen to the messages as "you don't like to hear about nasty things"

Your great new future, everyone's futures have never been so dependent upon taking the right actions as is needed now as all our futures hang in the balance, one way or another. By not taking the messages of the book seriously and not taking the right actions – we are allowing the unwelcome scenarios to continue and we will not remove our chains of deceit and this will prove to be the biggest mistake in history. The future of mankind literally hangs on making the right decision, that is no idle threat, it is the stark truth. By taking the right actions suggested throughout the book we will deliver to ourselves the greatest time in man's history which is rightly ours to experience. Forget negativity, forget the past, forget what you have been taught about life and how life "works", they are all negative teachings designed to cheat you – the real world outside of this negativity is a great place to be and to experience it you need to discard the old teachings and recognise you have a great future.

You must agree that if you have a problem you must sort this out before moving on or the problem remains and holds you back. As a simple example, I play over 35 soccer, football for over 35 year olds. I had a reoccurring injury to an ankle, my action was to go to an Internet search engine and seek out informative help. The information I uncovered gave me simple exercises to carry out to strengthen my ankle and the problem went away. This is what we need to do with failing lives, discover what is behind the failure, take action to deal with this and then move on. This book provides the guidance to find your solutions to the biggest problems in life and what to do to correct them.

The first task of this book in part one is to unmask the deceit which is used to fool us all and openly discuss this fraud, then these deceitful moves will be outlined in more detail in part two with links to back up the actions required. The solution to remove the fraud cannot be introduced until the fraud itself is fully unmasked (understanding the problem), we all have to know what we are changing before we make the necessary and appropriate changes (actions) for the better life we all crave and deserve – will you give this process a chance?

"There's none so deaf than those that will not hear, none so blind that will not see."

If I had one wish as you read through my book it would be that I was standing with you as you go from cover to cover, walking you through what must be some of the most eye opening and ground shaking text you will ever read. When the looks of shock and awe spread across your face I would look you in the eyes and say to you "take all of this seriously", "this is not hype". To experience the amazing great new life that awaits us all, we will first have to see the world and life in general for what they really are at this moment – a gigantic fraud. Yes, this will be so hard to do as we are in essence sleepwalking through life totally unaware that we are being fooled on a grand scale, we don't have a clue what is really going on behind our backs (which is a big part of the plan). The most subtle and most brilliant of plans has removed the lives we should all have been living and replaced them with a second rate replacement that hands all freedom into the grips of the plotters who know we do not suspect a thing. Surely you must have wondered why life is going so badly wrong around the world and why your own lives keeps hitting stumbling blocks? You, me, everyone have been hit with the ultimate fraud and we don't have the slightest clue its happened, you most likely "just get on with life in the best possible way in the circumstances". Which of course is what we all do, we all do what we can with what we have, we make do with the best that we have and we "get on with life". When your eyes are opened to this massive fraud you may still choose to ignore the stated facts, disbelieve the facts or block out the truth due to fear, none of which will help anyone. Until you open your eyes to the life we are enduring and take some kind of action to change the evil planning, *you are allowing the fraud to continue and not just for yourself, for everyone.* So you see we all have a huge responsibility, a very serious one at that as through our inactivity we are condemning each other to a life of fraud, slavery and loss of freedom when we can so easily be grabbing a sensational new life of unlimited abundance. This idea of mass fraud of the people all sounds like something from a Hollywood thriller film score, sadly this is not fiction, not a film script, this is your life – my life – everyone's lives and it is very real, too real. No matter how hard your mind fights to disbelieve what follows, the amassed quantities of detailed evidence available are pointing overwhelmingly to the only possible conclusion - that which follows is based in fact not fiction. Something I am sure of is that large numbers of people will reject the idea of mass fraud of the people, they will not be able to accept this at all as they have unknowingly been programmed this way. Some of my own family and friends will be no different, they will not accept the truth, they will find it impossible to take in and wonder if I have lost control of my senses. The evidence though is stacked heavily in my favour, piled high to the sky and I will not move from my stance – we have all been seriously defrauded.

What you do after learning of the grade one fraud is up to you, though I hope you will take peaceful and nonviolent action, but please do something. From here on the journey can get a little rough as uncovering fraud, lies and deception can rock your boat. Take your time to go through the book, don't pre-judge anything, then make up your own mind how much you want to believe, how much you want to reject, if anything. As you travel through the text that follows please keep this thought in mind as it is vitally important and it will help you from dipping into depressing moods – "the false lives that have been imposed on us are exactly that, false". Therefore to remove the fraud is a relatively simple counter action – expose the fraud. let the world see that we have all been deceived, reject the fraud and the true life we all were meant to have can be accepted in place of the deceitful lies. You have so much on offer to you that is good, a fresh beginning, a life full of freedom and free of the nightmares of the past, this though hangs on you keeping your mind open to what follows. Remember the saying "Your mind is like a parachute, it works best when its open".

Please read these quotes below slowly, keep them in mind as you read on:

- Life that we all believe in is a false impression, a fraudulent plot, it's all illusion
- Your life as you live it is not the life you were meant to have, your true life has been stolen from you and replaced with a second rate alternative
- Many people you think you can trust are secretly using and cheating you
- Those who you believe run your country do not, they are puppets on a string
- Your most likely reaction to what follows in this book will be to disbelieve it, <u>don't!</u>

* * *

**"If you learn one truth today, it should be that
you do not know the real world."**

Truth is often harder to accept than lies and deceit as truth can appear sensational compared to the smoothly glossed over hidden appearance of "silk tongued" lies. It is highly unlikely you have ever and will ever have your beliefs on life and how the world "operates" be so tested than the book you are about to read will accomplish. Writer Mark Twain said this of lies and truth "a lie can travel halfway around the world while truth is putting on its shoes". Within this text your basic understandings on much of the truth of life will be put under the microscope and exposed as a monumental deception that has been meticulously planned to rob you of the true life you should be living. At some point you may feel like screaming or shouting out in either rage or frustration as the truth slowly sinks in that we have all been severely cheated by many of the people we trust. We should all be wearing T-shirts with "I have been cheated" printed across them, because that is the full reality of our lives, we HAVE been cheated.

"we HAVE been cheated and we better wake up to this before it's too late"

Let me forewarn you, it will be very difficult to believe that which follows as we have all been brainwashed all of our lives to accept the fraudulent plans imposed on us and if there is something guaranteed to upset us it is when we learn we have been used and made fools of. When lifelong beliefs are openly challenged we tend to recoil in shock at first and then come out fighting to protect our beliefs or try to cover up our embarrassment of being fooled. Nobody will welcome the news that we have been totally deceived, few will fully accept the truth of the situation, many will reject all the unwelcome news and still many more will shrug their shoulders and say "what can I do about it?". Yet it is only by fully accepting we have all been deceived that we can start to rebuild our lives and restore faith in life and go forward. Refusing truth is even more damaging than accepting lies, we must all recognise this and bury the lies and grasp truth to move to a more positive approach to life. There is much in our lives that is not what it seems to be, but then the worse things rarely are. We all trust what we see with our eyes, sadly though we tend to see what we want to see and can hide from ourselves the truth if it suits us that way. We can all be very selective in what we place belief in and choose to ignore or reject that which we do not want to personally accept into our lives, even when we know we are wrong to do so.

We have three major problems that are holding us back from the exceptional new life that is on offer, throughout the book it is these three problems that are being made clear to the reader that they are the blockages we must overcome.

1. <u>Ignorance of the truth.</u> The attitude that effects just about everyone in which we refuse to believe the truth if it goes against our deeply held ingrained personal beliefs.
2. <u>Apathy.</u> We have become so disillusioned with life as more and more goes wrong, we lose interest in life and accept whatever is thrown at us and we shrug our shoulders of all responsibility and concern.
3. <u>Fear.</u> We are too frightened to accept the truth if it upsets us and would prefer to stay "uneducated" and in the dark to truth, sticking our fingers in our ears to block out truth.

All three of these above are well known to the people who are defrauding us and they cleverly use these failings against us as they are experts at manipulation and use our shortcomings to their fullest. We have to recognise that it is these three failures above that are helping to hold us all back in life. Should we remove these blockages we will see all the fraudulent schemes fall apart and expose them for what they are, which in turn will cast off our chains that hold us back. The shift to a greatly improved new way of life is not a difficult move when you consider that it is a shift in our falsely created beliefs that is required.

As you make your way through this book, please understand that the uncovering of deceit is not a personal attack on you, it is simply part of the process of re-building life, rebuilding faith in mankind and cutting the chains of deceit away. Forgiveness of those who have deceived us is a large part of the change to a positive future we all need, without forgiveness there cannot be closure on the past and this will hold us back. Please try to control any feelings of anger and desires for retribution, these emotions do not help the situation we all find ourselves in. When we can all accept that we have been fooled for most of our lives and that one of the ways to change is to forgive the deceit, then we will open up many doors to a positive life that is going to greatly surprise us with its unlimited potential. A great new future awaits us all once we have dealt with the past, a new more positive chapter in world history awaits us, keep that in mind as you go from cover to cover of this book. Don't let the shadow of deceit dim the light of the bright future we are all waiting to experience.

Are you patriotic, are you proud of your country, do you stand with your hand across your heart as you sing out your national anthem, do you proudly fly your countries flag and like many before you do you love your country enough to risk your life fighting to defend it? **Isn't it a criminal shame that some of our leaders and bankers do not share our devotion to our countries as they bow down to the real rulers of the world who take complete advantage of us and mock our patriotism and devotion to our homeland?**

It is time for you to wake up and see the truth sitting in front of you, staring you in the eyes, this is an "us and them world" which will be gradually explained to you. There is no doubt that what follows in this book will severely test your powers of belief, your mind will fight to reject the suggestions it raises, therefore I will try to present the book and its messages in as gentle an approach as possible. You do not have to be a practicing psychologist to understand that most people are very reluctant to change their minds on their deep held views of life and their personal belief of how life works, which make up parts of the chain that binds us to a fake life. Have faith in the old saying which states so well, "the truth will set you free". Mahatma Gandhi said "You must have faith in humanity, humanity is an ocean; if a few drops of the ocean are dirty, the ocean does not become dirty". The text of this book does return often to this theme of reluctance to accept challenges to our beliefs on life and I try to make it clear I understand why we are so reluctant to change our beliefs about life. The reason I return to the subject often is that it is one of the major keys to why life is failing us and more importantly, the route to unlock change for a better life. By accepting that we have had false and/or the wrong beliefs installed within us we can replace those faulty beliefs which are holding us back with true and more positive beliefs that will help us move forward.

At this early stage of the book, I ask you to test your powers of belief and reflect on these details that I have learned of to experience for yourself how you personally react to them, **believing them or not**: Each day across the world 24,000 people die from poverty – 13 to 18 million children die each year, of which 12 million are aged under five, depending which charities figures you read it is claimed a child dies every 10 – 15 seconds from starvation or malnutrition, many of these deaths are avoidable if we change our ways. How does that make you feel? Do you believe the figures (they are from reputable sources) Here we are, more than a decade into the new millennium and children are dropping like flies to preventable and curable illnesses, they are starving to death while obesity is rife in the western world. Why don't you know about this? Why is it happening when we are such a modern caring society (supposedly)? Think also on this, since the year 1900 there has been over 167 wars around the world that has slaughtered almost 200 MILLION people and to this day wars are continuing and the casualties mount up. Can we really claim to be the civilised race we like to believe? we fool ourselves that we are civilised but how can we be when faced with details such as these? In truth we are fooling ourselves when we believe we are civilised. Think also on this detail, considerable sources state that our news reporting services are heavily controlled and we are only allowed to learn the propaganda news that is deemed suitable for us to learn, *important news is withheld from us* – you will find out that this is as close to truth as any of the comments above.

Consider these details, in the USA there are:

- 15000 newspapers
- 1100 magazines
- 9000 radio stations

- 2300 publishers
- 1500 tv stations

They are owned by just 3 corporations!

How difficult would it be to impose your rule over a nation if you own "The Media"? **not very!** Do you believe this is only an American problem? Think again.

Our news services are reputedly as sinister and devious as the propaganda led news media of the Nazi's prior to World War Two. How does all this information fit in with your beliefs of how the world works? Consider this shocking truth - we have a true golden age waiting for us that can put our present world experiences into the shade, this golden age can be the greatest period in the history of the world, how do you feel to find out that this golden age will be withheld from you and everyone, hidden from you by the very people you place trust in and the facts are buried by the media? Is all that too difficult to believe? See how you feel after reading the book that follows.

"We live in a them and us world"

Who is this book aimed towards? The book is aimed solely at what I call "The People" (as you will discover the people really <u>are</u> the "downtrodden" people we hear of so much) the workers – the housewives at home – factory staff – shop workers – farmers - office staff – builders – tradesmen – the unemployed – medical staff – the retired and many more. From hereon I will simply refer to this group as "the people". It is this group, the middle class and the lower class who stand to lose the most wealth and freedom in the very near future. Much sooner than people realise they can soon be dropped into a very undesirable new rounded down classification – "The Poor". In a time when the rich have never had it so good and are becoming the "Super Rich", the middle and lower classes are doomed to face a miserable life simply as "the poor". Will this be as a result of bad decisions by our leaders? Or more cynically, will it be part of a wicked long term plan? Read on to make up your own mind on that.

"Sooner than you think we will have a two tier world, the super-rich and the poor"

Our leaders are introducing ever increasing amounts of new laws and measures to take ever more control of us by any means possible and we do not suspect a thing. What is just as frightening is that at the same time they are trying to play at being God by interfering with the physical make up of our planet, which ultimately endangers us all greatly with the threat of instant destruction without any warning – here one second and gone the next! You are most likely unaware of all this and you will also fight the very idea that it could hold a grain of truth (ignorance of truth), the fact remains though that this is the truth and I will try all that I can to explain this to you so that you can make up your own mind. The worst action you can take is to put this book down without reading it, or to dismiss it as a crazy load of "mumbo jumbo", you owe it to yourself and the future of your family and every child in the world to read the whole of this book. Something I am 100% sure of is that mankind faces making the biggest, most important decision in the whole of history, a decision that will ultimately decide if mankind is to survive or perish. That decision must be made now and its simple enough "do we continue on our present (mis)-guided path to a possible end of life *as we know it*, or do we choose to change and experience the closest we are ever likely to get to Paradise?

"The biggest decision in history has to be made, now"

The answer to the above decision should be a no-brainer - go for the near perfect future by accepting we have got things hopelessly wrong and need to change as soon as possible. History tells us that it is very doubtful that mankind will take the sensible route, for the reasons I will explore within this book. Ask a hundred people in the street if they would choose a near perfect life against almost certain destruction or a life in chains and naturally you would have one hundred people jumping at the chance to experience a near perfect world, let's be honest, who wouldn't? One of the major problems we face is that the question will never be asked, those 100 people in the street mentioned above would never get this opportunity to make their key decisions known as we are all having this type of information completely hidden from us. That such an important decision is needed and our very future depends on that decision to be hidden from us is typical of the way the *real* world is being (mis)run. The consequences we face by remaining on our present path will never be revealed to anyone and the idea we can have a near perfect future, which we should all experience, will definitely be withheld from us. Do you find that difficult to believe? that a wondrous potential future is almost in your hands but it is being deliberately withheld from you in favour of an end to life as we know it. Emperor Julius Caesar said "men in general are quick to believe that which they wish to believe" – I would add that they are very slow to disbelieve that which they do not wish to! In truth, we have a true golden age waiting for us that will never be allowed to happen as things stand. By the time you get to the end of this book you should understand that these words are completely true.

Over a ten year period of voluntary work, I delivered lectures and ran hundreds of classes, plus I sent out thousands of e-mails to test reactions on people to gauge their response to having their beliefs of how life works challenged. On occasions I have to admit that I deliberately and mischievously targeted certain people who I knew held strong beliefs on a subject just to see how high they would jump when their beliefs were challenged. What I learned did not surprise me at all, it is that most people will fight hard to keep and justify their false beliefs (ignorance of truth) even when confronted with the truth that those beliefs are false. The people with deep held beliefs tended to leap up and challenge what I was saying and to try and overpower me with outbursts claiming their own brilliance, or reel off their qualifications and experience and finally there were those who said "there is nothing I can do about it, so why worry?". All in all though, the responses were closely similar and amount to the fact that people do not accept their beliefs and principles being challenged, even if those beliefs are proven wrong or outdated. Until we can overcome a very major problem, I call this "the ignorance of the truth" we will remain on course for an unpleasant and very sudden end to life *as we know it.* We are in real trouble this time, not a threat, a possibility or silly talk, this is a certainty and we are in so very deep. When things look normal we expect things to stay that way, we become complacent and do not prepare ourselves for when anything out of the normal hits. The wicked twist in this is that things stay normal right up until the point where they change to danger, which is too late for anyone to do anything about it.

"What man interferes with usually goes horribly wrong"

Man has to stop trying to play at being God as he interferes with the world and how it operates, as we all know "what man interferes with usually goes horribly wrong", man just does not know when to stop dabbling in things he does not understand. Even the bible tries to warn us and makes this point clear with the story of Adam and Eve. Adam was warned not to touch the forbidden apples, but Adam was a typical man and he gave in to temptation, he could not stop himself from doing something he should not do. Just like Adam, modern man does not know when not to touch forbidden fruit, the fruit being life, freedom and our planet, we go on and on interfering.

"There are many very dangerous games being played under a smokescreen of total secrecy"

Attempts at manipulating the Earth's atmosphere could at some point prove disastrous and destroy our eco systems (you will learn about this later) *it is an experiment that is seriously endangering all life, everyone on the planet and could destroy all living things at any moment – without warning!*

Controlling the people by deception, mind control and brainwashing must eventually explode in the faces of the plotters as their deceitful schemes are publicised. There are many very dangerous games being played under a smokescreen of total secrecy, games kept from the sight of the people because it is not in the interests of any of the people, it only serves the governments and the secret organisations making the deceitful moves. There are far too many offensive secret schemes and secret organisation's being run in our world to cover in the pages that follow, I have chosen to look at those that I feel offer the most serious and immediate threat to the lives of the people of the world.

"Mankind's evolution is reversing as we lose contact with reality"

We are led to believe that mankind is advancing in evolution, technology certainly is, but man? No, not at all and as I will attempt to explain in many ways we are backtracking, our evolution is reversing as we have lost touch with basic reality. You will soon see that human decency, respect for our fellow man is waning fast and we have learned nothing from the abominable treatment subjected on those who perished in the Holocaust or the horrors of the Dark Ages. From what I have learned we are as barbaric now as the time when the Dark Ages were being imposed on the world, we have not advanced forward at all. Man has to grow up, to come of age and stop playing power games while striving to be the best or the first to achieve fame and carve their name into the history books. Man has got to start to behave as the respectable civilised race he claims to be. I know though that this is unlikely to happen, we are probably too far down the wrong path to make an about turn now, those leading us astray will never willingly change their plans. Should those who carry the mantle of leadership not be able to see they are ultimately endangering the world with their secret plans (I am sure they can't as they are so lost in their own power insanity), they should step aside and let someone more responsible take over. World leaders must raise their heads out of their power plays and wake up to the fact that what they are doing is leading to a calamitous and sudden end of mankind and that they have lost control of their own actions and their plans are too dangerous to carry out. Time and time again man has shown he is incapable and untrustworthy to be a custodian of power as in the hands of man power is a drug he becomes addicted to, the more he has the more he wants. History is full of records of corruption and disasters caused by the abuse of power, the dangers threatening us all now could be man's last steward-ship of power as everything disintegrates, a fitting epitaph to the end of mankind would surely read "we never learn to leave things alone". Why do we seek to emulate God when we have yet to learn how to look after what we already have? The world is in disarray on many fronts and we concentrate on trying to understand the universe, shouldn't we understand our own world and ourselves first? We can only hope that man does not find out too much about the universe as he would probably destroy that as well. Why are we dabbling in energy manipu-lation? After the freak mistakes from the Philadelphia Experiment, I am surprised we would give a second thought to this arena (for those who are not familiar with the Philadelphia Experiment look it up on the Internet). The experiments and actions taking place with energy manipulation, to be discussed later, are just so typical of the wild quests for power and control that have littered man's past with failure, only this time a failure could so easily destroy our earth's atmosphere. So why do it? Because we never learn to leave the things alone that we do not understand, we have to tinker and be the first to achieve the results, to try and gain fame for our work and to gain more power. This is taking us back to the scenario of the little boy who cannot stop playing with fire, he knows it is dangerous, he has been told not to do it, but he cannot stop playing and he gets burnt fingers. Our problem is that the fire being played with can engulf the world and we all get burned. Daily we actively seek the almost mythical Higgs Boson par-ticle, or the God particle as it is nicknamed with potentially danger-ous experiments, we actually try **(and are) to create mini black holes in a laboratory environment!!!,** why – why - why? Did anyone ask the people if they want scientists to try and create black holes here on our Earth which could destroy everything in seconds? Why do we want this, why do we need to know the details of the particle that sparked the origin of our planet and the universe, the particle responsible for what is known as The Big Bang? Can anyone imagine what the next step would be if scientists were to find this particle? Yes, to try and replicate it. Because that is what man does, he does not know when to stop and the obvious next stage would be to try and produce the effects of the original "Big Bang" that created our universe, who knows what would happen should that occur (though I think we could guess that one). While man tries to play at being God, we are all under threat of instant destruction in the blink of an eye. Whatever your religion or how much you believe in the existence of God, don't you think that God is at the end of his tether with man's meddling? Will God stand much more or will God either terminate man or remove those responsible for ruining the Earth? Another Mahatma Gandhi Quote "When in despair I remember that all through history the way of truth and love has always won. There have been many tyrants and murderers and for a time they seem invincible. But in the end, they always fail. Think of this always."

"We never learn to leave things alone that we do not understand"

Personally I believe that things started to go wrong and fly into a downward spiral from around the start of the 1900's as man advanced too fast, growing ever more and too powerful and began to use new increased powers such as faster travel through greatly improved aircraft, vastly improved communication systems, nuclear power, much more powerful weapons and also the power of globalisation which created massive industrial and retail empires. To many these are good positive moves and they would be except they brought with them a new problem, as man advanced he became more secretive and protective of his new found power, man developed a mania to "keep it all for himself and not share it". This mania has grown and grown until it has become a rampant disease as individuals, organisations and even governments seek to hold onto and hide their new depths of power and control.

"How can the slaughter of 200 million people be the action of a civilised race?"

Has a more modern world contributed to making man more civilised? No, no, no. Look at the number of wars that have been fought since 1900, has there ever been a period in this time that there was not a war, civil war, battle, fighting of some kind? From researching the Internet I can confirm that between the years 1900 – 2006 there were a total of 167 wars. The world has lost something like 200 MILLION lives to war since 1900, that is 200,000,000 people slain while we deceive ourselves and boast how we have grown and how civilised we are. How can the deaths of 200 million people in terrible circumstances be considered the actions of a civilised race? How could the serious abuse of those slaughtered in WW2 concentration camps be the actions of a civilised people? Have you ever been unlucky enough to see film footage of the allied troops entering the concentration camps at the end of world war two? The scenes are soul shaking in their total horror as living skeletons were shown and piles of dead bodies were scattered all over the place, the filming showing an excavator pushing mounds of limp bodies into hastily dug trenches – this was not that long ago and it was the work of a modern nation with civilised people who had been ***brainwashed by clever government programming, propaganda and manipulation of the media***, **which you should keep in mind as you read the latter chapters of this book**. In this same period in our history we have developed chemical and germ warfare that can massacre huge numbers of people without destroying infrastructure and buildings, are you aware that throughout the world there are stockpiles of chemical and germ warfare amounting to hundreds of tons? These are the sort of wars that we can see, that are obvious, what about the wars being fought against the people that cannot be seen? The turn of the twentieth century coincided with the start of another war, an unseen war that claims many lives around the world each and every day – one you do not know about, a war you will definitely find it hard to believe exists. Later in the book you will find a chapter that looks at secret organisations who are regarded as the real rulers of the world, these organisations grew in strength over this same time period to such an extent that they control every aspect of your life and *you do not have a clue they are doing it*. I know how hard you will find this to believe, I was informed about these facts over thirty years ago and would not believe it, for the last ten years I have been bombarded with information about the presence of secret societies and I still refused to fully accept they exist until the volume of evidence proved too hard NOT to believe. The chapter on these secret organisations you probably will need to read more than once, I doubt if the full implications of what you will read can sink in on only one read. If you follow the recommended reading and Internet options listed in that chapter, you will have no doubts that the existence of these secret organisations is real, very real. In the thirty years I rejected the possibility that our world is run by these secret organisations I did not have the books that are now in print or the many millions (yes, there are oceans of data and information logged on this) of articles published on the Internet to browse, you do.

"A glorious future will not be allowed to happen"

While some attempt to knowingly ruin our world, our world is actually standing at a potentially glorious crossroads where a true golden future awaits, incredible innovative new products are ready to go into production, new energy sources are coming on stream and mind blowing inventions are primed to transform life as we know it. There is also a growing awareness and intensity to life with what is commonly termed a "raised vibration of humanity", humans are presently evolving much faster than ever on a spiritual level, growing in their awareness of life. All around the world people are waking up to new realities of life and its deeper meaning. The accelerating leaps forward in our all-round quality of life that are due will be far in advance of anything we have previously witnessed. But! (isn't there always a but?) forming an almost insurmountable barrier to the bright future we all deserve is - the present, or to be more precise – the present way our lives are shaped for us, which will also be explained within the book.

The people of the world who make up 99.99% of the population have been grossly deceived by the power hungry controllers that really rule our world, our so called leaders. The whole set up of the systems the world runs on is designed to control the 99.9% masses while bleeding away their money and turning them into slaves. To put it even more simply it is a case of "us" and "them", us being the people who make up 99.9% of the world population and them being our leaders who make up the 0.01% of the population, The 0.01% have complete control of the world and protect their bounty with an iron fist approach. Nobody would blame you if you were to completely disbelieve what you have just read, it would be very understandable for you to throw out these statements – because that is part of the programming and brainwashing we have all been exposed to all of our lives and a large part of the overall deception imposed on us by the 0.01%. In order to exercise control over their electorate, governments throughout history have made people dependent on government handouts. By providing more and more benefits to a larger and larger share of the population, governments can control the population who become more and more dependent on those handouts. If your food supply or living accommodation is funded by the government, you are not likely to attack that government in fear of losing your benefits. A system controlled by unknowing deceived electors being manipulated by a fully controlled media which publishes fraudulent propaganda on behalf of a corrupt political establishment can hardly be the path to a lasting positive future. Governments do not want full employment or large numbers of people not dependent on benefits, they would lose their control of a large part of the population should we all be in employment and something governments crave is control. We foolishly believe we live in a democratic society because we freely elect our government representatives – **wrong!** In fact we have just one minute of democracy every four to five years when we collect our election voting paper, walk over to the voting area and make our cross against the person of our choice. Once leaders are elected, democracy goes out of the window, we believed we were electing the candidates to serve us and stand up for our rights – **wrong again!** As hard as it sounds to believe, many of our leading politicians have been groomed for their posts from an early age and promoted with help to their place on the election voting paper, once in power they are the representatives of those who put them into power and not the electorate, **remember that**. The last thing many of our leading politicians represent is the country they govern, **remember that too**. These last two comments are something that everyone is going to have to wake up to, it is not mischief making anti-government talk, this is fact whether you can believe it or not.

The life you believe you live is fake, a bundle of lies tied up with a very long string of deception stretching back to the fully controlled and manipulated news reporting agencies. The control freaks that have authorised this deception to be woven into life have worryingly lost all sense of reality and have become too power crazed, the whole fraudulent system will crash like so many schemes before it that were lost in forced power grabs. Our worry must be how much damage will be done to the world as their scheming unwinds? Deception is lie based and these lies need to be embedded deep into our subconscious minds, this is achieved by constant repetition of the lies as we are brainwashed by our "trusted" news reporting agencies.

"The next economic crash will be monstrous and devastate world economies"

All empires eventually self-destruct and crash as its leaders over reach and greed distorts judgment, Rome crashed, the British Empire self-imploded, The Ottoman Empire, the German empire over reached and burned and this unseen "world control empire" is about to go the same way as once again over reaching and greed bite into it. Who will suffer as the crash takes place – we all will, of that there is no doubt, it is after all already happening and the world's economic markets are wildly out of control and only surviving by fraudulent measures. The USA will not be able to prop up the world this time, which it has done before as it is probably in some of the worst trouble of all with massive deficits (yes, I know many people will fail to believe that comment, it is easily confirmed though). Many of the "alternative" economic commentators (nearly all American citizens) predict that it will not be long before the USA collapses and becomes a third world economy, if you had said that to me two years ago, I would have laughed loudly in your face, but now I have seen so much to say that it is so. Many western government economies have been propped up by heavy borrowing and money printing to cover the shortfall of money coming into their coffers. Money has been borrowed at rock bottom interest rates around 0.5%, that's just a half per cent, these rock bottom rates cannot go on forever and must rise soon. Our massive levels of borrowing brought on by rock bottom rates, will then be an anchor around our necks as suddenly the interest our governments pay back will balloon and they will not be able to repay the debts. What will that do to government budgets? the choices facing our governments would be to either cut budgets again (more austerity, only on a massive scale) or default on the loans. This does not paint a pretty picture, you should start to get the idea though that all is far from well. Why do we keep borrowing on top of already record amounts of debt? It's like putting your foot on the accelerator when your car is headed at a brick wall - you hit the wall faster.

"Mankind is the real danger to mankind"

Please be clear about this: this book is not another ridiculous "end of the world prophecy" warning book that forewarns of impending alien invasion or strikes on the earth by giant asteroids or powerful waves of solar radiation striking earth and knocking out electric supplies. No, what we are endangered by comes from much closer to home, we - mankind *are the threat to our own futures,* and we *are the ones imperiling life on earth.* I am not saying the world will end, I am saying that the chances of the world ending are at the highest we have ever experienced and that this could happen at any time because there are so many dangers threatening us all. Most worrying to me is that the means to end our world appear to be in the hands of power crazed people who have lost all control of reason and normal thinking. As the book unfolds you will see that in reality this is one of the most positive books you are ever likely to pick up as it presents a very real solution (the only real present solution) to most of the world's more serious problems. This it seeks to achieve after clearly defining exactly what those potential major problems are. A strong belief I have is that people need to identify where and what perils face them, you cannot fight against an enemy you cannot see. Being prepared for problems is half the battle, knowing what problems you are battling against is the other half. Even those among us who refuse to listen to bad news (fear) will have to come to their senses and not block out truth, **we are talking about the future of mankind here and walking around with fingers in our ears to block out what we do not want to hear will only hasten the ending**. So yes, on the surface and on first impressions this would appear as yet another "doom & gloom" nightmare scenario warning, you will learn though it is anything but a negative alarm call.

The book and I the author are sure to draw much criticism, my sanity will be questioned as will my judgment and probably I will be accused of naivety in accepting such details as those which follow. Attacks on my words I expect to come thick and fast from all corners as the organisations this book unmasks start to defend themselves from unwelcome exposure to the truth. The loudest and most prolonged attacks will surely come from those with most to hide and lose, they will publish all kinds of statistical propaganda to try and debase the words of this book as they fight exposure and cling on to their control. To the critics I would simply remind them that we live in the Information Age "nobody can argue against hard evidence and there is too much hard evidence available not to accept the points highlighted in this book". Just as important, there has never been a person or organisation anywhere that is willing to publicly stand up and say that the background of the evidence offered is incorrect or even distorted. Therefore, on one hand there is a mountain of evidence backing up the reasoning and on the other there is a complete lack of denial that the evidence is true or false either way, which leaves only one possible conclusion to most sensible people. I fully expect a series of attacks on the books contents from many corners of what I call "The Establishment" and the "Intelligentsia". I do not expect many, if any attacks to come from the people who the book is aimed at helping. The attacks will come from people who will be protecting their own interests and have something to lose, they will fight to retain control, *control over the masses – the people*. We should all take note of those who attack the words of this book, and then delve down and look closely to see what and who they are protecting or who they are representing. Alternatively, another tactic may be used – silence!! Not saying anything is a recognised tactic of the people and organisations that secretly run the world, they believe that to speak out is to give unwelcome publicity to things they do not want to be publicly aired. Sweeping unwelcome exposure under the carpet is the usual approach of these people, which they can do easily as they control all forms of news reporting. It will be interesting to watch which way this swings. Silence is also a sign that they do not care as they have the control and can handle any criticism because they are the masters.

"None of the information within this book is secretive"

None of the information discussed and put forward within this book is of a secretive nature; it is all readily available if you know where to look. There lays the problem, due to the subtlety of the overall deception, few people even suspect that "something is wrong", so why would they look for confirmation or answers that there is a problem? In this day and age nobody has to be an Oxford or Cambridge University educated graduate, anything we need to know is right in front of us and at our fingertips, those fingertips will be touching the keyboard of a PC that is connected to an Internet search engine. As long as you know how to ask the right questions of the on-line search engine, you can access whatever information you require. Many Governments are taking hostile actions against both the hosts and those uploading information onto the Internet as the governments secretive actions are exposed for all to see on-line. The freedom to place the information exposing unscrupulous actions must be protected as this is how a true democracy works. This book will open many people's eyes and shock a huge part of the population as it unrolls. Key points are repeated regularly throughout the book, this is to ensure the key points are not missed and to ensure they are fixed into the readers mind. Something else I have purposely aimed to do is break up main points into paragraphs and separate the paragraphs as I want to keep the book from dragging a theory on for too long. By breaking it up, the reader is not going to be bored by long weary pages of the same text subject, my subjects do jump around a little, this is by design. By breaking the information into paragraphs and not presenting pages in long blocks of type, I am attempting to keep the readers eyes and mind active, trying to avoid the readers mind wandering.

"This book will provide considerable resources to facts and data to back up its claims"

Naturally there will be people who will accuse me of using fear to press home my points, to them I say that I am no fear-monger, I regard myself more as a patriotic "people person" in exposing hidden threats to all our futures and it is detailed truth I use, not fear. The reader will see that I do not cover conspiracy theories, which are rife across the Internet and elsewhere, why I avoid these (even though I believe many) is that they are theories and I prefer solid fact. My book is backed up with connections to massed files of fact available for all to read. Unlike end of the world "theories" which are mostly prophecies and opinion, this book will provide considerable links to resources of facts and data to back up its claims. With the amount of subjects covered here, it would be impossible to provide what would be endless pages of data and keep it interesting, therefore I make the valid point and then direct the reader via recommendations throughout the book to back up information in order to prove the points of this book. The amount of information available to back up the principles of the book is truly mountainous thanks to the vast levels of information stored on the Internet and as you will soon discover there is one subject alone that has over ten million articles published on it via the Internet and yet crazily this is a subject that is still something of a closely guarded secret. If I am to be honest with you, though I have carried out ten years of research to write this book, the book relies on other people's detailed research and other peoples work for its factual reference base. I am not stealing, or as it's called plagiarising other peoples work, I am directing the reader to this research and recommending the reader to track down the original work. This book can be compared to a TV guide that directs a person to the programs and information available. The role I gave myself has been to bring together a balanced, easily readable and easy to understand introduction to those other people's research and encourage you the reader to look deeper for the factual truth. My aim has always been to present the text in a simple worded formula that nobody should need a dictionary at hand to understand the message in the text. From personal experience I have read far too many informative books that required me to re-read paragraphs or pages as the text is just too complicated and I missed the point on first reading. Something I pride myself in is the ability to "dumb down" information from complicated text to much simpler wording so that everyone can take in the main points of the text on a first read. As well as being an introductory book, this is also a reference source to enable the reader to "open their eyes" to the illusions of life, to see for themselves that life as we believe it to be is an enormous fraud and nothing at all like we believe it to be. I would go as far as to say that it is only the physical side to life (bricks & mortar – land & sea – hills & mountains, trees & plants etc.) displays any reality, our lives as we believe them to be are very false, as I will attempt to prove. Something else I will try to prove is that we have no true freedom of choice, no real freewill and that what we actually equate to is a walking, talking programmed human robot, a humanoid. Worse still is the realisation that the robotic programming is not at all in our interest, anything but, the programming is designed to run our lives and deliver control of our lives to others.

"I try to present the book as if I and the reader were sitting face to face"

An important aim for me is to present the text as if you the reader and I are sitting face to face and I am walking you through the text. The last thing I want is a stuffy, over complicated text that loses the reader's attention, there's just too much at stake for that. I make my points, and then I direct the reader to back up information which has been accumulated by highly skilled researchers (which is important).

With all the wars man has fought, we have never faced so much danger than today, world peace is at its most fragile ever and the stakes have never been higher - our freedom and our existence

Throughout the history of mankind we have never faced such outright personal dangers to life as we know it than we do today, our personal financial wealth has never faced such threat and our freedom and freewill has never been so endangered in all of man's history. We have faced thousands of wars, been ravaged by plague, suffered foul weather of all kinds, been hit by earthquakes and volcanic eruptions by the million – today though we are staring into the eyes of our greatest ever threat, one that can easily end mankind's stay on this planet. It should surprise nobody that this threat comes from mankind himself, the ultimate betrayal of man has always had its greatest chance of being an "inside job", carried out by man himself, and so it is. Today we are staring at either total annihilation or certainly near annihilation when we should be experiencing the greatest time in our history. The saddest facts of this idea are that we have not recognised this as we are too programmed by our media, second and much more worryingly we will not believe it to be true (ignorance of truth), third, we are so apathetic in life we just cannot be bothered to do anything about it and accept whatever is thrown at us. A greater part of the overall problem is that we have become so automated, brain washed and pre-programmed in our thinking, to challenge our ingrained beliefs is going to meet with heavy resistance. Where does that leave us? Exactly in the position mentioned above, staring destruction in the face. Unless we come to our senses fast (very fast), let the penny drop and realise our errors, there can be only one potential end result which nobody wants. Should we decide not to act and disbelieve what is written here there will be no "I told you so" from me, because I will have shared the same fate as everyone else. You would think that as we were are in such peril, our leaders would inform us and declare a state of emergency. But what if it is our leaders who have got us into the mess in the first place? Do you really think they will admit to getting it so badly wrong or that they have plotted against us? Later in the book we will look at the role of leadership and how it can transform a person into a power hungry ogre.

"It would be typical of mankind to face the end of the world totally clueless"

There is not a shred of doubt in my mind that the total or near total downfall of mankind is not only a major possibility, it is imminent, maybe as soon as tomorrow. Should the end of life "as we know it" happen tomorrow, it would be so typical of mankind to face the end without a clue it was going to take place. We have become so complacent, so arrogant in our belief that we are indestructible and we are here forever, we have let our guard down and as any fighter will tell you "when your guard is down, that's when the killer blows are landed". You are guaranteed that a person will laugh in your face if you tell them that the world is about to end, they will call you crazy or say you are drunk or on drugs, but believe you? no chance. We have made ourselves sitting ducks for what we face by drifting through life with our eyes closed to what's really going on around us – we won't know what hit us! If we were warned, we just wouldn't believe it. As already mentioned we have become too arrogant in our outlook on life, another major factor leading to our downfall is that we have allowed ignorance to run our lives, ignorance of the truth. When confronted with truth that goes against our beliefs & principles, we would rather choose to ignore truth than accept we are wrong, this even though we know were wrong to do so. Arrogance and ignorance, such meaningless traits alone, but combined they have the ability to destroy us. In this day and age truth is hidden because truth loosens the grip of control, it unbinds deception, weakens false influences, exposes lies, and it removes the blindfolds placed upon us by the deceivers. Truth is also taken by the deceivers and twisted to appear to be lies, ignorance of the truth has been forced on us all and we have tamely accepted it. The points in this paragraph above are easy to prove, your mind at this moment is most likely searching for any number of reasons to "put down" and dismiss the ideas listed, you will either try to laugh off the claims or simply get angry enough to reject the truth. Your mind will scour itself for reasons not to believe what's written and will not be happy until it does so, or you will simply hold up your hands and say "there's nothing I can do about it, so why worry?" (apathy). This is all due to the effects of the constant outside programming and brain washing we have faced for most of our lives, forcing us to reject anything that goes against the programming. We become very uncomfortable when we learn we have been fooled, especially when the teachings were given to us by people we trust, such as our parents, friends, school teachers, politicians, religious leaders etc. We can behave so stubbornly when confronted with the fact that we have been deceived and our beliefs are wrong, the longer we have held those beliefs the more we will defend them even though deep down we know we are wrong to do so. When we learn just how massive and how deep the deception has been, we are going to feel very foolish not to have seen what is going on. It is said that "pride comes before a fall", is though the fall of mankind worth such misplaced pride?

"We travel towards ruin with our leaders at the forefront"

Presently we are on a fast track to a serious downfall, we are here by following our leaders through misplaced trust (we elected them) and belief that they had our interests at heart (that is what we thought we elected them to do). We travel to downfall with our political – religious – industrial – financial & banking leaders at the forefront *knowingly* guiding us all to failure. Thomas S Monson said "The power to lead is the power to mislead is the power to destroy". It is safe to assume that some of these leaders are clueless that we are on a path to failure, such is the sad lack of forethought given to the important decisions they make. Eugene Victor Debs said "In every age it has been the tyrant, the oppressor and the exploiter who has wrapped himself in the cloak of patriotism, religion or both to deceive and overawe the people". Euripides said "When one with honeyed words and an evil mind persuades the mob, great woes befall the state".

While our leaders stick to what have become the "tried and tested" practices of the past, we will never go forward. We need fresh ideas, new incentives and not more of the old. It's plainly clear that the old practices do not work or we would not be in the mess we are today. Albert Einstein is one of the people credited with a very poignant saying that applies so well here: "insanity is to keep doing the same thing and expect a different result". Were all in dire trouble from a number of directions and all we keep doing is trying to resolve the problems using methods proven not to work (doesn't that make alarm bells ring in your head?) As an example look at the financial meltdown of 2007-08 which was caused by insane lending and borrowing, how are we tackling this? By insanely borrowing and lending more! Even a schoolchild can see the flaw in this strategy, why can't we see this, it is there in front of our noses – this isn't working and it never has. Hopefully all that you have read so far will start to make you think and make you realise that we have all placed too much faith and trust in our leaders who obviously, going on results so far, have lost all connection to reality and do not have a clue what they are doing, or they know exactly what they are doing and their plans are going very nicely thank you (again, to be explained later). The situation can only become worse and deepen as nobody is making any positive movement to stimulate growth in the various national economies, as the situation worsens, the people will finally react. They will not trust the banks, governments, law makers and the globalists, society will break down which unfortunately can only lead to the unwanted "mob rule" such as we saw in the 2011 London riots where gangs openly looted shops and torched buildings – that is not what we want to see as it benefits none.

It is time to accept reality and reality tells us that we are stumbling down a very dark pathway, it's time to swallow our pride before we pass the point of no return, if we have not reached that point already. Now is the time to change, not next year, not five years' time, not ten years' time, NOW is probably our last chance. Every-day that passes without taking the right actions draws us closer to the edge of the precipice when we should be experiencing life that we would choose for ourselves.

"We do not like challenges to our deeply held beliefs"

At this moment your mind is most likely spinning and searching for more suitable "put downs" on what you have read, you will be fighting to reel off words of derision and scouring your brain for ways to attack the reasoning of my words. This would be quite normal and expected behavior, we do not like challenges to our deeply held beliefs, and especially those we have held all our lives. Have you ever thought about this, *where do our beliefs come from?* Answer – other people! We learn our beliefs from others by either reading and learning, listening and learning or watching and learning, therefore our beliefs are NOT our beliefs they are other peoples beliefs we learned from them. If you can accept that, then you should be able to accept you need to change those learned beliefs as they are not your personal beliefs. Very few personal beliefs are learned from our own personal experiences, they are imposed beliefs from others. Let me state though that the rejection of challenge to our personal beliefs is one of the key reasons we have arrived at this time with such a negative future before us. The human mind is programmed from its early years to accept a life of "fitting in" to an accepted formula and that formula does not allow any movement away from its rigidity. We almost find it impossible to think "outside of the box" as we are so programmed to trust what we are told is normal behavior, normal practices, normal beliefs. We gave up on free thinking as early as when we turned age three, from that point we had imposed on us our induction into a false programmed life (more on this later). For me to challenge your beliefs is asking you to go against lifetime habits and more important to make you accept you are wrong in following those lifetime beliefs and habits. Nobody likes being proven wrong, end of sentence. We prefer to dismiss truth rather than suffer the pain and embarrassment of admitting we are wrong, rejecting truth is far less painful. Were about to fall off a cliff into a bottomless chasm and ignorance of the truth is a big part of the blame and even now you will be fighting that truth in your mind.

Later in the book we will look at the reasons our leaders have taken us down the wrong pathway, there are many reasons for their errors, treachery being one of them. As Lord Acton said in a letter to Bishop Mandell Creighton in 1887 "power corrupts and absolute power corrupts absolutely". It is a sad fact that mankind is in total disarray and it is our leaders that have got us here, it is also our leaders who are hiding the fact that we are in disarray, burying the sheer depth of our troubles in secrecy. Niccolo Machiavelli said "Never attempt to win by force what can be won by deception", something our leaders appear to have taken to heart. World economies have never been in such bad shape, the levels of debt is unbelievable, yet you would never know the full extent of the debt levels if you read the newspapers or tune in to television news programs, why is that? You will soon know.

In early 2012 a news item started to circulate on the Internet, it grew and grew with more and more articles being published and more and more attention being centered on it, what is this news item? The real possibility of World War Three! Why have you not read more about this in the news media? This threat is growing with the ever expanding turmoil in the Middle East, where will it really begin to take hold Israel – Egypt – Syria – Iran? We have to be very frightened of this as it is all being led by our leaders who have their own agendas and goals that they follow. WW3 is not to be dismissed, it is more likely than not (unless the people stand up and say no, we will not back this).

A shocking section of the book, will be the section on secret weapons, true weapons of mass destruction that have nothing to do with chemical or germ warfare, much more at home in the realm of "Star Wars". You will discover that weaponry exists, not theory, which can wipe out a whole countries population without destroying buildings and infrastructure etc. Also, have you wondered what's happening with our weather as it goes from bad to worse and we experience more earthquakes, more volcanic eruptions (almost weekly)? Most alarming is the fact that a weapon physically exists with this capability and is in the control of people who do not seem to have the slightest clue that it can cause the total destruction of human life on Earth. This explanation alone will really rock you on your heels.

At this point I think it is the right time to state clearly that I am not anti-government, I am not an anarchist, not a Fascist or Marxist, I am not anti-religion (any religion), I am not anti-politics, I am not a revolutionary and I am certainly not a pessimist. I am against all violence and street riots, I see little sense in violent street protest, I do not agree with hacking computer networks (whether by a government or an outside hacking group). Let me also confirm I do not seek fame and fortune from preparing this book, all I seek is for the people to have a future, a great future, which at the moment is just not possible. There are far more subtle ways to change history than by ousting a sitting government by revolution and protest, changes can be made peacefully, co-operatively and without any bloodshed.

There is not a person on the planet today that is not in real danger from an attack that could occur at any time, which is why we all need to see sense as we are all under threat. Co-operation and acceptance that things must change now is required, along with the courage to stand up and admit "we got it wrong, but we have learned our mistakes and we are putting them right". The consequences of not doing this are akin to signing our lives away and the very future of mankind are the stakes we are gambling with. That future includes EVERYONE on the planet, royalty - politicians – industrialist – clergy – military - ALL the secret service agencies – and all their families, we are all in this mess together, a mess that few have recognised is out of control. For the first time in history we are all equal and united across the world - all under the same threat, Americans – Russians – Chinese – Europeans – Africans – Asians – Arabia – Antipodeans, all facing serious danger and an end so sudden that we would not have a clue it was about to happen. We all need to unify and fight the same cause, super powers and minority countries alike, we all face the self-same threats, we are all fighting to survive by rejecting the power crazed people that endanger the whole human race. The next few years is going to see our nation's leaders in their true light and that is for sure, I doubt that we will be pleased with what we see.

That which follows from hereon will undoubtedly shock many, make many more very angry, some will still not be convinced that the ideas offered are real and as usual there will be those who just accept what is thrown at them without complaint. All that's asked of you is that as you read that you keep an open mind and do not pre-judge anything, then make up your own mind as to what you believe. Please read the entire book through to the end and remember, the book is designed to be a basic level introduction to the subject, I am not out to win any literary awards, my only aim is to get the message across that we have got to change course fast. If I could find a way to yell at full pitch to you I would and what I would yell is "we are all in serious trouble and it is getting worse by the minute, this is being deliberately withheld from you so wake up before it is too late!!!"

"To change now is the only way forward if we truly desire to experience a great future"

We have always known the world has its fair share of problems and imperfections such as greed, aggression, the desire to be top dog etc. We did not know how deep these problems went as truth is hidden from us by the people we mistakenly placed trust in.

US republican congressman Ron Paul (a much respected politician) said "freedom is defined by the ability of citizens to live without government interference". I could not agree more, this is especially so when some governments are ruled by self-interested sinister control freaks that are lost in dilutions of their own self-importance and their souls are being eaten away by a manic desire to increase their influence and power.

Before moving to the next chapter, here is a taste of the sort of thing that is to come: Governments have to lie. It is true, they have no other options than to falsify figures and statistics – which has become known as "massaging figures". Let me explain, governments and their countries depend on investment, mostly from outside of the country. This could be foreign governments buying the other governments debts or investing in projects in the country. Without this investment the country would stagnate and collapse, its future would be very bleak. The last thing a government wants is bad trade figures, high unemployment figures, bad news of any kind on debt etc. this will frighten off investors. The only option is to cover up bad news by "massaging figures" and it is widely accepted that items like unemployment data is heavily reduced and growth figures are heavily increased to produce a more rosy outlook for that country. Most governments do this if they are dependent on outside investment, they do not have any other option as its "lie or die". Next time you see government figures, such as unemployment levels – think back to this paragraph. Another reason governments "massage figures" is that many government payments are tied to the inflation rate of the country, winter payments, pensions etc. can be falsely held down by announced lower inflation rates. Personally I cannot condemn the governments, I condemn the system that requires governments to "stretch the truth" and it is yet another area that needs changing. How do you feel on learning this news?

Let's end this first chapter on an interesting thought, "are there many people that believe the world is in danger?" The answer is a resounding yes. There are many people who believe that disaster is waiting to hit us and have been taking actions to be ready for that time, they have become known as "Doomsday Preppers", those that prepare. Amazon.com has a section in its book sales department devoted to survival guides, how many book titles are advertised on survival? Answer - **50,902**. Satellite television broadcasts a regular program dedicated to the "Doomsday Preppers". There are an estimated 3 million "Preppers" in the USA alone. It seems then that there are many other people who believe that something unpleasant is heading our way, soon.

What if: So!!! one hell of an opening chapter for you, how have you handled all this? Are you sitting there stunned, are you sitting there heavily doubting what you have just read? What if it's all true? What if everything you have just read is not a conspiracy theory or the thoughts of a deranged trouble maker or the words from some anti-government anarchist? What IF it's all true and you are discovering the real world?

Summary

We all face a very uncertain future when we should be looking forward to a glorious chapter in our history, yet we find it impossible to recognise the threats we face and to compound the danger we are extremely unlikely to believe we face a sudden downfall (there's none so blind than those who will not see). The model our world runs on is hopelessly broken and at the moment nobody knows how to fix it. For many the revelations revealed in this book will come as some of the greatest shocks of their lives, the book is not using shock tactics without good reason – we have to wake up, take action and not become overawed. Life has become too busy and our thinking too automated to be able to "think outside of the box". Mankind could disappear from the face of earth and he would do so without suspecting a thing until it is too late, how typical would that be? Nobody is exempt from these threats.

Take a look into the eyes of a child, see their innocence – then consider if you want to dismiss the topic of this book as beyond belief, or do you want to make sure that child has a decent world to grow up in?

"The great future on offer may not come if we do not change today"

two

What Are The Worse Problems We Face?

* * *

**The worst problems we all face are the ones we do not
believe and those we do not know exist - until they hit us!**

It seems unimaginable that mankind is either teetering on the edge
of oblivion and there's hardly a person from within the people that
suspects it and would be able to believe it, or alternatively mankind is
on the edge of the greatest period of positivity in our history .

Virtually nobody has "connected the dots", added 2 + 2 to equal
4, seen through the mist into the future and recognised the twin path
choice as we run blindly into a brick wall. How could we be so foolish? The signs are everywhere, the information is stacked up to the
moon and back and yet we still don't see it – we are on the edge of
destruction of human life as we know it, or staring at a great future.
How could we have arrived at this situation, after all we have incredible minds spread throughout mankind, yet here we are staring an
un-ceremonial finale in the eyes as against a great future? Mankind
has managed to arrive at a destiny with fate in such a short space
of time, we have been evolving from caveman status for millions of
years, and all that progress could be destroyed in something like a
man's normal lifespan unless we act to stop it and choose a near
perfect future on offer.

The more advanced and educated we have become, the more self-destructive our nature has grown, and we have become too smart for our own good. We fail to see the twin path future even though it is quite obvious if we were to stop crashing through life at light speed. The pace of human life has become too fast, were all too busy and we do not stop to catch breath anymore or take time to sit back and assess our actions or to reflect on whether we have got our actions right. While the rest of us have been rushing through life at breakneck speed an undercover group have been crawling at snail's pace in comparison as they took gradual stealthy control of our world, we could not notice their moves as *we were too busy*. We fail to look deep enough at what repercussions can happen from all our rushed actions, we blindly plough on regardless and adopt an attitude of facing problems when they occur. Yet this is a true recipe for disaster and that disaster is ready and waiting to happen. How many times have we heard people say of a problem "where did that come from?" or "I didn't see it coming" or "I didn't believe it", or "it was too late to do anything about it". Far too often we rush through life with only a plan A on our agenda, plan B is not an option even if there was one. Greed has not helped either, the more we have the more we want seems to be the order of the day, greed is not one of the "seven deadly sins" for nothing. Greed is a disease, it infects us and we too often throw caution to the wind once we are in its grips. The pursuit of money and power are definite causes that contribute to the thoughtless attitude permeating society today and contributing to society's ultimate downfall. We can count greed as a major factor contributing to our failing approach to life. Refusing change also counts highly on a failure scale, we are too set in our ways or we are frightened of change as it means we have to try new ways of doing things that we might not be good at, making us look foolish and we do not like looking foolish, do we? But to me the biggest problem of all is our ignorance, the ignorance of the truth. Greed is a major problem, failing to accept change is a major problem and there are numerous other similar problems, *failing to accept truth though lies at the heart of all of these problems, I consider this to be our biggest failing.* If we were to be honest and admit greed is not good or that failing to make changes is detrimental, then we should be able to alter our lives for the better, we don't do this though. Until we drop the refusal to accept truth, we will continue on the slippery path into the abyss. Ignorance of truth has delivered our past, present and future into the hands of the secret rulers of the world, they knew we would not believe they existed as they helped us into that conclusion with their brainwashing and programming, ignorance of the truth has delivered us "like lambs to the slaughter".

Has it ever occurred to you that with all the great minds in our world that mankind should be much further ahead in evolution than we are?, disease and serious illness should be a thing of the past, alternative green energy should be mainstream, wars and fighting should have been assigned to the history books, food shortages and famine should be a thing of the past as should water shortages, worldwide financial stability should have been established, the environment should not be under threat, so why has none of this taken place? Greed is an obvious choice for many reasons as profits are placed higher on corporate and government agendas than people, but what if the pace of evolution has been deliberately held back? would we believe this is possible? the refusal to accept this to be possible is what allows the process to take place and survive. Should we accept that greed is holding progress back, then we just may change our ways. If we look at the law of "cause and effect" we will be able to see that greed and failing to make change are <u>effects</u>, refusing truth is the <u>cause.</u> We would not tolerate greed and failure to change if we understand that they are failings, we in our wisdom cover up this conclusion and refuse to accept that greed and failure to change are detrimental. At the heart of all our problems is the stark realisation that we reject truth when it does not suit us, rejecting truth is the cause of all our negative actions and beliefs. We could not take greedy actions or refuse to make changes if we understood and accept to do so would be wrong. Our politicians, religious leaders, industrialists, bankers and anyone in a position of power would not make the majority of the decisions they do if they were to accept that their actions are based on greed, a fear of change and that they are in the grip of power mania (as well as a myriad of other reasons). To accept that the consequences of their actions and decisions may not benefit anyone but themselves would be to accept truth, which is why they refuse and hide truth. We are all standing perilously close to the edge of a bottomless chasm which mankind can so easily plunge into and 99.9% of people will refuse to believe it, 100% of our politicians would refuse to confirm it and therefore nothing will be done to make the situation stable. As I said earlier in the book "you cannot fight an enemy you cannot see", I am sure you would agree that for mankind to perish due to such a ridiculous scenario would be the worst kind of madness and therefore it should be a fairly simple process to stop this situation playing out. We have to change our direction by admitting to our mistaken beliefs and own up to the principle of "ignorance of the truth" which damages all life.

Let's go off at a tangent here to try and prove the point above: The world is in a mess, man has wrecked our home planet by interfering with Mother Nature, we are polluting the rivers and seas by pumping sewage and effluence into them, we are polluting the land by creating huge landfill areas and filling them with our poisonous refuse, we are cutting down the rain forests at an alarming rate and destroying natural habitats, we are polluting the air with our industrial chimneys belching out all kinds of chemicals into the atmosphere, we are destabilising the earth itself as we sink mine shafts miles down into the earth's crust or scour the surface with open cast mining, we are over working the soil with intensive farming techniques that are causing soil depletion and draining the soil of its growing ability. What will happen when thousands of holes are simultaneously bored into the earth around our world to allow fracking is another major cause for concern. Also at any time there is a war being fought somewhere. We have little respect for human life, racial and religious prejudice is rife, we can send space-craft to the Moon, to Mars and all around the universe, yet we can-not feed the world's population as tens of thousands die each week from starvation. Drink and drugs have become commonplace in the Western World, overdosing turning people into psychotic murderers, a person will brutally attack their partner while under the influence or beat up a neighbor with a baseball bat, people will have drinking glasses smashed in their faces for no good reason. *Yet we call ourselves civilised, we actually believe we are advanced modern people* – that cannot be true when you look at the catalogue of minuses above. What we really are deep down below the surface amounts to savage barbarians who care little for the wellbeing of the planet that supports us and we disrespect the lives of our fellow human beings. While this may offend you to admit to this, facts speak for themselves and yes not everybody takes drugs and drinks too much alcohol or attack our neighbours, but we all let the world's eco systems be treated badly. We ignore the truth, put it to the back of our minds and get on with our lives. So! If we do this to the facts we are aware of, what will we do if we find out that our greatest problems are the ones we do not have a clue exist? Most likely dismiss those as well. We all know, when you keep taking and do not give anything back, or you constantly abuse something, somewhere, sometime "something's got to give". We are rapidly approaching that somewhere, sometime in the world, what will be the first thing "to give way?" who knows. There is no other option available to us than to learn to live differently, without greed, without ego, with truth not lies and deceit, most important we have to learn to live within our means. We will also need to re-learn many of the older "values" we have abandoned that previously served us well, values such as respect for each other and for the environment, good manners, politeness and ….. respect for ourselves. This last point is very important as we are showing plainly that we care little for our own bodies and minds, we push ourselves physically and mentally to the limit with long working hours, fail to take enough rest physically and mentally, we drink too much alcohol, do not take enough exercise and we have adopted a terrible diet full of chemicals, sugar, salt and very little "goodness". It is so true to say that "until we look after ourselves and respect ourselves, we will not respect and look after others". Change always begins within ourselves, we cannot change the world or other people while we stay the same, and we have to become the change we want to see in others. We have to set the good example we want others to accept, there is too much of the attitude of "do what I say, not what I do" in our world today, which is a very poor example to set anyone. This next comment is very important, please read this sentence several times until you have it imprinted into your mind – WE MUST BECOME THE CHANGE WE WANT TO SEE IN OTHERS.

Do you still consider we are civilised beings? Or are you seeing that we bury truth for our own convenience and to satisfy our conscience? Can you see that our principles are mis-guided when we send exploration craft around the cosmos while allowing millions to starve to death on our own planet in places like Africa? Our priorities are hopelessly wrong, our beliefs are tainted and our attitude to suffering is appalling when we ignore the truth that it is happening, which is unforgivable. Will you accept this or will you simply turn the page over and forget what has been said? which amounts to taking the easy option. Having put many similar questions as these to many people I know that the most likely reply would be "what can I do, I am nobody, I can't change anything", this is not a true reply, it amounts to a "get out clause", an "I can't be bothered clause" or "it's not my problem clause". When the world descends into chaos, all those "get out clauses" will sit very heavy on the shoulders of mankind. If all this sounds too ridiculous to believe, consider this, if I am right and life as we know it is in danger, isn't it time to wake up to the truth and put skepticism aside? Or will we wait until the air we breathe is unfit to sustain life, the seas so poisoned that all life within it is killed or the great rainforests have all been cut down?

Returning to the original text: What are your thoughts on this idea? That we could all "meet our maker" in the near future and it could be avoided by simply admitting to the truth of our actions which have placed us on the verge of destruction. To accept this idea would be the clear signal to our leaders and policy makers that we demand to change and take a safer more sensible direction, now. Such a small step to take, accept truth, but in doing so we can change the world and pull back from the brink of an inglorious ending.

How we came to face an inglorious end and what the actual dangers are that could be the instruments of our demise will be covered in later chapters, for this moment we have to be clear in our minds that though it took us a single lifetime to put ourselves on the brink, to pull back from the edge would take a much shorter period of time, perhaps measured in months. The complete re-designing of how we run humanity will naturally need longer; the process of stopping our fall into the chasm will be surprisingly quick once we accept all our many serious failings. To many, this will appear too easy that all we have to do is accept we have denied truth and can change our whole destiny. This is an understandable reaction, but sometimes it only takes a small shift in thinking and belief to alter our future.

During 2012 a significant landmark was achieved, world population reached seven billion. That is seven billion people all destined to live false lives, with no real freewill, no real freedom of choice, no control over their own lives, hardly a person in seven billion that will live the life they deserve. What we have is seven billion people living the life of slaves to a fraudulent system that so far has remained impossible to detect due to its subtlety and our loss of interest in taking our lives forward. If we were a spacecraft, we could say that we have "dropped out of warp drive", lost forward momentum and we are drifting in space aimlessly. We can resume the forward motion of warp drive thrust if we recognise that we have allowed ourselves to lose our grip on life and that we are drifting without a destination. I had to face the realisation that we are in deep trouble, I had to accept that I had been fooled along with everyone else and I had to accept that unless I took action I too would suffer. This was not a difficult task, it took a lot of soul searching as I began to see what is going on and how foolish I had been, that is though all it took, the acceptance I had been wrong and that the world is not the place we all believe it to be. Is that such a tough thing to do, to accept that our lives are not what they appear, and to agree we have all been made fools of and that the way back to a more rewarding life path is to make changes? but most important of all is to accept truth even when it goes against our personal beliefs.

None of the changes suggested in this book are difficult to achieve if we are honest with ourselves, that is why accepting truth is the first step we must take, all else will slot smoothly into place once we begin to allow truth its rightful place in our lives.

<u>Summary</u>

Our biggest problems are the ones we do not know exist as we cannot defend against something we do not know and we cannot see. Excessive greed and failure to make changes are major problems in life, they are though effects and not cause, failure to believe truth is the cause and until we accept truth we will continue on the path to destruction. Failure to accept the truth is the major problem we face, yet we are unaware of that failing and how it is causing us to endanger life.

three

Life Delivers A Double Dose Of Reality

* * *

Two life altering incidents hit me in quick succession and thankfully my life has never been the same again. These two incidents opened up my eyes to the truth about life and the fraud of life.

Middle aged and still a "lifelong teenager", a true Peter Pan character that did not want to let go of youthful endeavors. My week revolved around playing pub league darts, weekend football and "clubbing" at disco´s, show me a dance floor and I would be on it all night until the music stopped. I was still holidaying in the top European dance hotspots like Ibiza, Crete or flying to Amsterdam for long weekends. Then whammy number one stepped in and changed all that. A new partner introduced me to a new life which I took to like a duck to water as I became deeply immersed in the world of spiritualists, psychic mediums, alternative healers, I began mixing with top psychics, but the biggest shock was to discover that I myself am a natural clairvoyant and always had been. What a shock! From Peter Pan to "Insight Man" in no time at all. Though I had lived what I believed was an entertaining life of sport and clubbing, this new direction gave me much more fulfillment and I soon realised I had wasted most of my life so far, forty years wasted! Can you imagine that you too could have wasted great swathes of your life as you allowed yourself to be swept along by the tide of what life presents you and that you just may have a hidden talent?

When I sat down to consider that I had wasted so much of my life I was able to recognise that I had used the previously unidentified talent of clairvoyance often, but not to its full potential and without realising what it was. I recognised moments of deep "knowing" things in advance or tuning into people's emotions that were around me was commonplace. Looking into my life I could recall that frequently I had a knowing inside of me of how proposed actions and plans would work out well in advance of those plans being put into practice. This was not always welcomed by the people putting forward the plans as I appeared to be casting doubt on their plans, on one occasion I was bawled out during a managers meeting as I had asked sensibly if there was a backup plan for a proposed action. The actual comment aimed at me was "I am fed up with your negativity, if you don't have something positive to say, don´t say anything". Well that plan and that company fell flat on its face just as I had told everyone it would years in advance. But I was not me being negative, I just "knew" the plan and the changes would not work. You may or may not believe in fate, but when I lost my job with this company, as I predicted, it was the greatest favour I have ever received in my life so far as I was able to "spread my wings and fly". As so often happens, "good things come from bad", which should give you hope as we face so much in the way of bad news at present. My ability to sense how a plan or situation would work out has intensified with experience. Naturally I began to develop my new found clairvoyant abilities, first I trained with an excellent Scottish teacher named Fiona Smith, who also introduced me to the world renowned psychic college in Stansted England, The Sir Arthur Findley College. After a number of residential courses at the college I began to teach an expanded version of the subject myself and over a number of years I taught several hundred people on the fundamentals of psychic awareness, self-improvement, positive thinking, the law of attraction, Karma, personal development and much more. Throughout this period of time I kept up my life long quest to learn from new research, for seven days a week and up to twelve a day hours a day I scoured the Internet, read educational books, attended lectures and I started to use a new service to me, webinars. A webinar is a live Internet interview with an expert in a particular field of knowledge, the interview lasting around ninety minutes. At one point I was listening in to three webinars a day, taking down pages and pages of notes as I listened, mainly new information I had not learned of before. My eyes were being opened to many new theories and facts about life that the average person just does not get the opportunity to discover (unless they knew about webinars). The ideas and information given out were fresh, innovative and challenged many of our established "imposed beliefs", they also made complete sense. As I learned more and combined the new learning with my own clairvoyant senses, a new clearer understanding began to form within me about life in general, it was not an understanding I liked the look of. This led me to research deeper still into what I had found and sadly my worst fears were confirmed, millions of pages of information and data are freely available to substantiate my suspicions, pages I will introduce you the reader to as we go along. Another incredible process started to take place at this time as more and more people dropped into my life to reveal information to me that was previously not available. People I had known for years suddenly offered me introductions to insights about the world – people I had never known before started to offer insights – books I read gave me insights – websites "appeared" from nowhere that gave me insights – I started to be given access to financial websites that taught me about the economies of the world. Day after day I was receiving more and more data and information until I reached the point that I had to sit down and decide which sources of information to keep coming and which to stop. I know there is no such thing as coincidence, I was meant to have the information, and it was just amazing how the access to the information cropped up from all sorts of places. Some of the sources of information were extreme in their message giving and stretched my powers of belief, but then we all need extremes to stretch us which helps us to form our own opinions. Throughout the receiving of these sources of information there would always be a common thread tying them together, they had connecting themes which were easy to see. These common threads though were also extremely worrying as they showed up as they spelt out a different view of life than we all accept to be our way of life.

One question started to really bother me "why is nobody reporting anything about the serious problems of the world?" The answer to that one is actually a part of the problem; it is all being hidden from us by the people who have rigged the whole system in their favour. Hiding truth, concealing what is going on is very easy if you either own or control all the various news reporting agencies such as TV & radio news and daily newspapers, as hard as that may seem to be to believe (ignorance of truth), it is true, as many books, on-line videos, search engine results will inform you. It will shock reporters and news program presenters to discover that their work is heavily controlled propaganda, biased and a great many news items that should be broadcast are withheld by their superiors.

Whammy number two therefore is the realisation that the world is not the place we think it is (at all) and that life as we know it can be destroyed at any moment in time.

Returning to my newly discovered clairvoyance, clairvoyance is not fortune telling or forecasting the future, I do not claim to be a Nostradamus or able to predict lottery numbers or horse racing results. The definition of clairvoyance is "clear seeing". I gather the facts and I am able to see and sense the likely outcome of an action or plan by looking at the direction something is heading, mixed with details of the plan, I mull over the possible outcomes of the movement and "sense" the end result. This is not crystal ball reading or anything like that, no misty apparitions forming from behind a curtain or tarot card reading, nothing closely linked to the impression of a person going into trancelike states. I do not wear stars or pentacles around my neck, no flowing robes, no mystical tattoos and I do not give psychic readings. My "abilities" are considerably boring in comparison to the aforementioned; I search for data, look at the likely outcome of an action and "sense" the end result, which is hardly wizardry in anyone's eyes, it has been though surprisingly accurate! Something interesting I uncovered while researching is that throughout the world there are more and more people "waking up" in a similar way to the realisation that they too have hidden abilities such as clairvoyance and that the world is not the place they believed it to be. My surprising "double whammy" is therefore quite a common awakening.

<u>Recommendation</u> The subject of webinars was mentioned in this chapter, to find out more about this highly enlightening subject please look up "New Wealth Revolution" hosted by Darius Barazandeh, which is in my opinion the best of the webinars available. The webinars run for about a three month period, so you would most likely need to register your interest and wait for the new season to start.

four

How Did We Get In Such A Mess?

* * *

How did we get in such a mess? we drifted into it as we sleepwalk our way through life, blissfully unaware what we were doing and where we were headed, like a boat that has lost its moorings we drifted with the stream just as everybody else has/does. Later in the book you will discover that we were helped along in our drifting by an unseen secret organisation.

Complacency and over confidence, two of mankind's failings, as the saying goes "you never know what you got until it's gone" and as always we find out when it is too late to do anything about our problems. Why do we find it so difficult to believe that because something is running smoothly, it can go wrong? We move through life without thinking of what tomorrow may bring and that maybe tomorrow our lives could crash around us. The financial crash of 2007-08 being a perfect example, property values were sky-rocketing and wherever people gathered they were loudly boasting how much their home value had shot up in a month. Homeowners borrowed more money against the increased value of their home, never for one minute considering the fact that property values can plunge faster than they can climb. All we could see in our wisdom was rising values, we became intoxicated with our new found wealth and we spent our new money – which of course we did not really have. When the inevitable crash took place, we were hit hard and found ourselves up the proverbial creek without a paddle, we had allowed ourselves to drift into a situation that we should have seen coming. We are all guilty of making this misjudgment, we are all too trusting, too complacent, too busy in our lives to see what is going on around us – until it is too late, we sleepwalk. We have allowed our lives to drift as we believe nothing can do us any serious harm, we believe we will always survive, we believe that mankind is here on earth forever and never give a thought that one day that might not be true. In fact, even after reading the last comment, most people will not change their attitude and it will take something such as a major disaster or war to snap them out of their dream state. We have allowed our freedom of choice, our freewill, our control over our own lives, our present and future to be taken away from us and we don't have a clue it has been filtered away as we aimlessly drifted (if that has confused you, all will be revealed). Just because we have always done certain things all of our lives does not mean we will not have those things taken away from us, nothing is permanent and we should all remember that, often.

Our free lives ended at about age three, which is the time that the first of our "free life robbers" began to steal our free lives from us, these free life thieves being our parents. Our parents are the first in a long line of people who *shape our lives for us*, they believe they are doing this for the right reasons, unfortunately they are misguided in their intentions. Our parents start the process of placing strong boundaries around us which we must stay within for the rest of our lives – "you must do this, do that, behave this way, dress this way, eat this way, play this way, learn this way, not make too much noise, go to sleep at this time, get up out of bed at this time" etc. etc. After this initial home-spun "programming", we are handed over to the education system, here the rules and restrictions are delivered thick and fast – "you must do this, do that etc." Also about this time we start to be programmed by laws and law keepers (police and judicial services), we learn to obey and conform to laws that run society, equating to more programming. Wherever we go and whatever we do, there are rules and laws we must adhere to, go to a shop and we must obey their rules or we do not get served, go to the cinema, the zoo, a swimming pool, ride a bicycle, play sport, own a house and its rules, laws, must do this, must do that. Our workplace carries all sorts of rules and regulations, you will start work at such and such a time, have a break at such and such a time, leave work at such and such a time. Go to a restaurant to eat and not only are there rules to meet, you can only choose to eat what the restaurant is prepared to cook for you on their menu, so your choice is not your choice, you eat what they are prepared to serve you. Should you dare to be different in life, you will meet with strong disapproval from just about everyone you meet and be accused of being a trouble maker or weird! Punk rockers being a perfect example, their part shaven heads and spikey hair brought derision and disgust as they were daring to be different and people are uncomfortable with anything that does not fit "the norm". Our friends, our relatives, our workmates, our neighbours, people in the street, will all shun us if we dare to challenge the accepted "norm" and be different. Who is taking away your freedom, who is taking away your freewill? It is not just your parents/friends/workmates/neighbors, it is EVERYBODY. Who makes us slaves to a system that removes our birthrights? EVERYBODY. You do it to the people you know and meet by rejecting them if they do not fit into your programmed "norm" and they do it to you. We are robbing each other and you are doing this as well to everybody you meet, we are all caught up in this malicious game where we must all conform and fit into an accepted formula or be accused of being different and risk the threat of being made an outcast. Whichever way you look at it, you have no freedom of choice and like everyone else you allowed this to happen as you drifted through life instead of taking a grip of life and "saying no! I am in charge of my own life". You, me, everyone, we gave away our lives, or to be precise, we allowed it to be stolen from us. Each day new laws are forced upon us and our money is taken away by ever more taxes or eroded by inflation, our control over our own lives grows smaller all the time and we continue to drift as it happens. We blame the politicians, we blame the police, we blame everyone else, it is ourselves though that is the real cause of our downfall as we have kept our eyes closed for too long at what is going on around us – we drift, we sleepwalk.

Why do we drift into situations we would not choose to enter? Life as stated is a made up by a long process of being programmed and brainwashed, laws & rules – expected behavior – expected dress codes – parental control etc. Deep down within us there lies another unexpected reason for our submission to giving away our lives – our brain and our mind!! Already mentioned before is the fact that at around aged three our lives are stolen from us, in fact from our birth to around aged three was the only time we were in control of our own lives. How do you like that idea, that the only time you had control was when you were a near helpless baby? Our brains emit brainwaves of different frequencies depending on what we are doing and how old we are, the brainwaves change if we are using our conscious mind or sub-conscious. From birth to around age two to three we are in the brainwave pattern known as Delta, this equates to our lowest brain-wave pattern of only 0.5 to 4 cycles a second, adults experiencing deep sleep have lowered brainwave patterns of Delta. From age two to six our brainwaves step up a gear to between 4 to 8 cycles per second, this is known as Theta and at Theta we begin to automatically accept outside influences on our thinking, we learn to do what we are told – *our parents and early life school teachers start us on our long road to life programming.* This part of our lives is the most formative period of our whole lives, should we suffer bad experiences at this time such as the death of someone close or our parents separating, it will affect the rest of our lives. For a short period of our lives we were in charge, we were "the boss" – we cried for food and our parents responded, we cried for a nappy change and our parents responded, we cried because we were ill and our parents responded, anything we demanded, we got. From here on in, it's all downhill as the life programming swings into overdrive and our say on how our lives are run is snatched away. Our brain accepts the programming as it knows nothing else, at this early stage in life our brain accepts this as normal to "do as we are told", unfortunately the brain also accepts that this is how life works and never changes that mindset, freewill – freedom of choice, gone and never to return.

The last paragraph was a much shortened explanation on a very interesting subject area, I would highly recommend at this point that for a detailed explanation of this and related subjects that you read an enlightening book "Breaking the Habit of Being Yourself" by Dr. Joe Dispenza. Dr. Joe is a bestselling author and one of the presenters in the series of DVD's "What the Bleep and Down the Rabbit Hole" which explains such things as quantum physics. If you have the chance to attend one of his lectures then I strongly recommend you do it. The title above is a first rate book that will explain many of life's mysteries to you, published by Hay House and available from the Amazon.com on-line services. Also, search on the Internet for explanations of brain waves and their effects on us.

Our parents and our early life school teachers began to prepare us for life (that is life as they see it and how they have experienced it), the life being prepared for us is therefore based on the beliefs of our parents and school teachers, who is to say that those beliefs are correct? What if those imposed beliefs are wrong or outdated and no longer workable? We do not know if the programming is wrong or outdated, we are in the Theta state, we accept whatever is presented to us. The worrying thing is that our parents were programmed by their parents and school teachers, it's all second hand beliefs (worse still is that these beliefs have been handed down from generation to genera-tion and could be third – fourth hand or more). If our parents had a rough life, a life of poverty, a life of mistreatment, do they make good role models for us? Are you setting a good example to your children, or are you continuing the programming you received from your par-ents? Did your parents often say to you that "money doesn't grow on trees you know"? do you repeat this to your children? Can you imagine the modeling I received from my father, he had to start working at aged twelve down a coal mine, walking several miles on foot to get to the mine. He worked a long shift and then walked home again and for his efforts he had to hand over his meager earnings to his father at the end of the week, earnings spent by his father in the local bar. What sort of a role model do you think my grandfather made? What sort of role model do you think my father made to me after suffering this terrible tortured early life?

We have drifted into the mess we find ourselves in, too complacent – to smug to believe we have got it wrong – too blind to the facts that are right there in front of us and too apathetic of life. We crumble when confronted with major problems as we are not programmed to deal with anything that is outside of our programming, we just do not know how to respond as it's not in our personal programmed hard drive. This lifetime of programming suits nobody other than those who seek to control us and we blindly accept the programming because!!! *we have been programmed to do so!* This is why we reject truth that goes against our beliefs, beliefs that have been programmed into us from as early as age three. Challenge a person's beliefs and you challenge their life, their reason for being here, holding a belief is good, just be sure that the belief is based on fact and is a good belief to hold on to. Only defend a belief when you know it is a belief based in truth. Be wary of beliefs that are imposed on you by others, they may be wrong – they may be purposely misleading you, make up your own mind after you have investigated what is being proposed, just as I recommend you check out what is being suggested in this book.

We may see a very different world if our leaders were to check on their beliefs and accept that they reject truth if it goes against their personal beliefs.

Summary

We find ourselves in the mess we are in because we have drifted aimlessly into it, we never challenged anything because we have been heavily programmed all our lives to accept what we are told to do, to obey. When we accept we have drifted unknowingly, then we can correct this problem easily and start to live the life we would choose for ourselves.

THE MOST IMPORTANT BOOK EVER WRITTEN

WRITTEN

Part Two

The reality of pathway two and why we need to step off of it NOW

five

So Much Deceit, Yet So Much To Gain,

Where To Begin?

* * *

Part two of the book could have begun with any of six or seven different interesting and contentious subjects, finally I settled for something of complete importance, to try and prove to and convince the reader that what follows is more than a possibility and not conspiracy theory. Everything in this chapter is very acceptable to believe as it is based on man's previous history – history as we all know is a detailed record of past facts, actions and more disturbing, has a habit of repeating itself. Part two of the book details the life planned for us without us having a say on the matter, it is pathway two and you are not going to like it. If you already decided that you much prefer the switch to pathway one, part two of the book will confirm what a great decision that is.

Man's wickedness knows no bounds

When you first started to read this book you would surely have been disturbed and found it almost impossible to believe that mankind faces either total, or close to total wipeout and that this fate would be delivered by man himself. As discussed in part one of the book, people are drifting through life on virtual auto-pilot and everything in life for them has become very mundane, boring, one day is just like any other. This shows me they are probably also so lost in their mundane lives that they are unaware of the other surprises to come in part two of the book. What you will learn in part two is that man's wickedness knows no bounds, mankind still has a foot entrenched in a very dark past. We believe we have advanced and in many ways we have, we do though have some dark past actions that will not release us. Should you think about man's history you will realise that we are a war-like race, our history is littered with details of wars and fighting. Deep down we are still barbarians, we always have been and always will be and it is this deep held trait that rises up when stimulated by leaders who force us to war. There can be no other conclusion than that we are at our human core still barbarians, just look at recent history for numerous wars, the slaughter of innocent people by terrorists or insane people like the maniac who killed so many teenagers on an island in Norway etc. etc. etc. We still think nothing about cold blooded murder for no good reason, we are barbarians deep down. Keep this "barbarian" thought in your mind as you read part two of the book, it will help you understand why some of the details that follow are very acceptable. When you find yourself doubting that actions to be discussed in later chapters are beyond human possibility, remind yourself we **are** still barbarians deep down.

If you think also of man's aggressive actions in their home countries you will see that we will attack each other for any of many different reasons and this is of course one of the reasons we why we have large police forces. Nobody can escape from the fact that deep down we are an aggressive race who will attack and murder our own countrymen, our neighbours, work colleagues and even our own family. One of the reasons many become aggressive when they have drunk too much alcohol or taken drugs is that drink and drugs awaken our buried barbarian instincts, our brains slip back in time. We can commit terrible atrocities against our fellow men, women and children, we always have and we always will, because we are not as civilised as we like to believe. At all levels and scales of life we display "warrior instincts" with murderous intentions just under the surface, this is what history clearly shows us, whether we like to admit this or not. The rioting, demonstrations and killing taking place around the world today more than confirms this idea, nobody can argue against this conclusion. Look at today's news and see wars all around the globe and see the blood on the streets after demonstrations have erupted into violence. There is not a single sensible person in the world that can truthfully state we are not a race of barbarians, the thirst for blood may be under control, it does though still exist and can flare up on any given signal. You have to see the truth in these statements and then perhaps you will understand that we do face a precarious situation as our leaders are stirring up the buried emotions within us to further their deceitful plans. WW3 is not as far away as we all might imagine and many astute people are warning that we are on the verge of more destruction and desolation. This is one of the dark secrets that pathway two delivers to us and why we need to ditch it as soon as possible.

Of course we do not all venture out to harm and kill someone, the instinct though is not as deeply buried inside of us as we think it is. When this instinct is over shadowed by power insanity from the roll we assume in life, it can rise up to the surface again, as any military action will surely prove. Place a person in a position of power, a position of control, a position of authority and the instinct to "protect", to "conquer" to "rule" will rise up, it's not that far under the surface. People who murder other people have not had this instinct buried deep enough, it rose up and the barbarian inside of them took control. No matter what you believe of yourself, this instinct is inside of you and should someone in authority "push you" to defend yourself or attack others, eventually you would obey. Aggression is inside of us, murderous actions live within and it is just a matter of how deep it lies that will decide if the intentions surface or not. This will appear to many to be something which they could never consider doing, that is because they have never had to face a situation that the warrior instincts inside are needed to be used, to survive! In the right circumstances and under enough pressure our "warrior survival and protection instincts" will surface. Unfortunately the "warrior instincts" are more than obvious in too many of our leaders today and we are sadly approaching a time that could easily see a third world war erupt or serious fighting on a large scale. The only people who can stop this are the people of the world who must rein in their leaders before many millions of innocent people are slaughtered in terrible conditions. We really do not have any bounds to our wickedness and that wickedness is rising to the top fast, only the people can stop this by choosing to leave pathway two of the twin path scenario.

From my research and experience I have uncovered some very disturbing details of unthinkable horrors that man is capable of committing against his fellow man without remorse, details that left me reeling in shock and I had to drop the information I was studying to take a walk to clear my head. What shocked me as much was to realise that basically we have not changed much from our darker days and we are still very capable of handing out some wicked inhumane actions and again, for no good reason. For us to doubt that the dark deeds and negative actions being suggested in this book are impossible is to accept and give our go ahead for them to take place (ignorance of the truth). This is why I have started out in section two to look at history and remind the reader to the depths man can sink and the wickedness man is very capable of inflicting on innocent people.

It is very probable that you like me will be disgusted at actions that are taken in our name by our governments that is killing innocent people each and every day, actions you are unaware of but will learn of later. As we look at man's past dark history let me suggest to you that this last comment is the proof that nothing has changed that much, a repetition of such dismal past acts is not as difficult to imagine as you may at first think. History informs us that in the past man had no worries about wiping out his fellow man in any quantity and by any means, to this day nothing has changed even if we think it has. World War one resulted in the loss of life of around twenty million lives, eight million soldiers and twelve million civilians which took place less than a century ago. Twenty million people dying in terrible conditions and for what? We learned nothing as world war two followed in just thirty years. World War two casualties are estimated at an incredible sixty million and again more civilians perished than soldiers – SIXTY MILLION DIED and again for what? In Cambodia the rebel army led by Pol Pot slaughtered an estimated 1.7 to 2.5 million innocent people, the Bosnian civil war figures are around three hundred thousand. All manner of atrocities were carried out in all these wars, torture and slaughter of innocent people, bombing, shelling, chemical warfare, gassing etc. Consider also that most people only associate The Holocaust with the death of Jewish people and it is true that around six million Jews were killed, there were many others who died at the hands of the Nazis. 3.3 million Soviet POW's – 1.8 million non-Jewish Poles - 220,000 to 270,000 Romani's (gypsies) – 200,000 to 250,000 disabled – 5000 to 15,000 homosexuals – 2500 to 5000 Jehovah's Witnesses, the figure of total fatalities is often given at eleven million but that figure is regarded as being too low. We should not move on until we consider a very important and stark point – these mass murders and wicked deeds were carried out by what was a modern and supposedly civilised nation and not that long ago. The people of Germany were stirred up by propaganda campaigns and transformed into a nation of war mongering barbarians. The German press and media were used extensively to "whip up patriotism and devotion to their leaders" and that alone was sufficient to turn them from a peaceful nation into a barbaric nation committing terrible acts and atrocities. Do you see that this is something achieved by corrupt and power insane leaders and all they had to do was utilise the media and press to carry out their aims. Today we have the exact same scenario, the press and media is completely controlled and issuing government propaganda and we are on the edge of another massive war (these are too many similarities to the last world war to be ignored). We do not like to believe this, but the conclusions are obvious if we put aside our "ignorance of the truth". Do you want to go to war or do you want a great future? Will you reject pathway two and accept pathway one? Only you stand in the way of the deceitful future and the choice to accept a great future – but will you believe this or choose to disbelieve this? Don't you think we had all better find out what is really going on? We must also see the truth that we are suppressing the barbarian side of our emotions and that this can easily rise to the surface if the right buttons are pushed.

What a lot of people are not familiar with is that former Russian leader Joseph Stalin waged a campaign against the people of his own country that is estimated to have killed as many as sixty million. The upper suggestion was that one hundred million died. While that figure is likely an exaggeration, many millions did suffer under his repression. Hitler / Stalin / Pol Pot/ Bosnia etc. all slaying millions and millions of enemies and *their own people*, don't you find that difficult to imagine that leaders would order the mass murders of their own people? Do you think that this does not continue today? Sadly it does and each and every day, and do you think that a major nation could not do something like this today?

Stalin is noted for his refusal to give mercy to his prisoners and it is believed he oversaw the total death of thirty million prisoners of war from various nations. Stalin is infamous for killing political opponents and sending huge numbers of innocent people to concentration camps in Siberia. Many historians believe that Stalin was following the policies of his predecessor Lenin who used fear as his control system over the people of the Soviet Union, Lenin is quoted as saying "I prefer to rule my people with fear than conviction". Stalin certainly ruled by fear, during the 1930's he sought to remove all barriers to his complete and total power. He created the Central Purge Commission which publicly investigated and tried members of the Communist Party for treason, between 1933 and 1934 1,140,000 members were expelled or shot, including 25 per cent of the army officer corps. 139 members of the Central committee were arrested and 98 were shot. All defendants were forced to confess publicly, and then were shot. Stalin accepted no resistance during his reign of oppression and reportedly ordered the killing of as many as three million of his own peasant farmers for rebelling against his forced seizure of their land.

We probably find all these details unimaginable, it is though the way many died that we should be most shocked by, gassing in concentration camps, firing squads, bombing, land mines, chemical warfare. How can man do something like this? to deliberately wipe out fellow humans simply because they are of a different religion, different nationality or have different principles. Do you think this does not carry on today, the wiping out of innocent people for no better reason than that they believe in a different God? or that those people being murdered might cut off oil supplies to the western world? People are dying every day and in the same type of way that it has always been, only now by more sophisticated weaponry, nothing has changed and the only difference is the scale of deaths is lower – (at present). The truth has to be faced though, we are still killing each other for no good reason and nothing has changed. Could we see a war or military action that could dwarf even some of these excessively high fatalities? Undoubtedly and sadly, yes, as I will describe to you later. Are we capable of carrying out a barbaric mass murder of hundreds of millions of innocent people at once? Absolutely yes! We are still trapped in the mentality of the Dark Ages whether we like to admit that or not. Please realise we are not as far down the road of civilisation as we like to believe and the mass murder of hundreds of millions of people is no idle threat and that includes you. We choose to turn a blind eye today as women and children are hacked to death by machete wielding rebels in parts of Africa, how can turning our backs on this awful suffering be the actions of a reputed modern civilisation? This becomes especially wicked when we send the might of a fully equipped armed force into areas that threaten our oil supplies such as Iraq while ignoring human suffering elsewhere. There lies our true issue of importance, **money**, people can die horrible deaths as they are sliced up alive, but do not threaten our oil supply or we will attack you with everything we have! Money obviously counts more than freedom and life.

Can I at this point recommend a truly exceptional book to all those who enjoy a strong read, this book is better than any paperback thriller I have read, full of factual details and it is more shocking than any horror book or movie I have ever sat through. It is this book that I had to put down on many occasions to take a walk to clear my mind of what I had just read due to its shocking details. This book is head high above any other I have read and will leave you in no doubt whatsoever that man is capable of many hideous actions against his fellow man. This book goes into graphic details of the horror of what must be man's worst treatment of his fellow man during what is known as The Dark Ages. This book, The Master Game by authors Graham Hancock and Robert Bauval is subtitled "unmasking the secret rulers of the world" and covers many other subjects beside the wickedness of The Dark Ages. Should you read this book you will no doubt have a different opinion of mankind than you possess now, you will see the world in a very different light - its true light. Should you want to understand the truth about man and his total disregard for life, this is the book. If you enjoy reading a good thriller, order this now, but if you have a weak stomach, this is not for you. Packed full of data, where, when, who, how and what, you will not be left in any confusion.

We think nothing about murdering enemies during warfare, we are simply told that it is "kill or be killed", "it´s us or them", but who says that is true? Why are we fighting in the first place? Who made us pick up our weapons and trudge off to war? Answer, our leaders. Would a bank clerk, a farmer, a butcher or a builder prefer to be at home with their family or sitting in a bomb crater as bullets and shells whistle past their heads? The millions who lost their lives in the trenches of world war one, living in nightmare conditions, fearing bullets and mustard gas, where would they have rather been? Next time you are sitting in your local restaurant, bar or laying in the sun, think about where you could be – dodging land mines, air attacks, artillery shells etc. which would you prefer to be doing? Our leaders "pick a fight", our leaders send us to the battle front, our leaders sit at home as the fighting is waged and we the people die. Let us be very clear here – the shop workers – factory workers – office workers – builders – cleaners – farmers etc. would not start a war, they do not want to go to war and they most likely hate the whole idea of war – our leaders force or trick us to go to war – we would never choose to go to war ourselves. War is man's worst invention, nobody wins, one side merely loses less than the other, so why do we keep doing it? because our leaders say so. We hack each other to death, stab each other with bayonets, roast each other alive with flame throwers, blow each other up with grenades, land mines, artillery, rockets and bombs, we slit each other's throats, break necks with our hands, why? because deep down we are still tribal barbarians and we do as the tribal elders tell us to, **we are still attached to dark ages**. When the suggestions are put forward later that we could destroy hundreds of millions of lives in one easy action, do not dispel the idea, it is real, very real.

Think on this, If our leaders used the age old trick of telling us that a marauding army was headed our way that would abduct your wife, rape your children and murder you, you would also fight to the death and run them through with a bayonet, blast them with a flame thrower etc. That's leadership for you and we dutifully obey.

History is crammed full with details of wars and fighting, The Conquistadores who wiped out the Inca Indians, early settlers who murdered Native American Indians, The Knights of The Templar crusades against Moslems, The Battle of Trafalgar etc. etc. What makes anyone believe we are past all of this behavior? The Bosnian War, The Falklands war, the war in Iraq and Afghanistan, the wars in Ethiopia/ DR Congo, the Middle East struggles are all "modern era" wars and some continue to this day, so why would we believe that WW3 is impossible or that a whole nation the size of the USA or Russia or Europe or the UK could not be wiped out in a swift action that nobody saw coming? Remember, when Japan entered the second world war they did so from a surprise attack on Pearl Harbour, who says that another nation or terrorist organisation could not use a secret attack to achieve mass destruction on an unprecedented scale against one of the countries mentioned above? Don't forget, "when your guard is down – you will get hit".

We do not believe we could be attacked, we do not believe a whole nation could be wiped out at once and that is down to our habitual rejection of truth, our politicians would never inform us it is possible, yet as I will soon show you, the threat is so very real. Something we are known for is to be "caught with our pants down", reacting when it is too late, undone by surprise, the stakes are too high this time to be caught out, it is time to wake up. All of this will seem a million miles away as you walk through your supermarket or your local shopping street, it will appear to be a load of hot air as you sit and enjoy a drink in your local bar or you watch TV at home. The millions who died in world wars one and two thought like that as well, that war would not break out, that they could not be facing bombing of their own home – it happened and it can happen again and you need to realise this.

What if? How hard was it to accept that we all are still barbarians deep down? That put into a situation that requires aggressive response or misled by our leaders propaganda that we will attack and seek to kill supposed enemies? What if this is true, even though we will not admit this?

<u>Summary</u>

Though we do not like to admit such details, man is more than capable of some hideous actions that go far beyond the idea that we are civilised, modern thinking and peaceful beings. We should not write off the possibility that a whole nation could be erased by an out-side attacker in one action. Should this happen we should not be sur-prised as history tells us that "getting caught cold" is a failing we have always had. We believe we are a modern civilised race, in truth we are still as barbaric as we ever have been, no extent of "ignorance of the truth" can hide this fact, frighteningly we now have the power to take our "barbarism" to new un-paralleled levels – as the next chapter will explain.

six

Secret Weapons Primed And Ready To Destroy Us, Now

* * *

This will most likely be a very unsettling and disturbing chapter to you when you learn for yourself that our governments are covering up information that true weapons of mass destruction are not only fact, they are primed and ready to be used. This is one of the most important chapters in the book as it clearly exposes man's modern day barbarism, it will aptly show you that everything in the book is acceptable reality. Secret weapons that can wipe out a whole nation in one move exist, super power countries have them, they are weapons straight out of a child's science fiction comic book. This chapter will show you the deceit that is performed on us all and will demonstrate that the subjects in this book are based in fact. Again I could have chosen any of a number of subjects to cover in this chapter, my decision to cover secret weapons at this point was based on the fact that these weapons are already in position, primed and could be used as early as NOW to destroy us (that comment is as close to reality as I can make it). That's right, today could see one of these secret weapons deployed and just as I have tried to force my point home so frequently I remind you again, **we would not expect a thing – we would not believe it is possible** - we are oblivious that such weaponry is primed with the potential to destroy us, or our reaction would be to shrug our shoulders and say "what can I do about it?".

There are many secret weapons of many different types, germ warfare, chemical warfare, nuclear warfare, high intensity energy beam weapons and a myriad of aircraft having special attack equipment. Here we will look at two weapons that although they are secret to the vast majority of people, they are reported on the Internet if you know how to search and if you have an idea they exist. Both weapons are deadly and capable of wiping out a whole nation with one easy action, both are true weapons of mass destruction. Governments cannot deny the weaponry exists as the Internet carries too much detailed information and photo's about these terrible weapons as whistle blowers uncover the secrets we're not meant to know. The general public is mostly unaware of these weapons as news reporting agencies are under strict control and prevented from reporting that the weapons exist, but the Internet is another case and reporting on the net is much more free and open.

Nuclear armaments have been around for a long time, nuclear weapons are regarded primarily as deterrents that have stopped one Super Power from starting a war against another Super Power. The theory behind a nuclear deterrent being that, "if you fire nuclear warheads at us, we will fire our nuclear warheads at you", destroying both sides and so it is prevented from taking place. The great fear we have in this day and age is that nuclear weapons would fall into the hands of the wrong people who would use them against a Super Power and thus start a war that nobody can win. It is true that detonating a nuclear device in a city would bring devastation and heavy casualties by the millions, there is a far greater fear though that a nuclear device detonated in the right place would kill hundreds of millions. That place is in the air, miles above a country and the blast would not be the cause of the massive loss of life or the resulting radiation. A nuclear detonation high above a country would leave buildings and infrastructure untouched as would the people at first, what happens next though is terrifying, goes beyond human belief and enters into the horrors of Armageddon.

By setting off a nuclear device high above the land, a massive Electro Magnetic Field would be generated and released which would send a wave of destruction raining down to the countries below. This high frequency EMF wave would instantly fry and burn out all electrical equipment – circuits – wiring – electric supplies. Anything with an electric operating system would be useless. All forms of communication would be burned out, cars/trucks/buses would be useless, there would be no electric supply to anywhere as the national grid system would also have been burned out. There would be no water supply as this needs pumping, no sewerage disposal and shops would be closed meaning no food supplies. Can you imagine this scenario? No communication, No food supplies, No transport other than by foot or bicycle so no food chain supplies, No water supply, No sewerage, No electricity, so no way to cook or keep warm, we would be back to living conditions of pre-Victorian times overnight. It is said that "man is nine missed meals away from anarchy", after that he will become savagely murderous through hunger pains, when he has a family to feed his mindset will become even more desperate. People will kill each other out of desperation and madness driven by acute hunger, they would try to violently steal each other's food to feed themselves and their families. Civilisation will break down faster than you believe it possible. Neighbours will attack and steal from neighbours, driven on by hunger and desperation. One estimate I have seen predicted that in the USA alone, approximately 230 million people could die if a large enough nuclear device was detonated above the land. Buildings and infrastructure would be untouched by the EMF burst. Electricity supplies could not be restored as there would be no way to transport the hundreds of thousands of miles of cables to rewire the grid if trucks are inoperable. It would take an outside force to come to the rescue of a nation doomed by an EMF attack (a foreign army, perhaps a Russian army ?).

Could it happen? Make up your own mind. The weaponry that could do such damage is probably already in place, circling our heads at this moment in the form of nuclear armed satellites sent up into space by super powers as a deterrent, just as missiles were used as deterrents. The old "fire one at me and I will fire one at you" principle. Only this time there is a big difference from those days because those weapons orbiting the planet are controlled by computers and as we should all know by now – any computer can be hacked into. A rogue nation or a terrorist organisation could hack say a Russian satellite over the USA and detonate the nuclear charge, or it could be the other way around, or a satellite orbiting The UK or Europe could be hacked and detonated. All it would take is minutes to override control and press the detonation button. It would also be possible to hack into and launch a missile from its ground based silo carrying a nuclear device that could achieve the same deadly results. We have to ask ourselves "what have we done?" why have we created such potentially destructive weapons? Did the people say to their leaders "go and make weapons of mass destruction?" No, No, No. Was it the people of the countries who drew up plans to build such terrible weapons? No, do the people want such weapons? No, was it our leaders who put these plans into action without telling the people who put them into power? Yes. It all amounts to "power games" and misuse of power, leaders and military chiefs caught up in their own power, using bluff and double bluff against each other without seeing where they have landed, **they have endangered the world, the whole world and its future.** They have taken actions without a suitable plan B, they have taken decisions without exploring the full implications of their actions, they have taken decisions without consulting the people who they represent, so you see whatever level a leader sits at, manager of a company or leader of a nation, the same problems persist - leaders lose control of their senses when too much power is rested upon them. This "oops, I didn't see that coming" situation is one we must work as fast as it is humanly possible to remove before we need a plan B and that is if there is anything left to save after plan A fails.

Me, you, everyone are being kept in the dark about decisions that have been made that directly affect our lives and endanger our safety, these decisions are hidden from us by the very people we put into power to represent our safety. They carry out their plans under a "top secret" approach, concealing their decisions and actions under a cloak of secrecy by using the excuse that the population would suffer mass hysteria if they knew what was going on. If the leaders of the world stopped making such frightening plans in the first place, there would be no need to cover up the potential dangers and the fear of spreading panic to the masses. If nobody created a fearful situation, there would be no fear. But leaders feel the need to "show whose boss" and the military need to play their big boys games and exercise their power and influence, and so it goes on under a veil of secrecy. We the people are "kept out of the loop", totally unaware that our safety is being risked, that our whole way of life is under threat and that our lives, our families, friends, neighbours, workmates lives are also in real danger. How does that make you feel? We all know that there are top secret projects going on and that there always has and always will be, but did we ever think that these top secret projects could easily bring an end to life on earth as we know it? Don't you agree that it is time to rein in our leaders before they commit to ending all life?

Let's now look at the second secret weapon

This one is going to rock your world as much as the first mentioned weapon.

We all must have recognised that the weather across the world has gone haywire, record breaking weather conditions of every kind, drought – record rainfall – plummeting temperatures – polar ice caps melting at record speed – incredible storms and tsunami's etc. We put it all down to global warming, movement of sea currents or air currents, what though if it was all as a result of manipulation by a secret weapon? Okay, you will find this one harder to accept than the previous details, we always say that "man cannot control the weather", what if that's untrue and man has been changing weather patterns for some time? Welcome to H.A.A.R.P. **H**igh Frequency **A**ctive **A**uroral **R**esearch **P**rogram.

Let's start out by directing you first to Amazon.com on-line who have around 200 titles for sale on this subject, You Tube has hundreds of thousands of related on-line videos, Internet search engines have over TWO MILLION related articles. This is a difficult subject to describe, operating experiments with HAARP could prove to be the equivalent of opening Pandora's Box or it could be a way of improving communications and much more. Conspiracy theorists are having a field day with this one, claiming it is a top secret program with many potential serious dangers. They claim that it can induce earthquakes and volcanic eruptions (which may explain why we are seeing so many high level earthquakes) it can destroy aircraft (reputedly up to 500 at once) and incoming missiles, alter weather patterns, destroy communication systems (very handy in a war to be able to disrupt an enemy's communications). The conspiracy theorists blame the Japanese tsunami of 2010 and the Indonesian tsunami on the use of HAARP due to photographic evidence of unusual cloud distortions synonymous of HAARP being seen just prior to these disasters occurring. Whatever the truth, the program is funded by the people via the US navy and air force budgets, so shouldn't the people know the truth, shouldn't they know that HAARP exists? If the USA and Russia both have this capability, as well as other nations, it is hardly a reason to keep them a secret as each side knows the other has this and what it can do. If these systems are a protection as stated, shouldn't the people it is supposed to protect know they are being protected to take away the fear of attack? If there are other reasons for burying the program under secrecy, this goes against the principles of democracy, the people pay the costs, the people elect the politicians and the people should have a say what their money is paying for and what the elected politicians are up to.

How does HAARP work? This is the description that authorities would like us to believe: HAARP is a scientific endeavor aimed at studying the properties of the ionosphere, with particular emphasis on being able to understand and use it to enhance communications and surveillance systems for both civilian and defense purposes. The Ionospheric Research Instrument, a high power transmitter facility operating in the High Frequency range. The IRI will be used to temporarily excite a limited area of the ionosphere for a scientific study.

Put simply, the apparatus will zap the upper atmosphere with a high focused electromagnetic beam that has a range of between 40 to 60 miles above the earth's surface. The extreme high intensity beam targets a section of the ionosphere and heats it up, electromagnetic waves then bounce back onto earth and penetrate everything living, everything solid – that's how powerful it is. A 1990 US government document indicates that the radio frequency power will drive the ionosphere to unnatural activities. The reasons the military give for the need of these experiments are sound, can we though trust military reasons for anything after the debacle of the weapons of mass destruction that Iraq was supposed to possess and was never found? It is claimed that by using this technology it can disable an enemy's complete communications system while allowing the user to use their own systems, which is a very understandable key advantage. Missiles would have their guidance systems knocked out and aircraft could be downed by it, all great defense advantages. Patents for the device state … molecular modifications of the atmosphere can take place so that positive environmental effects can be achieved, for example, ozone, nitrogen, etc. concentrations in the atmosphere could be artificially increased. Which probably means that they can also be decreased? Other patents said they could make "nuclear sized explosions without radiation". The worrying data is the widespread belief is that the device can be easily used as a mass mind altering program which so disturbs the brain that people would be unable to function normally, soldiers unable to think yet alone fight. Going one stage further, it is suggested that the system could be used to target a countries own population to influence public behavior, that's mind control to you and me.

You are recommended to read one of the 195 books Amazon. com have on the subject "Angels Don't Play This HAARP", by Jeanne Manning and Nick Begich. Also read HAARP: The Ultimate Weapon of the Conspiracy (mind control/conspiracy) by Jerry E. Smith.

So why are we playing at being God again? Trying to manipulate the Earth's atmosphere? Supposedly as a defensive measure against foreign enemy's missile attack, what though if our reckless use of something we do not exactly fully understand is potentially more dangerous than an enemy attack? Have we weighed up the pros and cons? Is this a viable proposition? Shouldn't we be using civilised means to remove the threat of attack, like peace talks, instead of endangering the lives of every living thing on the planet? Does any of this make any real sense to anyone? Will man ever grow up and stop playing war games, games that can easily go wrong at any minute? Will we ever learn? HAARP is more than capable of destroying our natural upper atmosphere protection against harmful solar radiation which would cause the sun's rays to fry the earth to a crisp in no time at all – do we really want that? The upper atmosphere is very fragile and if HAARP pierces a large enough hole in the protective sheath keeping harmful solar radiation out, the consequences can only be disastrous, there is no other conclusion. So why do we allow the system to be used?

* while looking at secret weapons on-line, type in "chemtrails" (113 books available on Amazon.com and numerous videos on-line), this is yet another shocker.

Why do we need weapons and their vile potential to kill en-masse if we are a civilised race? why do we need "defense" measures? Isn't the negotiation table a better place to be than an underground concrete bomb shelter? It certainly is to the people of the world who do not have concrete bomb shelters to protect them, but of course it is not the people of the world that make the decisions, it is the people we elect to represent us, so maybe it's time that they took notice of what we want. There are just too many unknowns with these weapons, too many good reasons to stop their use and development. The people, the population, the masses, call them what you will, they are supposed to be the ones these "defense" weapons are in place to defend, has anyone asked us if we want such unstable devices "supposedly" protecting us?

American President Dwight D Eisenhower gave this speech: Every gun that is made, every warship launched, every rocket fired signifies in the final sense a theft from those who hunger and are not fed, those who are cold and not clothed. This world in arms is not spending money alone. It is spending the sweat of the labourers, the genius of its scientists, the hopes of its children. This is not a way of life at all in any true sense. Under clouds of war, it is humanity hanging on a cross of iron.

Which country has the largest and best equipped army the world has ever seen, a "defense" budget that is greater than all the other major countries "defense" budgets added together, has military bases in almost one hundred and fifty countries around the world, spending billions of dollars on the development and manufacture of the two weapons described above and also has 12.3 million people "officially" jobless,17 million people are receiving food stamps as they have no money for food – 1 in 4 people are so poor they cannot afford health insurance, which means they have limited access to medical care such as a doctor/hospital/prescription drugs, government debt has increased from US$5 trillion to US$16.5 trillion since the year 2000? It's of course the USA, the "greatest nation in the world". Doesn't this make a mockery of President Eisenhower's words? Hasn't somebody got their priorities wrong somewhere? The US is the greatest country the world has ever seen without doubt, has its leaders though lost contact with reality, would the American people prefer to spend some of the astronomical "defense" budget on other areas? Do the American people want access to a doctor or another assault rifle to be purchased? Would they rather have a table with food on it or another tank rolling across a desert? Would they rather have a job than cruise missiles being fired in their names? Apart from obvious terrorist organisations, who in their right mind would want to attack the USA? So why does the USA have such massive armed forces? With the huge level of government debt and budget deficits, why continue to support the largest military the world has ever seen? If we were not so over focused on war and defense, the extreme costs of these areas could be spent in much wiser places that would benefit "the people, for the people by the people". Is the USA any different to other countries on this subject? Of course not, they just spend more than everyone else, the principle remains the same. All countries spend far too much on "defense" while their people suffer, if we were all to be more trustworthy and truly civilised we would not need to spend more than a fraction of what we do to remind other people we can defend ourselves. So we arrive back at a re-occurring theme, if we are civilised as we say we are we would not need to channel obscene amounts of funding into "war machines" or "defense".

There is a saying that says "if the only tool you have is a hammer, everything looks like a nail" spending so much money on "defense" looks like a hammer to me

You will see why we do overspend on war machines and defense in chapter eight, I want to make it clear here that I am not at all anti-American, having visited the country a number of times I consider it an amazing country with equally wonderful people, though the direction the government is heading and its aggressive policies do worry me considerably. My greatest fear is that the country will suffer the same fate as other Empires that over spent and over reached, **the world needs a strong vibrant USA,** it must pull back from the brink. Let us all hope that commonsense will prevail sometime soon.

The mind behind HAARP and so much more in the field of energy manipulation etc. is someone that few know much about, he should rightly be as well-known as some of our other brilliant scientists like Albert Einstein. This scientist, Nikola Tesla, I recommend should be searched for on the Internet or via any one of the 1632 books about him available from Amazon.com. He was a genius so ahead of his time and his inventions spurred on many of today's electrical implements. He is also considered the true pioneer and inventor of using radio waves before Marconi. Tesla was truly brilliant and his list of inventions is considerable, you can find details of one of his inventions on line that creates a free supply of electricity enough to power a home that has nothing to do with solar panels or wind turbines. Just imagine that, a simple device that creates free electricity, the question you must now be asking is "why haven't you heard of this?", "why is this device actively hidden by governments?" good questions and the answer is that our leaders do not want us to know of this, I will let you guess why. There are other devices capable of producing free electricity for the home, there are batteries able to power cars for longer runs than we are led to believe, again hidden from us, why? Something that is sure to shock you if you look it up on the Internet is a fusion torch, you will wonder why you not know about this equipment when you learn of its potential?

HAARP has to be taken completely "off line" now and not as its claimed "mothballed", in my opinion it appears the chosen weapon for mass destruction. Should this weapon be decommissioned and taken apart, the world should celebrate on a level that was last witnessed when WW2 ended. This is an evil piece of mechanisation that should only exist in the pages of a child's comic book. HAARP is not a defense weapon as we are lead to believe, it is an offense weapon and it can be turned against the people who unknowingly paid for it.

Please remember that these are physical weapons, one other serious threat that is being spread around the Internet is a growing worry about microbes being introduced to our food and/or water supplies. This would be the easiest of all the methods to kill en-masse, undetectable, easy to administer. There's NO protection on our water and food chains which adds up once again to being unprepared and unwilling to believe such a thing is possible. "Caught with our pants down" and "I didn't believe it could happen" are words we should be printing on our T shirts as it sums us all up so perfectly. When are we going to wake up to truth, to the real world?

What if? How do you feel? You have just learned of subjects that should only be at home in the plot of a sci-fi or disaster movie on a cinema screen and not reality. What if it is true, how do feel now towards our leaders who hide these sort of details?

Summary

Secret weapons abound in many shapes and forms, experimenting with weapons that "bend" nature should worry us all, as should weapons that can wipe out whole nations. We also need to know if these secret weapons can be turned on the population of the people they are "supposed" to protect and "mind bend" the population's senses of reality. If all sides know that these secret weapons exist, they are therefore only a secret being kept from the population, does that seem right to you?

seven

Corrupt From Top To Bottom

* * *

"Power corrupts, absolute power corrupts absolutely"

Rest power on someone's shoulders and watch it change them, slowly at first as they get accustomed to their new found influence, then it will gradually run away with them as the addiction to power eats into them and destroys their very soul. Far too many of our leaders are acting as if they are possessed by evil entities as "Power Insanity" destroys their basic senses of decency, this must be recognised before one of these people destroys our world with their thoughtless and insane actions.

**"Some leaders change their attitude, others sell
their soul, but all change in some way."**

The greater the power a person has bestowed on them, the greater the negative transformation they will likely go through. Try to think of someone you know who had power of any level placed on their shoulders and did not change in some way, it will be difficult. Of course if you were to say to a person who has taken a position of power that they have changed, they would strongly disagree and vehemently defend themselves, such is the strength of deception that power casts over people as they do not realise that they have taken on a new loathsome persona. From a lowly factory floor foreman to the President/Prime Minister of a country, rest power on them and see the changes creep over them. Power will corrupt the most honest of people, decent people become anything but decent, they lie, cheat, misuse their power, take on an air of aloofness and above the people under their charge, they can become traitors to people who were friends and they become attached to the coat tails of their superiors as they seek to cement their position (and plot to overthrow their superiors). Disrespecting and victimising their staff is quite normal as well as refusing to socialise with them. Protectionism is openly practiced as leaders hold back potential understudies who are showing too much promise that could threaten their own position, they will blacken the work of the threatening person. Leaders are friends to nobody and trust nobody, none are allowed too close unless they are superiors. Naturally there are exceptions to the rule and a few people can retain most of their normal attitudes when they rise up the leadership ladder, they are rare, few and far between.

"Trust a leader, trust the devil"

Leadership decisions have put the world in the mess it is today, **which nobody can argue against**, corrupt practices, protectionism, greed, bribery, power insanity, loss of reality brought on by power insanity, decisions made without enough thought for possible error margins, being stubborn and sticking with outdated practices. While too much power and responsibility is rested on the shoulders of one person, there is always going to be the chance that that person will not be able to shoulder that extreme amount of power and responsibility. On the other side of the coin is the fact that too much power is too much pressure to place on one person, too much responsibility rested on them and the person may become ill and/or delusional. A more workable formula has to be established that takes the final decision making away from a single person, making it more democratic and not dictatorial, a system where a group decision is arrived at after careful consideration.

Our world today is on the edge of vast destruction and it is there as result of decisions made by leaders, which leaders are making the major decisions you will soon find out

Think on this: Did a father of a family in Baghdad choose to have his city bombed by cruise missiles and constant aircraft attack night after night. Does a Russian baker want to kill an American butcher – does a North Korean tailor want to shoot a British street cleaner – would a Brazilian librarian want to cut the throat of a Chinese cook? NO, absolutely not, all each wants to do is their job and to go home when they have finished their work. It is our leaders who make the decisions to kill and maim, we either follow them blindly or we are told it is our duty to slay an enemy through campaigns of government propaganda - we would not choose to do this by ourselves. Wars, battles are picked and started by leaders, political and military leaders, the forces under their command have little option other than to obey. Wars are never started by the people of a country, that decision to risk the lives of millions comes from our leaders who mostly have their own agenda and reasons for fighting wars. Who wouldn't rather be sat at home watching TV or eating with their family than crawling along on their stomachs through swamps or ducking for cover from bullets and artillery shelling? How often would we see our political or military leaders crawling through swamps and dodging shells? NEVER. Is there any real purpose in war? Usually it is one side becoming too greedy or seeking ever more power over the other, trying to take by force something the other side has which they want. Worse still is the fact that many wars are fought over religion, one side has different beliefs than the other, how can that be a rightful reason to kill? Isn't religion about "loving thy neighbour as thyself", how can loving your neighbour mean killing them because they have a different belief? Wars over religion, when you think about it, are the worst kind of hypocrisy known to man. Wars over religion have always been fought, are being fought now and will always be fought, so is man a "God loving person" or is he a war monger that will pick a fight for any reason? If we were truly civilised, wouldn't we follow our own beliefs and respect people who have their own alternate beliefs? Do civilised people kill each other because the other person has a different holy book? Well obviously they do if their leaders tell them to kill the other person for having a different view. Personally I would be very happy to see every church – chapel – mosque – synagogue – place of worship full for every service every week and the people attending are allowed to follow whichever beliefs that they want from personal freewill. Is that though something our religious leaders agree with? again obviously not as history is full of details of wars and battles between forces of opposing religious beliefs and of persecution of the masses for not following "the right religion". Did the ordinary believers "pick the fight?" what is it to them if their neighbour has a different belief to their own? As usual it is down to leaders wanting more power and more control.

Many subjects in this book make me angry as we the people are being made complete fools of by the people we trust to represent us and look after our welfare, when you finally see through their mists of deception I am sure you too will get hot under the collar and feel very let down. Normally I am a very calm person, but this area of life makes my blood boil when I realise that many of our trusted past and present leaders are a sinister set of heartless thugs who are responsible for the killing of millions without a second thought. They think nothing of poisoning and blowing up their own countrymen and their families just as long as the action benefits those leaders in their pursuit of more power and influence. Our leaders openly demonstrate they have allowed the buried barbarian trait rise up inside of them. To explain this it would be suitable to take a recent incidence in our dark history which will show perfectly how our leaders behave and act in secrecy. The War in Iraq is so typical of the actions taken by leaders that endanger the people of the world in their power games without a single thought given to the lives of the people. To leaders, the people are "cannon fodder" to be used and abused as they wish. When it looked like Iraq was going to nationalise their oilfields in 1963 the Central Intelligence Agency of the USA instigated what they themselves called their "favourite coup", the head of the CIA in the Middle East is quoted as stating it was a "great victory" by disposing of the ruling government and starting a reign of terror by none other than Saddam Hussein who became the Iraqi top man in 1979. As we all know that relationship turned sour when Saddam raided Kuwait in 1990, and something else we all know is that "you do not bite the hand that feeds you", which Saddam forgot to his peril. Saddam used mustard gas and nerve gas against Iranian soldiers and Kurdish civilians. There were one million casualties in the Iran-Iraq war from both sides. After invading Kuwait, Saddam became the enemy and his country was subjected to tough sanctions which surprise – surprise, only hurt the people of Iraq, the leaders continued to live well while the people starved to death. Iraq was allowed to sell only a fraction of its oil, in return the money had to be used to feed the Iraqi people, this amounted to an allowance for food per person of just $100 a year, which was clearly not enough. The bombing of Iraq from British planes cost the British taxpayer £800 million (what could this massive figure have been better spent on? And how much was the total British outlay in the war?). At one point a reported 6000 Iraqi children were dying every week from being starved and refused medication by the coalition blockade of aid and supplies of food and medicines (anyone still proud of our victory in Iraq?). This is just a small snippet of what happened during the Iraq conflict, what should be considered is this, Saddam Hussein was brought to power, he killed huge numbers of his own people with chemical and biological weapons, he attacked neighboring countries which killed and wounded huge numbers on both sides. He was a tyrant leader who gave no thought to massacring his own people and the people of neighboring countries, he was a leader out of control, overtaken by his power, a barbarian. He became corrupted by power and moved large fortunes of money out of Iraq into his personal private accounts while living in the glorious splendor of his golden palace. The Iraqi people lost out heavily to Saddam, but they also lost out heavily to the leaders of the coalition forces who opposed Saddam, bombings wiping out electrical supplies, water supplies, sewage services - the blockading and withholding of food supplies and medicine supplies which starved half a million Iraqi children to death. The people lost time and again enduring hellish living conditions while leaders fought out their power games, it was the people who lost the most in lives, wealth and freedom. It is always the people who lose the most, which is something that you the reader should never forget. We tend to grow to hate and dislike a people when their leaders commit war crimes and attacks, yet it is not the people who are causing the atrocities, so why take it out on them? Leaders are the problem and not the people, do not hate the Iraqis for what Saddam did in their name. As we know Saddam lost his life in the end, what we should consider is, if Saddam had not become Iraq´s leader, would those millions of lives have been lost, millions of lives of the people. For in depth information of what happened in Iraq (which was not reported by the controlled media), truth that will I am sure worry you as it did me, read the excellent book from John Pilger - The New Rulers of the World. This book is a shocking read as it tells us of the hidden actions taken by governments that we do not have the chance to see normally. Let me warn you that this book will take the cover off of the secrets of all the coalition governments who blockaded and laid siege to Iraq and the depths that they can sink to in the pursuit of power. They are uncovered as causing child deaths on a grand scale, as thoughtless people that caused the deaths of hundreds of thousands of innocent people as they chased their goal of domination. At some point I would not be surprised if charges of war crimes are made against some of these people. I would make every coalition country citizen read John Pilgers book to discover for themselves about the actions taken and the huge number of deaths they're culpable for. I feel personally ashamed of the actions of the British politicians involvement from what I read in the book and feel they defiled and disgraced the name of the nation they were supposed to represent. I believe that many British people will share the disgust at the way their politicians acted towards innocent children, men and women, **all to keep oil supplies flowing**. The Iraqi conflict was a very dishonourable war on behalf of our politicians. Our military forces did their duty bravely and well, they just should not have been there at all. If you want to know how politicians behave in their roles as our representatives – read the book, just be ready for some major shocks.

Food for thought. If a disaster takes place it is blasted across our newspapers front pages, television and radio news will be full of reports, enquiries will be demanded and questions will be asked in parliament. For example, if a boat capsized and twenty adults with ten children drown, there will be massive coverage of the incident with national leaders announcing their sorrow at the loss of lives. Ask yourself this question, " if we make such a splash of news like this – why has nothing ever been said about the deaths of half a million children in Iraq?". Why were the facts hidden by television and radio news, why did newspapers fail to write a word about this horrendous loss of life? Why didn't national leaders read out a statement of regret and sorrow? Why was there no enquiry? Simple answer, as stated already, the press is under control and only releases what our leaders tell it to. Do you need any more proof that our news services are being manipulated and truth is withheld from us all? One child can die at the hands of a brutal murder in our homeland and the full fury of the press is released on the case, yet the death of half a million innocent Iraqi children does not warrant a single word. Are you waking up to the truth and reality of our world yet?

William Pitt the Elder said "unlimited power is apt to corrupt the minds of those who possess it"

The worst atrocities I have ever read about came from the period in man's history that is appropriately labeled "The Dark Ages" that lasted around 700 years and took the lives of an estimated sixty million people (depending on which estimate you read). The Dark Ages were a result of religious leaders fearing loss of power and control of the people, it was not from fear that their religion was being rejected. It was the leaders protecting their own status and not their religion. The "supposed" most holy people on the Earth at that time resorted to organising mass murder and crude torture in order to maintain their iron grip on the people. Horrors were committed on a scale never seen before and never repeated, horrors I cannot bring myself to describe here, such is their scale and intensity. Let me direct you for a second time to an excellent book "The Master Game" by Graham Hancock and Robert Bauval, full of detailed accounts of this terrible period in man's history. Should you read this excellent book, be prepared for many shocks to your system. The Dark Ages are testament to the depths man can sink in his pursuit of power and influence and once again aptly demonstrates that we are not really as civilised as we think we are.

"The word leader is missing three letters at its beginning – mis"

One more reportable issue of the Dark Ages I will briefly relate in my own words, for full details read The Master Game. A terrible army 30,000 strong was raised that more closely resembled something from the film trilogy The Lord of the Rings than a religious crusade, this army had few regular soldiers, most were blood thirsty criminals hired for their frightening brutality. This ragged army of cut throats would travel from village to village, town to town and subject the inhabitants to a terrifying ordeal. Each person of the town/village would be questioned (interrogated) by a representative of the church (the inquisitor) to find out if a travelling member of a breakaway religion had stayed in the village/town. If one of these break-away clergy had been allowed a bed for the night, the hosting family would be thrown on the street with nothing more than the clothes they wore, all possessions and livestock would be confiscated, any business would be taken away. If a person did not admit that one of these travelling clergy had stayed at someone's home in the village/town and this was discovered, they too lost everything and were thrown onto the streets. The fate that awaited those who refused to give up on their new found breakaway religion was to be burned alive (after being tortured), in one village alone 100 people were burned alive at once. Can you imagine the fear that entered the hearts of people when they learned of the approach of this fearsome army of soldiers, murderers, rapists, robbers who would torture and kill without a second thought? This army was raised and paid for by what was meant to be the most religious people on the planet, religious leaders using an iron fist approach to keep its people loyal. This brief example is one of the more pleasant (for want of a better description) episodes from this black period in time. This foul army and all the others that followed for 700 years was not raised by the people of the religion, it was not raised by the church of this religion, *it was raised by the religions leaders* to frighten its own church members into staying loyal. Thank goodness the dark ages stopped with all its severity and inhuman atrocities, though this did not happen until all of the break-away priests were slain. Did the faithful church goers demand that such barbarism be committed in their name? no, it was the church leaders and elders who made the fateful decision to slay and torture so many out of fear of losing power and control, religion and the church had nothing to do with it and should not be blamed for the leaders actions. Has anything changed, do church leaders still "look after their own interests and protect their personal power?", what do you think?

"There are no bounds to man's wickedness when it comes to protecting the reins of leadership"

Our only choice if we are to stop the misuse of power, is to limit the level of autonomous power of leaders or to find a fairer way of making important decisions. While we present too much overall control to one person, abuse will continue as power and control become an addiction leading to corruption and power insanity. Our ground floor overseers and managers must be taught to keep their feet on the ground and their heads out of the clouds, middle managers need to concentrate on their jobs and not eyeing up promotion to more lofty heights and our upper management tiers need a combination of all these mixed with humility. While we carry on as we are, there will always be conflict and a lack of cooperation which serves nobody. There is no room at all for an inflated ego when in a position of authority, playing office politics or assuming a "do as I say and not as I do" attitude will destroy working relationships and protecting a position of authority will always eventually blow up in a person's face. Work relationship psychologists and human resources officers must work together to formulate a new approach between leaders and workers if conflict is to be taken out of the workplace. A successful company cannot be shaped while worker/leader issues are negative. A very interesting article I read claimed that in The UK there are 5 MILLION managers! No wonder industry and just about everything else is going downhill. With so many managers using outdated methods, self centred in their outlook, it's a recipe for disaster. Once upon a time all we had was a factory and the owner overseeing things, now we have a managers for this and managers for that, layer upon layer of bodies all with personal agendas and personal beliefs, turmoil must ensue. In this day and age power sharing strategies at the highest levels are essential so as to remove too much power and control resting on the shoulders of lone individuals who may not be able to cope with such levels of responsibility. Until new approaches are implemented, we risk the threat of a megalomaniac leader endangering the world with warrior ambitions or insanity brought on by the poisonous thirst for power, these are leaders who are unconcerned with who dies and where or what repercussions will be caused by their decisions. The conditions that are brought on by too much power being rested on someone's shoulders must be better diagnosed and recognised earlier, before that person can do too much damage. A person diagnosed as suffering from this power crazed insanity should be relieved of their duties as they receive appropriate treatment, whether this is a Prime Minister or a shop-floor supervisor. There are many advisory agencies offering services for leaders to make sure they do not wander of course or become power hungry, would though a politician, especially a top politician, willingly request help?

Former UK foreign Minister and SDP leader David Owen is the author of "The Hubris Syndrome", a very interesting and highly recommendable book that looks closely at leadership in politics. Before entering politics David Owen was a specialist in neurology and psychiatry at St. Thomas Hospital in London. In the book, David Owen offers the opinion that former UK Prime Minister Tony Blair had fallen victim to a pathological obsession with his own political importance and moral righteousness. This condition of course is not just a politician's problem, it is commonplace wherever there is a prominent leadership post. Have you ever thought about this type of subject before, that leaders could be so seriously affected by the responsibility of their roll that all reality could be lost? How many leaders have found themselves being disposed of from their post because they had lost touch with reality and yet they still believed their people held them in respect? We think that leaders are obsessed with their post and the power it brings them, what though if it is something other than an obsession, what if it is a diagnosable illness? Unfortunately, whether an obsession or an illness, leaders carry on in their posts while doing untold damage and this is at all levels of leadership, not just at the very top. Ask yourself this "can we afford to have top political leaders and military heads in a position of making decisions that can destroy us all with their fingers on the nuclear button or deciding to "go to war"?" Can we have leaders who alone are commanding secret service agencies who assassinate targets of opposition, who control chemical and germ warfare programs, that are in charge of nuclear weapons, who are carrying out espionage programs, can we really trust one person with such massive responsibility? Who can honestly cope with this extreme level of responsibility alone? Can one man hold overall power of a nation alone? Look at history for that answer – Hitler, Stalin, Saddam Hussein, Idi Amin, and Muammar Gadhafi etc. etc. Too much power bestowed on them and they could not handle it, they became possessed by the power. Left alone with a medical condition that removes sensible judgment and behavior, just imagine what havoc a person can wreak, left alone too long and they can ultimately destroy the world. This is what I believe is happening right now, we are in an advanced state of destruction due to a long line of leaders creating an illusionary world for the people while they play their power games. The illusionary world is so well hidden and the illusion so complete that we still offer almost a worship of our leaders while they "fiddle as Rome burns". We offer adoration to our leaders simply because they are charming, they support and represent the political party we follow, they are the boss and we respect authority (after a lifetime of being programmed to respect authority), what we have to think to ourselves is "have they earned our adoration" or are we blindly falling in behind an image that is false?

We are programmed to adore our leaders by our parents, to respect authority, to do "as we are told", to give away our freedom of decision. Why do we blindly follow our leaders? because we know nothing else due to brainwashing, we follow their orders into battle and often almost certain death, why? because we have been brought up all our lives to respect authority and leadership. An old army joke is the sergeant shouting to his recruits "when I say jump, you say how high?", but this is what we all do, we follow orders just as our lifelong programming has been designed to achieve. The saddest part of this realisation is that you me and everyone are doing the same thing to our own children, we are feeding the same programming into them, which is again part of the overall program – *to be programmed and to program others.* We inter-connect and program each other to follow our leaders. Should a person not conform to the programming, the rest will stick together and make that person an outcast and label them as odd or a trouble maker when all they are doing is breaking loose of the shackles. A wonderful phrase was given me to sum this up perfectly: "you think I am mad because I am different, I think you are mad because you are all the same".

Personally I have not fully trusted our political leaders for many years, after reading several of the books recommended I can now say that I am completely disgusted with many of them and believe they have lost their souls, their decency. John Pilgers book is an emotional roller coaster, taking you from anger to tears with the abominable treatment of innocent people who suffered hideously just to force out their leaders by means that do not represent the actions of sane civilised government representatives. I felt embarrassed at the actions I read about that were taken by British parliamentarians and I would not be a bit surprised if war crimes and charges of treason are brought against them at some point. We cannot call people like this leaders, they are "mis - leaders", they are not representing the people of their country, none of the people of Britain would want to treat fellow human beings the way our leaders did in Iraq that led to the death of half a million innocent children. Having learned of many of the disgraceful and under hand ways political leaders act, It must be time to review how much power we can allow them to have, to stop them making secretive decisions without consulting with the people who elected them – that is something called democracy in case our leaders have forgotten. We should be arresting and putting on trial all the political and military leaders who had any part in war and blockades in the last 20 years, we need a modern day Nuremburg Trials as we cannot go forward until the past is cleaned up.

The speech that follows is in my opinion one of the greatest speeches in history, a speech from American President Abraham Lincoln on 19th November 1863, known as The Gettysburg Address. This took place at the dedication of the Soldiers National Cemetery four and a half months after the end of the American Civil War:

Four score and seven years ago our fathers brought forth on this continent a new nation, conceived in liberty, and dedicated to the proposition that all men are created equal.

Now we are engaged in a great civil war, testing whether that nation, or any nation, so conceived and so dedicated, can long endure. We are met on a great battlefield of that war. We have come to dedicate a portion of that field, as a final resting place for those who here gave their lives that that nation might live. It is altogether fitting and proper that we should do this.

But, in a large sense, we can not dedicate, we can not consecrate, we can not hallow this ground. The brave men, living and dead, who struggled here, have consecrated it, far above our poor power to add or detract. The world will little note, nor long remember what we say here, but it can never forget what they did here. It is for us the living, rather, to be dedicated here to unfinished work which they who fought here have thus far so nobly advanced. It is rather for us to be here dedicated to the great task remaining before us – that from these honored dead we take increased devotion to that cause for which they gave the last full measure and devotion – that we here highly resolve that these dead shall not have died in vain – that this nation, under God, shall have a new birth of freedom – and that government of the people, by the people, for the people, shall not perish from the earth.

As the next chapter will explain, these sentiments have not been honoured.

Leaders know they are committing treason against their country and their people, they know this is wrong, but they keep on doing it, why? Because they are in the grips of power insanity, a mania driven by an insatiable desire for more control, they have lost all sense of reason, all decency. Power insanity has driven many past and present leaders to abandon their allegiance to their country as they pursue their personal goals, they have been pushed to commit acts of treason against their country and its people. We should all see this and not treat the idea with contempt, one day we will have this proven and that day is not far off. Basically they have "lost it", their minds have been taken over and infected by wanton greed for more and more power, greater and greater control, they are more psychopath and zombie than person. When leaders plot against their own country and plan to slay their own countrymen, you know they are past the point of saving and the only action can be to remove them from their posts. Nobody with a gram of decency would plan to overthrow their own country and sell it out to outside influences, yet this is what is happening right now. The might of the USA is rumoured to be standing in the way of the takeover of the running of the world by a secret organisation, there-fore this organisation has decreed that the financial status of the USA to be destroyed – and this is what is taking place. The destruction of the USA economy is taking place from inside of the country, yet such is the dedication of the American people to its leaders – they will not believe this is possible. The USA has probably just a few years or so left before it crashes into a fiscal brick wall and will find it hard to recover from the crash, how many Americans are able to believe that? When this happens, remember it will be a pre-planned deliberate action.

We all have to realise this one fundamental and basic truth: **"At the moment our politicians are NOT our leaders, they are in fact our JAILERS!"** They have ruined our economies and smashed our savings, pensions and future prosperity to smithereens. They have imposed austerity measures on us, raised taxes, imposed more and more new confiding laws and legislation increasing their control of us, they are spying on our telephone calls – Internet searches – e-mails – our purchases – logging who we contact and building profiles of us and all *without our knowledge*, even though **WE elected THEM to represent US**. One report I watched stated that The UK is the worse for monitoring phone calls etc. with 600 million phone calls a day being watched throughout the world from its "spy base" in Cheltenham, GCHQ. Did you get that? 600,000,000 phone calls a day! What are they doing with all the results of this phone tapping? How much is it costing the tax payer per year to have their phone and e-mails tapped and their privacy invaded? Are you waking up yet to what your governments are doing without permission? Until you realise this is fact and not a conspiracy theory, you are giving them the permission to keep doing it. Do NOT be fobbed off with the fraudulent explanation that our privacy is being invaded to stop terrorism, that is a fake excuse – they are spying on us out of fear we may fight back against their treachery and that is all there is to it. Half the people of a country will back all this spying because they have fallen for the tales our government reel out that they are only looking for terrorists and criminals. Wake up!

Are **you** being watched?

Yes, you are, without any doubt. Your e-mails and phone calls are being monitored, not by tapping your lines personally, but by mass information accumulation. The content of your e-mails and phone calls is automatically read by listening equipment for "trigger" words. If you use words such as assassination – rebellion – revolution – bomb etc. you are red flagged by the listening equipment and a human operator will "look into you". They will use the electronic files stored on you, your bank files, who you connect to by e-mail and phone etc., to see if you mix with other known "red flags". Your banks records will be checked, social security records checked, criminal records (if any) checked, tax records checked and you may find yourself being pulled up by police on minor motoring offences – you are being watched by all the security cameras and motoring camera's and all because you used certain words. You will be considered a threat to national security if you get too many red flags. If you have unintentionally connected to a suspicious person via social media (let's face it you don't know who all are in your sphere of social media) you again earn a red flag. You will be innocent of any crime or plot, but the system identifies you as a threat and should people in your electronic profile prove to be a real security threat – you are automatically branded a threat as well. You would be very shocked at the list of very innocent words that are listed as red flag trigger words, they are words you probably use every day. Are you being watched, is your private life being scrutinised, oh yes, 100% fact. Your government who you elected, if you voted for them, is doing this without your knowledge and they hide it under counter terrorism and counter crime moves, when in truth they are just watching us all.

What if? What if your national leader is infected (infected is the right word, not affected) by power insanity? How do you feel about that, that you and everyone in your country is at the mercy of a manic leader with plans for your and everyone's future that you do not know about? They may appear sane, decent and honourable, what if they are fooling you and everyone?

Summary

Thanks to a life time of propaganda and brain washing we mistakenly trust our leaders because we wrongly believe that as we elected them, they represent us – WRONG! Far too much pressure is placed on leaders which leads to many of them cracking under the pressure. More worrying is that the more power a leader assumes appears to alter their personality and makes them what amounts to more Jekyll than Mr. Hide and many transform into callous murderers that give little thought to their actions. The world is in the mess it is because of decisions made by corrupt leaders and it is the people of the world who suffer - as usual. They are not leaders they are our jailers, wake up and see this before it is too late.

eight

When Is A Secret Organisation Not A Secret Organisation?

- Before you read this next chapter, please read this important opening paragraph first. A few people, but not many, emphatically deny the details that are set out in this chapter for many different reasons, yet tens of millions of people, probably hundreds of millions consider the details to be accurate, **which is a tough statistic to go against**. Some say what follows is a giant hoax to cover up what is really going on in our world, a double bluff. Take some time to think deeply on this information that follows - the world's leading Internet search engine carries ten million eight hundred thousand articles about just one of these secret organisations, there are millions of videos uploaded onto the Internet and tens of thousands of book titles published on the subject – which would mean that if this is a hoax it is the biggest ever hoax in history. As mentioned elsewhere in this book – you cannot argue against hard evidence and that is available in massed quantities. Be prepared for a number of significant shocks and to have your belief systems stretched to the limit. Consider also, If all the accumulated information is wrong or a conspiracy plot – **why doesn't one of our major world leaders stand up and say so and allay all our fears, which are plentiful?** I for one would welcome a reasonable explanation to remove my fears as I can only see solid information pointing towards the existence of these secret organisations that threaten our world. I know how hard it is going to be for people to believe the chapter that follows – it took me over thirty years before I accepted it. Though I did not have the massive files of proof available to me that is at your fingertips, you have.

When is a secret organisation not a secret organisation? Answer, when it no longer needs to hide itself under cover of secrecy. That is exactly what is taking place right now as the world's largest secret organisation "comes out of the closet" and is announcing itself to the general world more and more on a day to day basis.

- When a secret organisation has a massive granite block carving specially commissioned to stand on top of a prominent hill for all to see and read its intentions, it must be ready to show its true colours.
- When newspapers and television news reports carry open quotes from people involved in this secret organisation which are splashed everywhere, there can be no other conclusion than that they are coming into the open.
- When people involved with this secret organisation are pictured and filmed making the various secret signs associated with this secret organisation and making them very obvious, they have no fear of being exposed.
- When leading politicians quote this secret organisation openly, they are clearly showing to the world that they are part of it.

At one time it was risking a swift and certain sudden end to talk about this secret organisation, now it would appear it is content for all to mention it and even those who verbally attack it are ignored as they serve a useful purpose – announcing to the world it has total control and "has everything covered". This secret organisation has always used the whistleblowers to create rumours and has frequently employed its own whistle blowers as "double agents" that it could use to its benefit

- now it is using them all to announce its arrival on the public stage. Nobody can argue against this conclusion as this secret organisation goes public in so many ways and on more occasions, they are well and truly now a "public" organisation, secrecy is not needed when you hold overall control.

Please keep in mind as you read this chapter that this chapter and the last one dealing with leadership are not exposes to try and start "witch hunts" against those uncovered. The chapters are exposes of the frightening actions of leaders and secret organisations to highlight to these people that what they are doing has got seriously out of hand and "power insanity" endangers the very existence of the whole world and its people. That which follows is a summary of what I have learned from the detailed amassed information available.

It is understandably so difficult for the people of the world to believe that secret organisations and societies exist, yet exist they appear to do and by the hundreds, maybe thousands. For the average person in the street this idea will be near impossible to take in due to the lifetime of programming and brain washing we have experienced. When the public relies solely on the accepted route for discovering information, the tv/radio news broadcasts and daily newspapers, and these do not carry reports of subjects such as secret organisations – they can only find it all beyond belief. This of course is all part of the brilliant deception and how the overall deception has been carried off as our news media are an important integral part of the deception. What must also be considered is that many organisations are considered "secret covers" for what is really going on beneath the surface, they appear harmless and yet they have secretive hidden agendas. To me the implementation of the secret plans and schemes is to be greatly admired as it is probably the greatest scheming and planning in man's history, it is however also the greatest deceit in man's history and most worryingly it is the greatest threat to life in history. We the people are generally without the slightest clue what has taken place, what is taking place, we also would be unlikely to believe that it has and is taking place with so much fraudulent programming controlling our belief systems. We the 99.9% lose – they the 0.1% win again and again.

One of the most famous lines in history from the speech by President Lincoln that came from the Gettysburg Address was: "that this nation, under God, shall have a new birth of freedom – and that government of the people, by the people, for the people, shall not perish from the earth". Well it did perish from the earth and the last thing we can expect is a "government of the people, by the people, for the people". As details featured later outline with quotes from past US presidents who state that past US governments handed over the power to run their country to what are "the real rulers of the USA and the world" and this process of transferring power continues unabated today. This chapter of the book is the most pivotal and most important chapter of all, I have been building up to this one, trying to convince you the reader that the world is not the place we all think it is and that we have been systematically brainwashed and programmed to accept "ignorance of truth". You will now have your beliefs even more seriously challenged, your "ignorance of truth" will be stretched to bursting point and if you have never had any pre-knowledge of the subject matter of this chapter you will see that what follows is a slap in the face for all of us.

When I attended college as part of my apprenticeship qualification, my group was treated once a week to an hour long lesson from a member of the college's social studies department. At age seventeen I was informed by this tutor that governments do not run countries, the real rulers are banks, building societies and insurance companies, all of which went straight over the top of my head, though I never forgot it. Ten years ago I started to receive reminders of this early life awakening, only on a much stronger level with words warning that the world is completely ruled by secret organisations. At this time I was still not ready to accept any of this, it all seemed too hard to believe that our government ministers are virtual puppets dangling on strings being pulled by the banks and their associates. Over the last two years the whisper turned into a roar, evidence and detailed data piled up to back the claim of a system of world rule hidden under a veil of secrecy. To satisfy my own mind I began to dig and sift through the Internet and look for books on the subject, that is when the truth started to really dawn on me, the accusations appear accurate. One thing that nobody can argue with is detailed evidence along the lines of who did what, when, how and who to, this is available by the ship load. What I could not get my head round at first was that one secret organisation has over ten million related articles about it posted on Internet search engines, over 46,000 book titles about the New World Order and 1530 titles on the Illuminati available from on-line book sellers and millions of videos loaded on the Internet about it and yet it still remained a relative secret. (read those last sentences again, aren't they shocking?) When you understand the nature of this organisation and how far reaching it is, you will see for yourself why a "secret" organisation is also very public. Many USA Presidents have warned about this organisation, going back as early as George Washington on October 24th 1776, his warnings can be found in the Library of Congress: George Washington warns of Illuminati. Before looking at some of the comments of past USA Presidents let me state the secret organisation is known as either The Illuminati or The New World Order.

President Thomas Jefferson said, "I sincerely believe with you that the banking establishments are more dangerous than standing armies"'

President Franklin D Roosevelt said "a financial element in the large centres has owned the government ever since the days of Andrew Jackson".

President John F Kennedy said on April 27 1961, "The very word secrecy is repugnant in a free and open society: and we as a people inherently and historically opposed to secret societies, to oaths and to secret proceedings. Our way of life is under attack. Those who make themselves our enemy are advancing around the globe.... no war ever posed a greater threat to our security. If you are awaiting a finding of clear and present damage, then I can only say that the danger has never been more clear and its presence has never been more imminent. For we are opposed around the world by a monolithic and ruthless conspiracy that relies primarily on covert means for expanding its sphere of influence, on infiltration instead of invasion, on subversion instead of elections, on intimidation instead of free choice, on guerillas by night instead of armies by day. It is a system which has conscripted vast human and material resources into the building of a tightly knit, highly efficient machine that combines military, diplomatic, intelligence, economic, scientific and political operations. Its preparations are concealed, not published. Its mistakes are buried, not headlined. Its dissenters are silenced, not praised. No expenditure is questioned, no rumor is printed, no secret is revealed.

Many believe that it was the Illuminati that ordered the assassination of President Kennedy.

Vice President John C Calhoun in a speech on May 27 1836 said "a power has risen up in the government greater than the people themselves, consisting of many and various powerful interests, combined in one mass, and held together by the cohesive power of the vast surplus in banks".

President Woodrow Wilson said, "Since I entered politics, I have chiefly had men's views confided to me privately. Some of the biggest men in the United States, in the field of commerce and manufacture, are afraid of something. They know that there is a power somewhere so organised, so subtle, so watchful, so interlocked, so complete, so pervasive, that they had better not speak above their breath when they speak in condemnation of it".

New York City Mayor John F Hylan said in The New York Times, March 26 1922, "the real menace of our Republic is the invisible government, which like a giant octopus sprawls its slimy legs over our cities, states and nation. The little coterie of powerful international bankers virtually run the United States government for their own selfish purposes. They practically control both parties and control the majority of the newspapers and magazines in the country.

President J Edgar Hoover said "**the individual is handicapped by coming face to face with a conspiracy so monstrous he cannot believe it exists**. The American mind simply has not come to a realisation of evil which has been introduced into our midst. It rejects even the assumption that human creatures could espouse **a philosophy which must ultimately destroy all that is good and decent.**

Fourteen past US presidents are confirmed as freemasons.

Were all these famous named politicians wrong in their assumptions, had they all been fooled into believing a secret society exists, are they the original Conspiracy Theorists?

You could be sitting reading this and thinking "what the hell is going on?", " is this for real?" or any of hundreds of different expletives, just get used to the idea, the world is and has been for over 200 years run by an organisation more powerful than all the western world governments put together. It is said by many researchers that the NWO run all the western world governments and that they choose and groom every western world Prime Minister, Chancellor, President to take up the reins of government with their help and that in return the politician carries out their orders. (read that line again) It does not stop there, every aspect of daily life runs on the orders and command of this NWO, trade – airlines – oil companies – construction – publishing – insurance – investment – trade unions – employer organisations – secret services and much more. The whole hierarchy of life and business has been infiltrated, a stranglehold has been placed around all aspects of our lives and we generally are totally unaware it is so. Anything that is of an official nature such as the running of a town, county, country, business, trade, transport, investments, insurance, all forms of banking is firmly under control or owned by the NWO. Nothing is moved, sold or agreed without input from a NWO source, such is the complete control that has been forced on us all. Nobody can deny that the whole scheme is very impressive, secretly implemented, secretly being carried out daily and most of us do not have a vague idea what is going on. Naturally our leaders do know what is going on, if they are not part of it (many are not) they are aware that they are puppets dancing on the end of the NWO strings.

Perhaps now would be a good time to stop reading, sit down and take all this information in, no matter how hard your mind fights to have you disbelieve what you have just learned. The only conclusion from the massed sources of data is that the New World Order/ Illuminati is real and they have control of most of the world and your life – you are one of its unknowing slaves. When rarely a word is spoken to the contrary, we must naturally believe those who say this have it right. How does that make you feel, angry, frustrated, do you feel helpless in the knowledge of such absolute loss of control? Once more I state that I know how hard this all of this is to believe, it took me over thirty years before I accepted it and then it still needed a lot of persuading.

We are here in this position because we drifted, we turned our backs on truth, we are arrogant and believe nothing like this can happen and still many will fight the truth that this is all real and not a foolish claim or a conspiracy theory. Like fools we trusted our leaders because we thought they represented us. Our police and soldiers must feel the most let down as they risk their lives to defend leaders who spit on our patriotism and desecrate our flags. Perhaps now you will see the point made early in this book that "we do not know the real world" is accurate.

Do not totally blame all of today's politicians, industrialists, police chiefs, military heads, many have no choice other than to fall in line with the overall plan and they know that if they were to try and fight back against the NWO, they would lose. If the NWO wants someone out of the post they hold (this includes prime ministers, presidents and top politicians), then they will have them removed – one way or another! It is claimed that former British Prime Minister Margaret Thatcher was removed by them. (Opponents suffer fatal car crashes, airplane crashes, suffer **faked** suicide, suffer **artificially** induced heart attacks or are infected with cancer) Yes, politicians, industrialists and military heads work for the NWO, many hate to do it and would not carry out such deceit, they do not have any other choice than to comply with their orders. This is going back to the lifetime programming we have all received, to obey and do as we are told is second nature to us all, it is also back to tribal rites where we do as the tribe chief says. Our leaders are leading us astray, they are taking their orders from the NWO, do they really want to carry out the deceit of those that they supposedly represent and trust them? Some yes, some no. While I criticise our leaders, I also appreciate the dilemma they are in, the NWO is all powerful and will think nothing of crushing them should they rebel and a lifetime of programming has deeply embedded obedience into our leaders, so like us – they obey. Our leaders could secretly be crying out for change and find the whole NWO control of life despicable, what can they do though? Our leaders are probably aware of the threats to mankind's existence, how can they stop this happening without risking themselves? which is a true "catch 22" situation – let the world know the truth and risk their lives or let the threats play out and risk their lives! Lose or lose.

There are tens of thousands of good informative books available that deliver solid details on the NWO, how it first formed and who formed it, its history from the start and how it spread and by whom – DETAILED FACTS AND FIGURES. There are confirmed facts and data logged in massive amounts, who did what and when and how. There are too many facts logged for this to come under the heading of a conspiracy "theory", theories are based on thoughts and opinions not hard facts. Here is a list of some of the books I have read that are full of information and data:

This is a good starting point and a brilliant book from an accepted authority on the subject which I would rate ten out of ten: The Trillion Dollar Conspiracy by Jim Marrs, a New York Times best seller (also there is an on-line live edition of this, type in Trillion Dollar Conspiracy into your search engine, the book is better, the on-line version is a good intro) Everyone should read this book, it should sell by the tens of millions – totally brilliant.

*** My highly recommended next step would be to watch a DVD titled "THRIVE, what on earth will it take?" I not only recommend this I would just say – WATCH THIS AS SOON AS POSSIBLE and then tell everyone you know to get hold of a copy. *** Also available on the Internet as a free download, but not the full film version.

One World by Tal Brooke

The Master Game by Graham Hancock & Robert Bauval

Human Race Get Off Your Knees, The Lion Sleeps No More by David Icke (600 pages of facts, pictures & data)

The New World Order by Mark Dice

The Mark of the New World by Terry L Cook. Published in 1996, some of the data is out of date but what information there is I would give 10 out of 10 to, it is packed full with statistics, data, information and it even managed to shock me and leave me numb with horror (and a few sleepless nights).

The New Rulers of the World by John Pilger, a book I have only recently read – you need to read this one to understand what really goes on in life around our politicians.

The true story of the Bilderberg group by Daniel Estulin, another highly rated book and this one is an absolute must read, full of pictures and details – you are sure to be shocked by this book.

Another scary on-line video is "The Illuminati goes public on the new world order", look it up and watch it in half hour sessions, I watched the full one hour forty eight minutes as I could not stop watching this one. Look this up on your Internet search engine.

These are just a few of the 46,388 titles about the NWO and 1530 titles about the Illuminati I found on Amazon.com, so much for a secret society.

*another very good learning point to finding out the hidden facts would be to search out a very charismatic "whistle blower" called Jesse Ventura who fronts an American TV show called "Conspiracy Theories" on TruTV exposing all manner of topics. Jesse Ventura is an ex US navy seal, professional wrestler, mayor and former independent governor of Minnesota, he also does not care who he upsets in his search for truth. His shows can be over the top in dramatising his investigations, but he does get to the bottom of things and causes considerable embarrassment to those hiding dark deeds.

Turning to the Internet and you could choose to watch videos on the NWO subject that are loaded onto YouTube in their hundreds of thousands or read any of the over TEN MILLION articles posted on search engines. With the YouTube videos, some last as long as three hours, my tip is to watch them in snippets, I normally view for half an hour and write down where I had reached and then fast forward to that place when I wanted to watch more. IMPORTANT, please realise that anyone can load videos onto the Internet, so you will have all extremes, the NWO can load a video to discredit other videos or those who loath the NWO can load untrue propaganda about the NWO that could be outrageous, so viewer discretion is strongly advised. Can I recommend you start with a three hour documentary that covers a few subjects as well as the NWO, Jordan Maxwell "exposes the Illuminati", I guarantee this video will severely shock you and it is absolutely **not to be missed**. Please also watch David Icke "humanity is awakening" and any video by David Wilcock, look up his website – www.divinecosmos.com. From any of these on-line videos you will be made aware of the millions of others loaded onto the Internet as trailers for other videos are posted alongside the video being played. Any search engine with its millions of articles just needs you to type in "Illuminati or New World Order" and a "new world" will literally open up for you as you discover the depth of deceit and secrecy that has been imposed on us all. Some people would argue that there is merit in a few of the NWO ideas, such as a world bank that would set rules for the rest of the banking industry, world law setting so as to standardise laws which can make sense and a one world army to sort out problems, it is some of the other reported aims that worry me. The most frightening issue has to be that the majority of information available that lists NWO goals is the goal of reducing of the world population by over 90%. Is this really a NWO goal? who knows but there are many who claim this to be true, it does crop up time and again and is repeated throughout the combined Internet and published information available. **That would mean that six and a half billion people would be "culled" to achieve this suitable figure,** how does that make you feel? (okay if this is the first time you have seen this quote I _know_ how hard it is to believe as I struggled at first). "Culling" by war would have to include the type of weapons described in the chapter about secret weapons, those that destroy people but not infrastructure. Using nuclear bombs would not be a good idea due to radiation contamination and the danger of destroying the planet by ripping it apart. How does that statistic make you feel? that six and a half billion people face cold blooded murder just so the NWO can establish complete rule and control over our world? If I was reading that for the first time and without back up information I would surely dismiss the idea as a very sick joke, unfortunately I have seen too much proof and data to dismiss the idea, information and data that is ready for you to check out – should you want to. In one of the books recommended above, The Mark of the New World by Terry L Cook, one NWO insider claims that the actual figure they consider to be manageable is five billion, that's comforting, only two billion people to be culled after all.

It is claimed were all going to be micro-chipped

Another widely accepted and often repeated detail from massed data is that the NWO will (not might, but WILL) microchip everybody, the technology already exists and is in production, the chip is the size of a grain of rice and its waiting to be used, remember we already do it to our pets. The chip would allow tracking of the person wherever they are, if a person commits a crime (in the eyes of the NWO) their chip would be switched off which would not allow them to buy anything at a shop – receive medical help – move outside of their home etc. etc. (sounds like Orwell's 1984 to me). (**RFID, get used to this terminology, it's going to crop up time and time again in the next few years**). Softly – softly the micro-chipping will be introduced to "get us used to the idea – to imprint into our brains that this is harmless" and then it will be made law and as usual we will allow it and we won't understand what is happening or what we are giving away. This microchip will replace money, the person will be scanned just as a barcode scanner in a shop works and their bank account will automatically be deducted. The removal of physical money is a prime objective of the NWO as it needs to be able to monitor all spending by everyone, which physical money does not allow. **We must all fight with all we have to stop any and EVERY attempt to remove physical money from the system.** Did you wonder why cheque books were phased/being phased out? Cheque books do not allow instant electronic tracking and your purchases cannot be tracked to help form the electronic picture of your life, so cheque books had to go. Something I personally believe is that soon we will have debit and credit cards with implanted RFID chips and either a photo of the card holder or another way to identify them. We will be informed that the micro-chip is to our advantage as it makes bank card fraud impossible and that will seem a good measure as we are bombarded with tales of card fraud. This of course is just another subtle way of getting us used to the idea of carrying a RFID micro-chip and why we have had card fraud waved in our faces so often – to brainwash us into accepting the RFID. From this point on you are fully traceable while you have your bank cards on you, you will not suspect a thing and it takes you that much closer to the implanted RFID we are warned about.

Another fact for you to prove this idea of tracking spending is that if you pay cash for something in a large enough amount – the bank or shop/supplier is bound by law to report this to the police. We are informed this is to stop money laundering, which is another (mis)-truth, it is to force us down the route of making our purchases traceable and fully logged. The whole idea of discontinuing physical money will be "sold" to the people as a deterrent for theft, drug dealing, money laundering and much more as without money these criminal actions cannot be carried out – and we will feebly agree (God help us when we do as life will be given away and slavery put into its place). Should you be doubting this, I can only say that it is your lifelong programming that is at work and not your free thinking mind, get it into your head – this is going to happen. What do you think about that, your every move traceable and recorded, you can be found at all times and any time via your implanted chip, misbehave and you are switched off and house bound (of course this is IF you are one of the lucky ones living after the great culling). You will be stopped from buying certain items if they are deemed a threat, items such as hunting knives – guns – baseball bats Etc. While you're at home you can be put under surveillance via your Internet glass fibre cabled monitoring system, just as George Orwell described in his book. The thing is, there will be people who approve of this scenario and consider it a good idea – they being those people who have had this attitude programmed into them by their parents etc. no doubt.

The Governing Stones of Georgia – **do we need any other proof?**

The governing stones of Georgia are an enormous stone fabrication carved from granite which is situated on top of a hill in Elbert

County, Georgia, USA. The construction of the stones was ordered by an unknown person using the pseudonym of R,C.Christian who hired the granite finishing company to build the structure, paying cash to avoid discovery of their real identity. Many believe the R.C. stands for Rosicrucian which is an accepted NWO organization, which makes this unknown person "Rosicrucian Christian" and would clearly show that the NWO are becoming bolder, more confident and "coming out of the secrecy closet". The Stones have messages in ten languages carved into its sides, a smaller sized message is carved around the top of this huge structure written in four unusual languages – Babylonian Cuneiform, Ancient Hellenic, Egyptian Hieroglyphics and Sanskrit. Why the secrecy, why carve a repeating message in such obscure languages? You shall see. The message is one of many that is showing up in some very public places and appear to openly broadcast the ever growing confidence of the NWO, see also several messages at the newly built Denver Airport (search on-line for an expose by Jesse Ventura on this and see for yourself)

<u>The message reads</u>

Let these be guidestones to an age of reason

1. Maintain humanity under 500,000,000 in perpetual balance with nature
2. Guide reproduction wisely – improve fitness and diversity
3. Unite humanity with a living new language
4. Rule passion – faith – tradition and all things with tempered reason
5. Protect people and nature with fair laws and just courts
6. Let all nations rule internal, resolving external disputes in a world court
7. Avoid petty laws and useless officials
8. Balance personal rights with social duties
9. Prize truth – beauty – love – seeking harmony with the infinite
10. Be not a cancer on the Earth – leave room for nature

By typing "The Georgia Guidestones" into your Internet search engine, you can see for yourself the inscription in pictures on the Internet. Here then is the apparent solid proof that the NWO do indeed plan to cull six and half billion people down to a population of just half a billion and install a world order that will have one language, one religion, one law book, one army, they will practice "selective breeding of all humans" (no mixed races etc.). When they are so open and public about their intentions, we can only assume they have achieved almost full control of just about everything, or as we might say "it's in the bag". I have to add a personal comment, I still shake my head in disbelief as I discover more and more details of the apparent NWO plans and think to myself "have we been living on another planet while all this was slipped into place?" How can such a complete takeover of the world have happened and nobody raised a finger to stop it? We have wars and battles going on all over the world, riots and demonstrations as the people fight for their right to freedom from despot dictators, people laying down their lives for the right to be free and for their families right to be free – yet here we are on what appears to be the verge of the biggest enslavement of humanity ever witnessed – the complete removal of all rights to free speech – the complete removal of all rights to freedom of movement – the complete removal of all freedom of any kind – the complete removal of all wealth of the people – the mass genocide of 90% of the world's population – we are all going to be micro chipped so that someone somewhere will always know where we are and what we are doing – and we are doing nothing about it? Not a word of protest. Not a word in anger is being broadcast by the media because they are under direct rule of the NWO, which means this will be the place to start a fight back by taking back control of the media and remove and replace the media with a fair independent news reporting service, that is **the** immediate main priority. It is clear that those working for the media as reporters, political analysts and news broadcasters do not know what is going on, they take their orders and do as they are told, but their editors and heads of broadcasting stations is another story and are most likely freemasons.

If these "leaders" are not part of the evil deception, they should publicly say so. Other key ideas that I have read of that the NWO seek to implement are the removal of all private owned property (is this why property prices are forced ever higher?), the family circle is to be destroyed, mass unemployment of our youth, drug culture to be promoted among the young and football (soccer) to be ruined through bankrupting clubs. All of which appear on course.

For all of our futures, we had better wake up damn quick, as the man in the street who carries his placard says "THE END IS NIGH". Never give up hope that we can turn this situation around, it will need hard work, but then that's something the people are good at.

Author George Orwell said "during times of universal deceit, telling the truth becomes a revolutionary act". George Orwell is famed for his book 1984 and the terrifying horrors of a controlled life with no freedom, from what I have seen for myself, the book is around 30 – 40 years out in its timing and that Orwell's ideas will be proven correct within the next ten years or so. Author David Icke claims in his book "Human Race get off your Knees, The Lion Sleeps No More" that Orwell and author Aldous Huxley were recruited into the NWO via their membership of The Fabian Society, but did not like what they saw and that 1984 is a warning to us all what is planned for us, as is Aldous Huxley's book "Brave New World". The Fabian Society, and the London School of Economics are named as prime recruiting agencies for the NWO, trapping young impressionable minds with their promises of unlimited power and a new world. In David Ickes book there is a frighteningly long list of past and present students and staff at the Fabian Society's London School of Economics, a who's who of political leaders etc.

As governments are run by the NWO then so are government departments, which includes education, yes our children and what they are taught. College studies are also under firm control, which ultimately means that we are being brainwashed from the start of schooling to when we leave the education system, which in turn means that the more and longer education we have – the more programming we receive (and the least likely we are at accepting that anything in this book could be true). We can assume that the more academic a person the greater the influence on their thinking and the more control the NWO exerts over them.

*David Icke has been the receiver of some of the most concentrated ridicule ever given publicly to one person, the BBC went out of its way to publicly crucify him, even people's hero "Uncle Tel" Terry Wogan got in on the act and pulled Icke to pieces on his show. David Icke was going through a major change in his understanding of the world and how it works, he woke up to the reality we need to discover, only a long time in advance of the rest of us, he is a pioneer we should all respect. What and who was the BBC protecting with its broadsided biased attacks? Why did they twist his words and pull out all the stops to discredit David Icke? Could they have been under orders from their puppet masters? I consider David Icke to be one of the bravest (and yes controversial) people in the world, he stands up to the NWO and openly publicises what is going on under the surface. Even I do not accept everything he claims, which is my freedom of choice, his work though is highly illuminating. Look up David Ickes's work on the Internet, watch his video "humanity is waking up", watch some of his other videos as they are always topical, read his books, yes he is extreme but then so is secretly controlling the world. His website videos are often blank as part of the targeting he receives is to forbid the screening of the videos "due to third party legal actions".

Who runs the NWO? Good question. Something that trademark's the NWO is that it never openly refutes it exists, it never states what its agenda and goals are, and in fact it is totally silent on all things, **or at least it used to be**. All that has changed in the last decade or so, we can only assume the plan to rule the world must be almost complete, the NWO operatives are mostly in place, total control has almost been achieved, so naturally the need for secrecy is now increasingly unnecessary and quotes from those operatives can be found everywhere. The Internet is full of NWO world known operatives who are pictured making the sign of the Illuminati (a raised fist with the two outside fingers extended and the inner two clenched). Previously you would never mention the organisation in public or by phone, e-mail, fax etc. for fear of meeting a sticky end, but now with just about the whole system ready, it does not matter who says what. Now the operatives are getting braver and braver, full of confidence and issuing open quotes including NWO intentions, they publicly make themselves known as an insider by showing the secret greeting wave of an "Illuminati". There are now thousands of quotes littering the airways about the NWO, read Terry Cooks book to read hundreds of them. The last thing that you can now say of the NWO is that it is a secret society, it is very public, if you know where to look, the unveiling of the Guide stones of Georgia more than prove this. Previously it was left to past members who had left the organisation to reveal what was going on underneath the surface or it was the work of the many investigative anti-NWO reporters that have infiltrated or spied on the NWO who release details. They inform us that the NWO has a hierarchy that is made up at ground floor level by all the many Freemason groups who also form the backbone of the NWO. When you consider that there are around five million Freemason's across the world, you can see why they would be the backbone. This is followed by an overseeing group who meet once a year called the Bilderberg Group, Author Terry Cooks book describes the Bilderberg's as "the power brokers of the world" who set policy and advance the plans of the organisation. The Bilderberg Group is made up of politicians, past US Presidents, British past and present politicians, major Industrialists, bankers, as well as members of Royalty. There are many videos online identifying and showing the members of the group entering their annual meeting. The Bilderberg Group openly contact successful companies to try and recruit them under its wing and influence. Prime Ministers, Presidents, all serving politicians whether in government or opposition must be barred from Bilderberg if the meetings agendas remains secretive. If we are going to claim to be a democracy – we have to be democratic and transparent.

As you can see, it's hardly a secret society anymore and most of those considered to be running the NWO are named time and again with four of the world's most well-known banking families mentioned throughout many books and on-line information. There are videos of members of these banking families being harassed and accused of membership of the NWO on line. There are many quotes given on the Internet that are claimed to originate from members of these banking families, quotes which are very worrying. One piece of the jigsaw is mostly missing and that is who is in overall charge and above the Bilderberg Group and NWO ? Is it a member of these banking families? One report I saw named the head of the NWO to be a person known as "The Black Pope", not because of the colour of his skin, it relates to the colour of his robes. Should you turn to the Internet to seek out this person I am sure you will be shocked again, many sites DO place him at the head of The Illuminati, they also talk of him being the head of The Jesuits, which is another must discover subject. This secretive person, Adolfo Nicolas, is not even known to exist by many of his normal church members, such is the secrecy around him and I have read speculation that he has been accused of being the much heralded last anti-Christ (having searched on-line for articles on the book of revelation, I dismissed this idea). Many books I have read draw a strong link to the Catholic Church and the upper hierarchy of the NWO, when you include this mystery character The Black Pope and one last surprise to be added next, you have to wonder if it is true or the work of anti-Catholics and or anti-NWO activists? Why do I say this? Because there are also many people who say that the NWO is based on Zionism. I am not at all convinced that the Catholic church is involved yet there are considerable details and opinion available that places the Catholic Church hierarchy in a prominent position within the NWO. This last surprise comes from an item titled "The Last Pope", it is widely claimed that the present pope will be the last pope before "The Great Tribulation", which again is something that you can search out via the Internet. It is though unsure if the present pope is pope number 111 or 112 as there was one pope who only served very briefly before dying and some say he was not in the post long enough to be called a true pope. Why so much opinion linking the Catholic Church to The Illuminati? Is it an anti-Catholic plot? What is the real role of The Black Pope, or to use his official title The Superior General of the Society of Jesuits, or as many call him, The President of the World. This is a very interesting field and well worth looking at, I have no personal opinion on the truth or otherwise of this as I do not have any concrete details available only theory which is not enough for my enquiring mind.

There is considerable speculation and accusations in books and on-line that the NWO is based in Satanism and atheism, also that they are devoted to communism/facism, is it true or is it mischief making? Many books on the subject of the NWO quote specific bible passages, mainly the Book of Revelations in the belief that the NWO is a satanic devil worship organisation and that they are closely following the Book of Revelations which outlines the end of time on Earth and the ruling of the Earth by Satan. The Internet is full of this type of speculation with several different suggestions who the last anti-Christ will be, they do though make it very clear that the NWO is atheist based even though many religious leaders are involved (which would basically confirm these leaders are fake). If as accused, the NWO are Satanists and that they are closely following the Book of Revelations from the bible as many suggest, they could well be manipulating events (as normal) and trying to bring about the prophecies from the book of revelations. This tells of the rise of the anti-Christ and the arrival of The Beast and so much more, which would make it a good idea to familiarise yourself with those prophecies. Think on this, it is reported in many articles that one of the aims of the NWO is to remove Christians – Jews - Moslems and replace their faiths with a "One World Religion", there is no comment about removing the Catholic faith, why is that, is it more mischief making trying to implicate the Catholic Church? Will the Catholic faith be this One World Religion? Or will it form the basis of this new set up?

Nothing mentioned here is secret at all, I am not revealing anything here that has not already been made public and I have not completed any of the researching to provide the data, all I have been doing is dig for the completed research and give the links to that research to a greater audience so they can make up their own minds. Though this type of information may be new to you, it is certainly not new, it has been suppressed by TV and newspapers under strict orders of the NWO, yet it remains public knowledge to those "in the know".

How far and deep does the NWO web spread? Once again, opinions on this are very consistent throughout books and Internet search results. As mentioned before the NWO pyramid of manipulation covers just about all aspects of our daily lives banking – business – military – politics – education – the media (TV and radio news and newspapers) – religion – intelligence agencies, trade unions, also included are medicine and drug companies – illegal drugs and organised crime – law enforcement and law making agencies. The NWO reputedly controls many International organisations such as NATO, the UN, World Health Organisation, the IMF and just about all "secret services" such as the FBI, NSA, Mossad, MI5, MI6 and this is repeated frequently on many websites and books.

The EU is reported as being set up as the pilot scheme of the NWO "union" idea with American Union (this planning is well in advance with the USA, Mexico and Canada to unite as one), Pacific Union and African Union to follow forming four large sectors of the world with countries losing their sovereignty to a "collective". This equates to each country losing its individual identity such as Spain, or France and replaced with the European Union, having one rule, law, policy making body (to Europeans this will sound very familiar). The large group of Euro skeptics will be pleased to learn that their much detested EU is not all that it seems to be. Above these Unions will be a world government that would dictate to every country international law and international regulations via the four Unions. There would be a world army of which various nations armies would be a sub unit, this on paper sounds to be a move in the right direction, what would the world army be used to do? A one world religion is also planned which should, apart from the mass slaughter of the world's population, upset more people than any of the other ideas. A one world currency is reputedly planned as is the complete removal of physical money and a one world language would be enforced on all. It took over 200 years of planning and secretly implementing the plans, today the web of influence is complete and the next phase will surely begin to roll out soon, will it be the mass "culling" of the population or the collapsing of world economic systems, war in the Middle East? Who knows, though I believe it will be the latter as this area is a powder keg waiting to blow. World economic systems are already wrecked and only survive by fraud waiting for the plug to be pulled on a given signal from the NWO, could it be this that is next? Let us not forget though that the world could meet an untimely unexpected end that the NWO has not planned for if insane projects like HAARP misfire and destroy us all accidently (which to me is also a very real imminent possibility).

It would be inappropriate for me to relate more here as the books and on-line services are far more adept at relating the details than I am.

Before we go on to the next chapter about banks and the mess world economies are in, I want you to think on something that has me beaten to understand. The USA is reported to be teetering on the brink of financial collapse that many claim will reduce it to third world status, yet what should be happening is that the USA is entering into a period of sustained growth that even their amazing history could not find an equal to. The USA is about to start producing oil and gas from its own shale supplies that will make it the biggest oil and gas producer in the world by 2017. The shale oil and gas fields in the USA are massive, at present the oil and gas fields available total around 21 billion barrels, the new shale fields have around 20 billion barrels each and there are over twenty of them. The USA will be producing more oil and gas than Saudi Arabia and Russia combined – what a future to excitedly expect. One estimate suggests that the USA will be producing a staggering 10.9 MILLION BARRELS OF OIL A DAY. Thousands of new drilling rigs are being put to work along with hundreds of thousands of Americans.

Fantastic new products, inventions, materials are shortly to come on-stream in the USA that can help turn the countries fortunes around. Standing in the way of this progress is the massive debt that the US government and the Central Bank of the USA (Federal Reserve) have stacked up between them. There have been a number of reports circulating that sour the news of the shale oil and gas wealth to come, these reports state that the level of debt is so great in the USA that nothing will save it. So many people are claiming that the only way for the USA to go forward is to default on its debts, the whole situation is insane as there is a great future ahead that is in danger through past mistakes and decisions of the Federal Reserve. The only way the new bright future of the US will take place is if a fresh approach is adopted, but will that happen? Will the usual barriers of leaders and banks protecting their power and control bar the way of this bright future or will they let the tsunami wave of cash happen and take a ride while picking up even greater fortunes?

One of the new materials mentioned above is a substance called graphene, one report claims that the development of graphene is "an impending turning point in high tech as important as silicon and integrated circuitry were a half century ago". This new substance carries electricity faster than copper and 100 times faster than silicon, conducts heat better than any substance known to man and is as transparent as glass, yet somehow it is 200 times stronger than steel while remaining elastic enough to stretch 20% without breaking. The breakthrough can lead to mobile phones that roll up, smart phones and high definition TV's as thin as paper, super-efficient computers, solar panels and batteries. Cars and airplanes could be produced at a fraction of their present weight and far superior in strength, with greatly improved fuel efficiency due to lower weight. Areas of medicine could be revolutionised as tougher than steel artificial limbs and metal pins would be made of graphene. The discovery was made by two British scientists who received the Nobel Prize in physics for their discovery. Don't you think that this product alone will be enough to turn around the fortunes of the USA? There are of course other such great new discoveries and materials waiting to make the USA great again, will it be allowed to happen? – that is very doubtful.

Often something will keep cropping up when I am searching the Internet or reading a book, this is a usually a strong hint to me that I should take notice of whatever is appearing on a recurring basis. Just such a situation is that the year 2015 appears to be an important year, it keeps on surfacing as I work. I believe this could well be the year that big moves to step up planning towards controlling the world will take place. With war imminent in The Middle East, the numbers of countries in dire economic problems growing, mixed with the approaching boom for the USA, this would be a feasible opportunity to make the big push for control. If the NWO do not want the USA becoming powerful again around the year 2017, a move to collapse world economies before that year is very much on the cards. The NWO will need the USA to collapse to carry out its grander plans. Once all of this is achieved, the NWO will send in its people from the IMF to take over the running of the failed nations. This is why we have had the problems of Greece etc. rammed down our throats over the last few years – to prepare us (brainwashing us) to expect Greece or someone to fail and start the domino effect on other nations. The people will blame the failing countries for destroying the world economies and will welcome with open arms the "saviours" sent and supplied by the IMF to "get us out of trouble", which of course is the opposite of the truth as from that point on our lives will be lost. Can you imagine that? We would have been conned by one of the biggest sting operations in the history of mankind and we will welcome in with open arms the enemy just like the wooden Trojan horse was welcomed in and proved to be the downfall of Troy.

This next section has to be the most important in the book, please read it carefully

Take your time to read this next section of the book, consider its ideas thoroughly and thoughtfully, no matter how difficult you find it to believe.

No matter how hard we all find it to believe that a secret organisation has taken stealthy control of the western world, the amassed oceans of data and convincing information point only that it does indeed exist. In the total absence of any formal denial that this organisation exists, again we can only consider it does exist. With almost eleven million articles and tens of thousands of book titles printed, huge numbers of on-line videos available, hundreds of millions of people who are convinced the secret organisation is real, who can possibly deny that our world has been taken over? From the massed information I have picked through, this that follows "appears" to be what we have hidden from us:

Over two hundred years ago the budding Freemason movement began to grow and control the direction of national politics and later economies. Through many twists the original Freemason movement split into two, one division becoming what we know as The Illuminati. The Illuminati were far more ambitious and aggressive in their aims than the Freemasons. Detailed planning set the ball rolling to control the world and this planning has been stealthily implemented over the last two centuries, it is set to culminate into absolute control in the very near future. To carry out its dirty work the Illuminati created the New World Order and the Bilderberg group to oversee and be the central planning for the NWO. Neither the NWO or the Bilderberg group are Illuminati, they are both "tools" to be used to achieve the plans of The Illuminati. Do not associate the NWO and the Bilderberg Group with The Illuminati any more than that they are tools being used by The Illuminati. Something all three of these groups are well known for is the ability to use and "set up" people to work undercover or without knowing who their real masters are. Many Freemasons etc. at ground floor level do not know they are "in league" with the NWO and Illuminati and carrying out their plans. The secretive planning is a masterpiece of stealth and deceit as few know what is really taking place. Even the most intelligent people on our planet have not recognised what has taken place and will refuse to accept any of the news we have all been fooled and used. The NWO has virtual complete control of everything in the western world, their most important "asset" being the control of the news reporting media which churns out endless propaganda to brainwash us all each and every day. Until quite recently the NWO have remained a secret organisation, now they are far more open, which suggests they have just about achieved control of all areas of our lives. The final push for control must therefore be imminent.

Who will carry out the final push? Go back to the paragraph above and read again the part that describes how the NWO expertly uses and sets people up to do their dirty work. This amounts to programming into people a sense of devotion and duty to represent and protect their country, when they are in fact working unknowingly for the NWO. Our politicians, police, military, lower ranking Freemasons, all the secret services believe they are working for their country when they are actually carrying out the orders and plans of the NWO. The whole system of government has been "set up" to deliver the people into what amounts to slavery and obedience to secret masters. Many reports state that the USA is secretly preparing for massive civil unrest by building large internment camps, FEMA is buying up all spare ammunition and many armoured cars priced at over two million dollars each are being purchased by police forces. Why buy up all spare ammunition, why do they buy large numbers of armoured cars, why build large numbers of secret internment camps? They can only be expecting problems.

The Illuminati have no allegiance to our countries or the people, they only align to their own secret agendas, they have no allegiance or loyalty to the NWO, Bilderberg Group or Freemasons, their aims are purely personal.

So we have to ask ourselves how anyone could be so crassly stupid to believe they are going to "inherit the Earth" when the final push takes place? The NWO and Bilderbergs must suffer the same fate they have worked hard to impose on the people once The Illuminati have used them and "set them up" to carry out their plans. There can be no other conclusion, The Illuminati are totally ruthless, have no respect for human life or suffering, does anyone really believe they will be invited to join in the New World? The only place they are going is into a grave. Political leaders, military leaders, economic leaders, business moguls will all pay for their deceit and they just will not believe it until it happens. You cannot "dance with the devil without paying a heavy price". When will they wake up to this?

Our police and our brave fighting forces are being used and have been set up by their top level chiefs to believe they are protecting their country.

Our whole system of government has got to be discarded and completely replanned, our political parties must be disbanded and new modern ones created.

Failed economies at national and personal level must be dropped to allow us to start again from the bottom up. Many countries are after all bankrupt and only getting into worse and worse situations, which must lead to its people facing financial ruin as the national economy collapses under the sheer weight of debt.

Can we fool ourselves any longer that "we can come through all this, as we always have before?" How many times do we need telling, **this is not a normal situation!**

All of this above is the glaringly obvious conclusions from the enormous amount of data that we can all sift through, the observations are mine, the information was gleaned by many.

Do you agree yet that "we do not know the real world?"

Deep considerations our serviceman and police should take

This paragraph that follows is a wakeup call to the military and police forces who are under as much a threat as the rest of the people, possibly more so. **If** all we read is true and that this secret organisation exists and does intend to not only take over the world, but to also remove 90% of the population, commonsense tells us that all military from a private to a five star general/field marshall and all police officers from police chief to street police must be very high up on the list of "expendables" when the culling of 90% of the population takes place. No matter what the five star generals, police chiefs etc. have been promised, they *must* be some of the first "culled", so they had **better wake up to the obvious.** When the culling starts, there will be no need for soldiers, sailors, airmen, police as it will be done on a mass attack of some kind, whether disease, nuclear EMF attack or by HAARP. The last thing the Illuminati will want after the culling is a potential threat to their command of power which a military mind would present, they will not need policing as they will have the greatest system of policing in place – fear. The very last thing they will want is people who are secretive, which can only mean the various secret services will be wiped away early as the secret rulers will not trust anyone experienced in undercover covert actions. This would be very ironic, the secret services who helped plot the downfall of so many will be removed so that they cannot secretly plan against the people they put into power. Anyone who contributed to the downfall of mankind will be erased as they obviously cannot be trusted and the ruthless Illuminati will not tolerate such a potential threat to them. "The biter being bitten". **There can be no other conclusion**.

Once everything takes place and the new order is in control, the military – secret services – world leaders - police will be rewarded for their treachery with an early grave. Just as Lenin said, "rule by fear" and having seen 90% of the population wiped out the remaining humans will certainly be full of fear, they will need no policing and no military. There will be no thank you or a sense of honouring the help given to The Illuminati, quite the opposite, all those contributing to the downfall of the people will meet the same ending. Police, military and secret services will be conceived as the only possible threat to the Illuminati and that is why they will be terminated early on, there will be no sense of loyalty for the contribution they made. So wake up everyone in uniform, commonsense says you are probably earmarked for the opening act, when you dance with the devil you pay a heavy price.

More deep thoughts on the subject above

From the mass of information that is readily available and opinions of true experts on this subject there can be no other conclusions than these that follow, conclusions that will at first anger many I am sure and then lead to the realisation that military and police have been totally misled, "set up" and used. Soldiers – sailors – airmen – police – secret services that tap phones etc. All have been seriously defrauded to believe their actions (some actions, not all) were ordered to protect their country. By using patriotism, devotion to duty and country, allegiance to sworn oaths to defend their country, brainwashing through repeated orders and instructions, leaders have used our brave fighting forces to further plans that do not benefit the country these forces signed up to defend. Personally I have many ex school friends, friends and family that have served in the British military and know they will be furious, enraged to discover they have been fooled. They all are totally devoted to "Queen and Country" and would die protecting both, they will be so angry to learn they have been misled by some politicians and military chiefs. One friend still suffers badly today from the trauma of being blown up by a "pop up" land mine in The Falklands War, how must he feel to find out this war was about oil and not defending British citizens and soil? When the cold light of day finally dawns on our fighting forces that they unknowingly were often doing the dirty work of the secret rulers of the world and not defending their country, they will be angry, very angry. We have all been betrayed, but apparently none more so than our military and police. Let's look at a few recent conflicts to explain this in simpler language. The UK sent a huge task force around the world to The Falkland Isles to oust an attacking force from Argentina, what was the real reason this armada sailed to fight,? "supposedly" to protect a small population of 3000 islanders. The Falklands has a small population of sheep farmers and fishermen, why go to so much trouble, so much expense and lose so many lives to defend a small island outcrop inhabited by sheep farmers? Simple answer – OIL. The Falklands has potentially some of the largest oil and gas fields in the world in its seas which is being drilled for right now. Argentina knew this and so did the UK and they argued about the oil rights for twelve years before the Argentinian invasion in 1982, it was for this reason the military was sent to re-take the Islands. All the lives lost and the injuries suffered were measures taken to protect The UK's interests and snuff out the Argentine interests relating to oil and gas fields. The Iraq war was along the same lines, not to trace weapons of mass destruction as claimed, but to keep open the oil taps to the western world which Saddam Hussein was threatening to turn off. Afghanistan conflict falls into another area of importance – drugs and vast natural mineral reserves. As many sources suggest, the war moved from Iraq to Afghanistan on the orders of The Illuminati as the Taliban had cut off the drug trade to the western world and was destroying the opium poppy fields. Drugs return massive profits and banks make money from laundering drug money (as proven by massive fines imposed on banks for laundering drug money). However hard that sounds to believe, if you think about it, it does make sense.

The Taliban are tribes people and were not attacking western countries with terrorism (though they were accused of giving homes and bases to Al-Qeada) , so why target them? Yes, they treat people badly in Afghanistan villages, is that though a good reason to send the might of combined super equipped armies to halt them? Lost revenues from oil and drugs is what made all this military might swing into action and it will only be the leaders at the top of the tree that know this, those lower down will believe the reasons stated for "going to war". Something else that is not public is that Afghanistan has recently discovered huge mineral resources buried in the country, good reason to occupy a third world country in anyone's books. If you find this hard to believe, ask yourself "why are we still occupying what is basically a third world country that is virtually penniless?" Again I remind you that the information to back these claims up is available in large quantities, none of the above thoughts originated from myself, I am simply repeating and passing on what appears to be very feasible thoughts.

How does this make you feel? That decisions made at the highest levels are camouflaged to appear as if conflict is in the interest of your homeland when all along it is being fought for money? Our servicemen and women go through hell, they are killed and maimed, they kill and maim supposed enemies and its not to protect their homeland as they are led to believe. Our brave fighting forces are steeped in devotion to their duties and will surely find all this very difficult to accept, it does though all make sense when you examine the background information on offer and not the reasons our leaders announced.

Once more it is leaders fulfilling their own private agendas and using the people to carry out their dirty work, just the same as it has always been in history. Our brave military must find out the real reasons they were sent to war before they are sent to fight another, **they do though need to be careful who they ask for answers!**

Let us for a moment assume the threat to cull 90% of the population is real. Whatever and whichever system/weapon is used to cull six and a half billion people, it can only be used indiscriminately, that is it cannot be targeted to only hit some people and not others, it is all or nothing and no grey area between. Therefore whichever area is the target, Europe, The UK. North America, China, Russia, everyone will be erased, there is no other way. Biological warfare - poisoning water supplies – nuclear attack – EMF attack – HARRP attack can only wipeout everyone, nobody can be spared due to the type of weapon needed for mass execution. Unless you are in a safe bunker, you perish. All those who are working against their country under cover (with or without knowing it), if you don't have access to a safe bunker, your plotting will come full circle and claim your life and your families with everyone else's. All the military, the police forces, secret services, politicians, freemasons gone in an instant along with their families. Now we should all see why teaming up with the secret rulers of the world is the biggest fraud and mistake in man's long history, everyone has been used, misled, fooled, conned, "taken for a ride". If you cannot see the truth and irony in this, then you are fooling yourself and openly practicing ignorance of the truth. After the culling, the only people left will be Illuminati and those who will be used to clear up the mess, they will be micro-chipped and slaves to their Illuminati masters. Do you think this will not happen and that such cold blooded people can be trusted? Are you *absolutely sure* of that? Remember, the German people trusted Adolf Hitler. You will be "the deceivers deceived", there is no other way. This is the plan, not a Hollywood blockbuster movie score, not a conspiracy theory or the words of a deranged writer, this is the future if we allow it to happen.

If you are laughing or ridiculing all of these details, just remember we are well known for being caught out with our pants down, open to surprise attacks and moves due to complacency and a belief we are here forever. **Ignore these warnings at your peril**. Stop for a moment and really consider all this, no matter how much you disbelieve these warnings, what if it is all true, will you allow your disbelief to interfere with your judgment and stop you finding out if there is any truth in these warnings? Will you truly endanger the future of mankind by not investigating further and ask the questions that need answering? Isn't it time to find out how much of the warnings are true, before it is too late? Shouldn't our military and police be asking their superiors for answers before they venture out again on a mission or sortie and possibly against their fellow countrymen? Laugh, become angry, do whatever you feel right when faced with these warnings – **just find out where the truth lays before you do anything else and before you ridicule the suggestions.**

Due to the careful planning, all the military, police services, secret services, news reporting services and freemason's, should the culling take place or whatever is planned happens, they will be directly responsible, all the blame can only be on their shoulders. The secret rulers may make the plans, plans though are useless without people on the ground to carry out the orders, whether the ground workers know what the full implications of their actions are or not. This shows how deadly devious the planners are, shifting responsibility and blame onto others who will not realise they have been "set up". **It's about time that those being set up – woke up!** Six and a half billion deaths must sit very heavily on their shoulders, can they handle it? Actions taken against your country is treasonable, again whether you are fully aware of the implications of your actions or not, how will it feel to be part of the mass murder of your countrymen and women? Shouldn't you find out what is going on before you commit this act?

* * *

Throughout this chapter I have banded together the Illuminati and the New World Order only for ease of my preperation and your reading as to type and read the full titles each and every time I mention them would be wasting space and time. The Illuminati are a separate body to the NWO as the Illuminati created the NWO to carry out its dirty work for it. The Illuminati have no affinity to the NWO, they see them only as a necessary part of the overall planning and when the planning is in place the NWO will meet the same end as everyone else (no matter what they have been promised). The Bilderberg Group I believe are also a separate entity of their own, they are the decision making and general running body of the NWO but under direct instruction and control of the Illuminati. This group can also fully expect to be "erased" once full control of the world is established as they represent a threat to the Illuminati due to the fact they are a secret organisation in their own right and that will not be tolerated in the new world structure.

Something else I have read often is that the Illuminati consider themselves to be a "Super Race" and not members of the human race, they see the human race as underlings, slaves, second rate beings who they use for their own purposes. The NWO is made up of people from the human race, some will be kept on after the culling to ensure that the Illuminati are catered for, just like the majority of humans there will be many NWO operatives that meet their end when the culling is carried out. Some of the deeper reports I have read on the Illuminati state that they believe they are descendants of early Egyptians, which is why they follow the Gods of that era and why Paris, London and Washington have so many buildings and monuments in honour of the Egyptians and their Gods (**yes its true**, they are everywhere in those cities, search for this on the Internet)). Want proof? Watch Jordan Maxwells on-line video "exposing the Illuminati" and see what you think about his news. This would explain why the NWO are also considered atheists, non-believers in the God that the rest of the world follows (whether that is Allah, Mohammed etc.).

Another detail that crops up often is that the Illuminati will not marry outside of its own bloodline, this to ensure that only pure bloodlines are produced within their children. Take a look at "The Thirteen Bloodlines" via your search engine, this is a very enlightening subject. Now you should begin to understand why culling 90% of the population means nothing to the Illuminati, they do not consider they will be killing their own, they will be removing lower breeds while keeping some on as slaves. This will happen because we "the slaves" will not believe it is possible, or that it will happen and we will take no actions to stop it as we are totally lost in the careful brainwashing we have been subjected to all our lives. 25% to 30% of the population won't even listen or read the warnings as they are too scared and do not want to know about "nasty things", just like an ostrich with its head down a hole in the sand, that will not make the problem or the end result go away, on the contrary it will bring about the end result much faster. The Illuminati have no affinity to the USA, the UK, Europe or any country which is why the people of these countries will not be spared during the great culling, it's time to wake up to this principle.

The Illuminati have set up base in the USA for understandable reasons, where would you go if you wanted to run the world? To the most influential country of course, the country with the most power, the largest military force and the world's leading economy. They are not Americans, they use America and Americans while pretending to support the USA, which is a long way from the truth.

Whistle Blowers

Whistle blowers who expose government actions are quickly touted as public enemies by the national press and media, it's worth a look at this to decide if they really are enemies. Most whistle blowers do what they do from devotion to their country and can see that their country is being defrauded by its leaders, so they announce this publicly. With more and more leaders walking a thin line between a real and unreal world, the people will depend on someone exposing the dangers created by walking this precarious tightrope between reality and lies. With the terrible weapons that exist which can wipeout huge masses of the population, we need whistle blowers to warn us. Think about it, a whistle blower knows that once their secret is out they will be chased around the globe, under threat of assassination, no longer able to see their loved ones, live in fear and probably have to move to another country. Yet they still do it as they want to save their beloved country from the fraud exposed. Therefore, whistle blowers are more patriotic than all the others who keep quiet about the dangers to their country. With the world in the mess it is now, I fully expect more and more people to speak out and expose government espionage and hidden actions. The whistle blower is not an enemy of the state, they are heroes standing up to the deceptions. The only "crime" they have committed is to expose leaders dark plans and actions to the public, therefore they are only committing crime in the eyes of those exposed. We are wound up to hate whistle blowers and want them silenced, this is hatred fuelled by the controlled press and our leaders who are those being uncovered – have you ever thought about this fact? One day we will thank whistle blowers and rightly recognise their courageous contribution to a new free society.

If you were to ask me if I believe the NWO, Iluminati and secret societies exist, I would have to say 100% yes. I will not try personally to influence the reader, I am reporting here what is available to learn and ask the reader to make up their own minds after discovering the facts.

Let me make this very clear – I WANT to be proved wrong that a secret organisation rules our world with terrible plans for us all, I would openly welcome looking foolish. It will though take a major national leader to stand up, put their hand on a bible and state categorically that we are not ruled by secret organisations to calm my fears, not a television presenter or a newspaper report and not a government minister. If this does not happen then like the hundreds of millions of others who believe in a secret world ruling organisation, I can only keep believing this. Is there a major world leader out there who will do this, to stand up before the world to say this is all wrong and there is no plan to take over the world? that will be interesting and if it does not happen then it will prove a large part of the case that a secret organisation is real and has planned many atrocities.

The principle of a world order has many points of merit, a world army to stop wars and fighting, a world bank that standardises banking rules and practices, a world agreed law book to standardise laws so that we all know what to expect. Having a one world currency would also save so much confusion, though I realise this would take considerable time to implement as it would face many problems. An International language would be a huge benefit, if it was a second language. These would be positive moves, but a one world religion is a no starter (as would slaughtering 90% of the population). Let's face it, we have got to do something to sort out the immense problems of the world and change is the only way.

Closing comment goes to President Abraham Lincoln "America will never be destroyed from the outside. If we falter and lose our freedom, it will be because we destroyed ourselves". If the USA is destroyed in the way described above, it will be from the inside as the NWO is very much now an American based organisation staffed by powerful Americans.

The more you look into this subject, the deeper it gets and the more there is to find out, just let me remind you again of an early quote, probably the truest quote anywhere in the book "you do not know the real world". We are walking a very thin line between reality and an unreal world of total deceit and the chances of us all accepting this are a million to one against. The irrefutable proof we need should surface soon when the next phase of the planning is unleashed. Only the people can stop this and only if enough are able to believe the threats we are under, which is not looking likely at the moment, immediate action is needed, will you do anything?

Two possible epitaphs for mankind have been suggested in this book, this third suggestion has to be the ultimate, **"what have we done?"** to be followed by **"God help us"**.

What if? For those who have had no previous exposure to details like these in this chapter, it must all appear so hard to accept – just ask yourself "what if it's all true?". The mountains of evidence, the belief from hundreds of millions of people that this is all true must point you at the only conclusion – this is fact not theory. When no denial is offered that the facts are untrue from any of those accused of being part of the plot, what other conclusion is there? What if this one world organisation has indeed infiltrated every part of normal life, are you going to sit back and accept it, to accept the widely held view that 90% of the world population will be culled, that we will all be micro-chipped, that all our savings etc. will be removed and we will be virtual slaves. What if this is all fact and not conspiracy? What if all western world leaders **are** puppets to this organisation, will you be able to see past your devotion and belief in your leader? What if all our brave military, secret services and police been used to fulfill the plans of corrupted leaders and this one world organisation and not their country? – **shouldn't we all make it a number one priority to find out,** so we can correct any deceit?

Summary

Secret societies certainly appear to exist, their aims were unclear as they were of course a secret, which does not appear to be true anymore, they are no longer secretive. They're goals are only of benefit to themselves while holding a smoking gun to the heads of world leaders that force the leaders to dance to their tune. All aspects of life appear to have successfully been "taken over" and the people of the world are at their mercy while the secret societies play out their plans. Should you have learned of all this 5 – 10 years ago you would have little hard proof, with the secret organisation "out of the closet", you do not have to seek truth anymore, its everywhere and now you will start to recognise it having been informed what to look for. Do you really still doubt that secret organisations exist?

nine

Your Money, Going – Going – Gone

* * *

Henry Ford who founded Ford Motors got it so right with one of his many famous quotes "It is well enough that people of the nation do not understand our banking and monetary system, for if they did, I believe there would be a revolution before tomorrow morning".

We are probably headed for the biggest financial collapse in history and it could be a "blessing in disguise". Why? Because at last we will see for ourselves what our leaders have done with their insane policies and we will be forced to start all over again from the ground up to construct a realistic workable system. Our present systems do not work, they are broken and rely on a never ending stream of increasing debt – **on a massive scale**. Our world economic systems CANNOT be saved as **they are swamped with vast oceans of debt which grow larger by the second.** This is not a wild claim, our economies cannot be saved while left in the hands of politicians, bankers and economists – end of story. The gap between money coming into our economies and that going out is widening all the time, **as more debt is added the gap yawns open even further, wider and wider the void grows every second**. The equation is as simple as $1 + 1 = 2$, when you add more debt your repayments grow larger which forces the gap between money entering an economy and that which flows out to expand. **It is only a matter of time until the whole system crashes as you just cannot keep on borrowing unlimited,** when will this be? soon. We cannot repay our massive debts, in fact there is only one real escape route – drop and write off the debt and declare bankruptcy.

A case in point to consider before reading the rest of this chapter: The USA is regarded as the greatest and wealthiest nation on Earth, the financial generator of the world. Get ready for this.

The US govt. spends $121,067 per second, of which $52,162 is borrowed

The US govt. spends $7,264,000 per minute, of which $3,129,756 is borrowed

The US govt. spends $73,221,917,808 per week of which $31,547,945,205 is borrowed. That's $73 billion spent and $31.5 billion borrowed in one week.

The US govt. spends $3,818,000,000,000 per year, of which $1,645,000,000,000 is borrowed. That's $3.8 trillion spent and $1.6 trillion borrowed. (all figures from 2011) For every dollar spent, 46 cents is borrowed. US debt stands at just over sixteen trillion dollars! Take a look on-line at the "US federal debt clock". The figures above do not include the trillions being racked up by The Federal Reserve. If the world's most successful nation is in this amount of debt, what is the rest of the world like?

How much is a trillion dollars? If you taped ten dollar bills together end to end, it would wrap around the world 380 times! How does that picture sit with you?

Can you imagine what would happen to the debts if interest rates start to climb to a normal level from their abnormal low present rates?

How about The UK? Thankfully The UK has nothing like this towering debt time bomb, but it's borrowing is still at record levels. In the hundred years before the present coalition government formed, The UK had total borrowing of £700 billion, in the five years of the coalition government they will add to and borrow another £700 billion. The UK's total debt still sits at £1.2 trillion, which is massive and all that happens is that this debt is being added to daily, which means the repayment costs grow larger daily. It would be correct to point out that it is not the coalition government that has caused this as they were left in a precarious financial system from the two previous governments.

But the facts speak for themselves, massive debts are building and not being paid off, only added to, which equates to a downward spiral. Do you honestly believe a recovery is possible under these circumstances?

The Eurozone, what about them? Well, with so many Eurozone countries receiving bailouts and others on the edge of requesting financial help, this is a disaster waiting to happen. Eurozone debt is estimated at just over ten trillion euro's and it is growing all the time just like The USA and The UK debt. How long can we keep inflating these debt balloons before they burst? We will find out soon, sooner than you think.

It is one sorry mess that is infinitely worse than we are aware of, how could this have happened? We're sending space craft around the galaxy yet we cannot run our own nation's economies. We have brilliant minds creating amazing inventions, but we cannot make our pennies add up, which must worry us all.

Our governments find themselves in situations so similar to individuals who fall into the credit card trap, borrowing to pay for services and only paying off the minimal monthly interest, that interest creeps up and up until it becomes impossible to pay even the minimum repayment. That's where many governments are finding themselves or heading to.

The whole system has got to be turned inside out and re-designed, it does not work in its present form, how much proof of this would you like? Consider this: if all you do is add to your debts and increase repayments, how can you pay off your debts? Can you argue against this fact, that we are up to our necks in debt and all we do is pile on more and more? Can you ignore the facts? Remember this old saying, **politicians lie, but numbers don't.**

Despite what our governments, bankers and economists try to tell us, world economies are in free-fall to oblivion, it is clear from recent results that world financial systems are broken unworkable models and when coupled with banking practices which are dubious, failure is more or less assured. The "race to the bottom" is at full throttle. There is not a national economy anywhere in the world that has any degree of safety due to the actions of bankers, governments and economists.

Naturally you won't read this in any of our newspapers or hear it on radio or television news reports, that does not mean it isn't true, it just means that its being hidden from us. China, India, Indonesia, Russia, Brazil and all expanding economies must be looking with great fear at what is happening in the USA, Japan, Europe and the UK as these nations' economies continue to nose dive into worse and worse conditions, more and more debt. The expanding economies know that should the other nations explode into financial oblivion, they will be dragged down with them by the knock on effects of collapsing confidence. The desperate actions to shore up failed strategies of the recent past are not working and cannot work as all that is happening is that the measures being taken are an extension of those which delivered these nations into trouble in the first place – irrational borrowing and lending. The enormity of the conclusions is frightening, we have got our theories wrong, we have got our sums wrong, we have got our motives wrong, we have got just about everything wrong and our sole solution is to keep doing more of the same. The world is awash with debt and poverty and every penny borrowed now is robbing from the future as it all has to be paid back at some time. What wealth and prosperity exists is under complete control of a small minority who gained their prosperity by removing it from the majority (this is not a comment, it is fact).

This is a lengthy chapter as this is a lengthy subject, if you are not aware of the sort of information that follows – you had better prepare yourself for more shocks. Please keep this in mind as you go through this chapter: there is considerable condemnation of banking practices wherever you look, on the Internet – books – on-line videos & even in the daily press (a big shock).

We must not "tar all banks with the same brush", there are many great and decent banks, they are mainly the smaller banks. There certainly appears to be a cartel of major banks that many people say are behind all the fraud and are actively attacking other banks with their underhand tactics to ruin the banks outside of the cartel. Therefore, though this chapter mentions banks and banking as if they are banded together, keep in mind that there is a sinister group who are the real scourge and not all banks.

After preparing this chapter of the book I was filled with doubt and wondering how am I going to make people believe what they are about to read? This chapter deals after all with what is an accepted part of "The Establishment" a "Pillar of Society", a service we have been raised to respect in its entirety, it has been part of our everyday lives for all our lives and here I am attempting to uncover this respected institution as far from honest. You will learn that our trusted banking systems are actually at the heart and the cause of all our financial woes and until the banks are returned to being banks and not investment risk takers playing with fire, our world financial systems will remain on the brink of collapse and in serious danger. Banks are proving themselves to be the proverbial "rotten apple in the barrel" that is poisoning our world, more and more people are waking up to this every day as more and more banks face charges for inappropriate practices.

Lord Acton said this about the banks: "the issue which has swept down the centuries and which will have to be fought sooner or later is the people versus the banks."

Bankers are some of the greatest magicians the world has ever seen as each and every day they produce money out of thin air without so much as a shout of "Hey Presto!!" At the press of a button credit literally appears out of nowhere and it is loaned out to unsuspecting borrowers who are unaware they have just been stung by fraud on a grand scale. If anyone else tried to pull this type of scheme together they would be put in prison and the key thrown away, such is the outright fraudulent deeds being carried out. Banks are some of the biggest fraudsters in the history of the world and they get away with it every minute of every day fully knowing they will not be seriously penalised for what they are doing because they control everything" they have always done it and have always got away with it scot free".

Get ready for some mind numbing details. If you sign up for a bank loan, mortgage or run up a credit card debt, the bank simply invents the majority of the loaned money out of thin air and transfers it to your account (electronically) little physical money changes hands, little physical money left the vault of the banks head office or your local branch. You are in fact mainly borrowing credit, the borrowed money physically exists in small amounts, usually around 10% of the loan - you have borrowed little physical money, the banks cannot lend what they do not have. As far as the bank is concerned your "invented" debt is a now a new asset on the bank's balance sheet and you owe them not only the fictitious money they invented, but also the interest they charge on top. What a brilliant scheme for the banks, they loan you money created out of fresh air (I call this FAM, fresh air money) you have to repay the banks real money that you have earned plus the interest they charge you for the privilege of borrowing FAM they have invented. How does that feel to you, your mortgage and or bank loans, credit card debts are false – fake – phony – "funny money" but you work hard to repay the banks back real cash with plenty of extras added on top? It's all an illusion, a sleight of hand and we the people are the stooges "the suckers". Now I am sure that like the time I first had this explained to me, you are either very confused, angry or you do not believe it is possible, by the end of this chapter you should understand and believe what you just read. Harry Houdini has nothing on these banking illusionists. They make him look ordinary compared to their daily trickery.

*** here is a "dirty little secret" that the above equates to: as the banks are not lending real money and they invent your various loans, this means there is nothing backing the loan, no equity, no cash funding. It would therefore only take a fairly small fraction of people to "walk away" from their loans and default to send banks spinning into collapse. This is why a failure at national level can destroy banks, should a national failure occur and people of that nation become unable to pay their loans, their defaulting would break the banks and leave the banks underfunded. With many national economies looking very fragile, how long can we play this frightening game of deceit? We the people would see our savings dissolve before our very eyes and all because the banks are playing with fire via fractional reserve banking (loaning money that does not exist). It's time to change these practices, don't you agree?

Remember this as you go through this chapter – the over inflated false rises in property values, soaring prices on just about everything we buy has been driven by easy borrowing, the lending of fresh air money. Had borrowing been harder to complete, the steady rise in prices would have been kept in check and we would not have inflation or heavy loan repayments eating into our finances. The woes facing individuals, companies and nations has been caused by insane easy lending/borrowing which is hurting just about everyone. Look no further than to the banks, economists and governments to understand why the world is in the financial mess that it is suffering today. Two key decisions led to this irreversible and calamitous situation, the setting up of The Federal Reserve Bank of America and the removal of "The Gold Standard" which is something I recommend you search for online. From these two actions, our world financial systems have plunged into chaos time and time again, today we find ourselves once more at the door of financial collapse with little hope of improvement.

The "reclaim the streets" protestors knew something that most of the people did not, that banks are ruining life for everyone (that really is everyone and includes communist countries that lose out due to western world banking practices). Our media, TV, radio and newspapers did their level best to picture the reclaim the street protestors as worthless "dope smoking, jobless lay-abouts" in their efforts to blacken the image of the protestors and to bury the reason they were protesting and at the same time appease their NWO puppet masters. **The reclaim the streets protestors were representing us all,** we did not know this as they were not allowed air time to state their true cause – protesting against the banking industries fraudulent ways.

Some of the mass rallies taking place around the world protesting against austerity measures imposed by governments make the news, showing that hostility is beginning to boil up within the people of the world. Would we be facing cruel austerity cuts if lending and borrowing had been sensibly handled? The news reporters attempted to picture these protestors as lazy and work shy, wanting easy money without working for it in an attempt to turn public opinion against the protestors.

The people of the world have also been making their displeasure known by forcefully protesting and removing sinister dictators running various national governments, this has become known as "The Arab Spring". Frustration is building across the globe as world economies crash and burn, debt levels pile ever up and up while government services are cut and taxes rise, which always hurts the people the most. Again these are repercussions of the easy lending and borrowing. The people of the world are more than ready to rebel against their leaders, their leaders know this and are ready to turn police and troops against their own people and have secretly prepared many internment camps capable of holding hundreds of thousands of the people ready for the inevitable protests. Riots and aggressive protests must be expected as the people are suffering so much due to the economic destruction taking place. Civil wars cannot be ruled out – anywhere! Which would be a mistake for all. The Arab Spring riots will surely spread globally with all the tension that is in the air, the people are getting angrier and more frustrated by the day, protest marches are growing in number (even in China) and spreading worldwide (though of course only a few details of these protests reaches us from our news reporting services). In my opinion, at some point soon somebody will take it onto themselves and begin to organise the many groups across nations of the world, that is what the Internet and improved communication systems can achieve and the only surprise is that it has not happened already. All rebellions and revolutions start with angry and frustrated populations, at this point in time the number of angry frustrated people across the world runs into hundreds of millions across many nations. The age old cry of "enough is enough" is the cry that will surely ring out again. When money is at the center of frustration and a person's family wellbeing is threatened, the frustration will eventually reach fever pitch and turn to bloodshed, it always does. Money woes lies deep at the heart of most of the world's problems and when wage rises are held down, inflation eats into the money people have to spend, leaving them with empty pockets. Rising unemployment – pension schemes failing or under-performing – savings fast draining away – currencies devaluing - benefit cuts, all on top of the austerity measures will surely be the final straw. When the fighting starts the governments will call on the police and troops to rally round and fight off the protests, will they do it?

Are the police and troops also frustrated with leadership direction and suffering as well, have they begun to see that the masters they serve do not serve them or their country? Could we see the greatest combined worldwide rebellion in the history of man? *I hope not.*

Nothing is ever really gained by violent means, at first it will seem as if a suitable result has been reached as jubilant protestors celebrate their victory, all that's happening is that the problem is being pushed back in time waiting to show up again. Usually the problems that caused the original rebellion will return as the newly installed leaders pick up were the disposed leadership left off. For lasting resolutions, *all sides have to sit down and accept the truth of the situation,* blame has to be admitted where blame is deserved, past wrongdoings have to be accepted and lessons have to be learned from those wrongdoings, forgiveness must also be part of the healing process, above all though it is truth that must be the major winner.

- Financial and economic "experts" have got to admit that their policies are not working and accept that cuts and austerity measures only hurt the people
- Banks must be stopped from carrying out fraudulent practices (severe fines imposed on major banks in recent years proves this is so)
- Investment is the way forward and not cutbacks
- We have to agree that the whole monetary system needs to be overhauled and re-designed

We cannot wait for this to happen, the process must start now, not five or ten years' time. A very pathetic and halfhearted review of banking practices was held in the UK post 2007-08 financial crisis collapse, this was all a show and designed to appease the people who were angry at what had taken place. The review agreed banking practices should change and that 2020 should be the starting point. Who says so, the government at that time who were in the pockets of the banks and know that come 2020 everyone would have forgotten the recommendations and nothing would happen.

There has been nothing concrete put into place anywhere in the world to stop a repeat of the crash of 2007-08 and not a single banker was imprisoned for their part in the gigantic fraud that caused the crash. In fact we never recovered from that crash as we are still suffering heavily from the extreme damage done. The crisis should read from 2007 – now, whenever now is, the crisis is not over, it lingers on running unchecked and hidden from our eyes, our leaders prefer to say it is under control – *it is not*. What would be nearer to the truth is that world economies are as out of control as a raging bush fire and the pathetic measures taken to end the crisis can be likened to when areas of a bush fire are doused only for another area to burst into flame. Economists will not admit this as this would be clearly showing that they do not have a clue what they are doing. Anyone can talk a good talk just as economists are, it is not talk we need, it is positive actions to stimulate steady growth and not "more of the same" unworkable practices. Now is the time to sweep away the failed economics, take a grip of the dire situation and attack it with all we can to squeeze failure out of the system. Remember "only fools keep following fools" and economists have more than proven they are fools by hiding their failures with deceit.

Why do national economies crash?

Why indeed? National economies crash because of something we cherish and rightly value very highly – democracy, no, I do not believe we should abandon democracy. Let me explain what I mean and try my best to do so in a simple way that anyone would understand.

Governments are elected on the promises they make during election campaigns and on their actions taken in the period leading up to the elections. The sitting government will be judged on its performance while in power, did it upset too many people with its policies etc. This creates the biggest headache for a sitting government, does it implement policies to benefit the nation but may upset the electorate who will oust the sitting government, or does it unbalance the national economy and keep the electorate happy and make sure the government is re-elected? This over-shadows the vital decisions a national government should take when economies are crashing. The model that our national economies run on is broken but will not be mended while governments fixate themselves on being re-elected. Democracy seen this way is seriously flawed as governments cannot take the required brave "tough calls" to drag a nation out of the gutter for fear of being kicked out at election time. Today the world has many nations teetering on the edge of collapse and the correct decisions to halt the collapses will not be taken and the cowardly way out is adopted – borrowing on a massive scale and hiding the truth.

A nation's economy boils down to a balancing act between money coming in (tax revenues and investment) and money flowing out (benefits – pension payments – services – investment in national infrastructure etc.) If there is more money flowing out than coming in (which appears to be the normal situation) governments have no option other than to borrow money to cover its deficits and pay its bills, or default. This creates another perfect example of a "catch 22" situation as when you turn to borrowing you then have the added expense of repaying the loan on top of your other expenses forcing the gap between income and outgoings further apart. Nobody can win when credit is so free and easy and debt builds to such a level that it gets to a point that the credit repayments are so high they cannot be repaid. This is where nations are finding themselves, at a point that they cannot repay their creditors and they are forced to go "cap in hand" for a bailout. The bailout comes at a price and failing nations have to force through severe cuts to government spending and this increases unemployment, which increases the benefit payments needed to help the unemployed and so the problem just goes around in circles. Debts are not paid off they are merely pushed into the future and at some point they must be faced (only they are now much larger debts) more people are out of work and so less tax revenues are accrued – all in all its one very sorry mess. The national governments lose, the people lose and all because nobody is brave enough to face up to the truth – we have got it wrong and we are attempting to put the problem right with the same failed policies that got us into the problem in the first place. Population growth adds considerably to all government problems and benefits will have to increase along with a growing population. Population growth also compounds unemployment as there are more people than ever looking for a job.

Someone somewhere is going to have to "stick their head up above the parapets" and admit the system is badly flawed and only a complete makeover will solve the problems, we cannot carry on with insane borrowing and money printing. This may mean we may have to put democracy "on the shelf" for a few years (probably around ten years) as we finally "take the tough calls" and get our world economies back on track. All political parties and trade unions will be required to back the tough decisions to get a nation back on track and an amnesty will be needed to commit all sides to doing the right thing to save a nations future. Yes it will be painful, BUT NOTHING LIKE THE PAIN WE WILL SUFFER IF WE DO NOT DO THIS. National economies are just a house of cards, when one is removed, the rest will collapse, or they can be seen as a row of stacked dominoes, knock one over and the rest cascade down. It benefits everyone when all are strong, we need all national economies to pick themselves up and grow. If you knew the *true* state of your nation's economy, which you will never learn from the daily press, you would surely agree with the above suggestions.

Do not believe the talk about signs of recovery

Governments, banks and building societies, economists and the daily press will do their level best to try and make us believe that a recovery is on the way, picking up on any little snippet of good news to try and fool us into believing "the good times are back", it is all propaganda. Of course they want us to believe this as it benefits them and shows them in a better light (especially if an election is on the way), the truth though is that a real recovery cannot happen. National governments are borrowing at record levels, their repayments on loans are at record levels already, unemployment is high, investment is fading away, confidence in our economies is sinking. It does not take a mastermind to see this is not a recipe for recovery when more money is flowing out of a national economy faster than its coming in and the problem worsens each day with every extra penny that's borrowed. Until the borrowing stops and debts are removed – <u>there will be no real recovery,</u> how can a recovery take place when nobody is addressing the cause and all we do is "paper over the cracks"? National economies could collapse in the blink of an eye and we would not have seen it coming or know what hit us. There is also sure to be considerable emphasis placed on a recovery in the property market, newspapers and government ministers will brow beat us into accepting that its "lift off" for house prices – **which would actually be the worst possible move!** If property prices take off, it will be short lived as the lifeblood of the property market will be squashed – first time buyers. For continued growth the property market must (absolutely must) have new buyers entering at the lowest level, a process that has been labeled and now known as "entering the bottom rung of the property ladder". If you cannot supply enough first time buyers to the bottom rung of the ladder, everything stagnates and people cannot move up down or sideways on the property ladder, it grinds to a halt and values slip downwards. Think about it, if property values begin to shoot skywards again all we are achieving is making the deposit a first time buyer needs escalate further out of reach and kill all forward momentum, it would be pure insanity, a real case of shooting ourselves in the foot. If values rise 5% or more, first time buyers will effectively be shut out of the market, which would shut down and shoot down the market – can nobody understand that? I expect all sorts of government stimulus to "get the property market going again" **which should prove to everyone just how out of touch with reality governments are**.

By stepping in to help first time buyers onto the bottom rung and lending them money for a deposit, governments will stimulate the prices upwards and push the average deposit required higher, therefore making it an impossible dream for all the first time buyers lining up in the near future. Will governments continue to help first time buyers for ever and a day? They will need to if they stupidly stimulate prices skywards. The days of easy borrowing are long gone, mortgage lenders require new borrowers to provide huge deposits compared to the past (around 20%), rising prices puts those deposits out of reach, its basic mathematics that anyone should be able to see. In the UK, to buy a house priced in the average price bracket will require a buyer to have an income of £62,000 per annum, yet the average national salary is a mere £26,000 per annum, whether your good at mathematics or not, that is a very obvious gap in what is required. What is going to happen to all those who are taking government help when interest rates creep up and they cannot afford the leaps in monthly repayments? An accepted fact in our present downturn is that wage increases are stagnant, rising slowly or even slipping back, this again is hitting first time buyers, rising property values do not equate with stagnant salaries – could someone remind governments of this basic detail they are overlooking. The trouble is that there is little point in warning people of all these facts as nobody took the blindest piece of notice of the warnings before the last crash, we were all too carried away in the euphoria of seeing our property values leaping higher and higher.

Governments have got to take a far more responsible attitude to property and forget about artificial stimulus which in the end helps nobody if it collapses the whole shebang. Unstable property prices destabilises the property market, mortgage lenders are reluctant to lend after being hit so hard post 2007-08 (due to THEIR insane lending) stifles first time buyers. Therefore, if you artificially stimulate the property market with special government subsidies and offers, prices begin to rise and the initiative will eventually have the opposite effect than is desired. The stimulus will be short lived as you push the chances of first time buyers acquiring a property further away as they cannot raise the extra deposit money required to step onto the mortgage ladder. The UK property market is on a knife edge like so many other countries because lending rates are at record all-time lows, they will have to rise at some point – they cannot stay low forever. When this happens huge numbers of people will find themselves with massive mortgages they cannot repay – where is the sense in that? This detail alone is enough to collapse the property market. Governments that artificially stimulate property markets are shooting themselves in the foot and have definitely not learned a thing from the last property crash which was caused by insane lending and values rising out of reach of the vital first time buyers. This is a sure way to create a property bubble (crash) and the higher the values rise – the deeper the crash when it hits. The only way to save the property market is to allow it to drift down to its true value level and make property more affordable – artificially induced increasing property prices kill the long term future of this marketplace, we need to wake up to this fact. Let's all be very honest here, property values are grossly overpriced due to all the giant leaps experienced when fraudulent money lending was rife, our properties are just not worth their over inflated values. At some point the overpriced property market must meet a correction down to their true worth (estimated at a drop of 20-30%), will we scream and shout that this is wrong as we protect our overpriced homes, or will we see that it is an inevitable correction based on the fraud of the past? To let values slip goes against the grain in the minds of property owners who wrongly see property as an investment instead of a home, the alternative though is **a complete collapse in property values if we keep "fixing" the values to only rise.** The idea of letting values slip will cause an outcry from homeowners with heavy mortgages who will be horrified at the idea, they just won't be able to see that there is a very real danger of a huge collapse in property values if prices are artificially stimulated, we are not talking about a fall in value of 10%, it can be three times that or more. We are playing with fire when property values shoot up above the true worth of a property, it can only end in tears. Home owners want never ending rising property values to pay off frightening mortgage repayments, that is only natural, there is though a much more suitable way to remove the fright, to allow values to slip slowly down to their true values and greatly reduce mortgage repayments to offset devalued property. Just like most everything else we have got our priorities wrong when it comes to property and matters financial, as usual it is the people who suffer the most at the hands of our leaders. I have a mortgaged property, the value of the house has slipped around 7% in the two years since I bought it, that slip could increase to an almost overnight 60% if we fail to deal with the problems of our world - allowing a controlled soft let down of values is a far safer route than a monumental overnight crash that could wipe away a large part of property values. * the value of properties in the country I now live fell 9.7% in one month in 2013 and for no obvious reason, this can happen anywhere at any time while we allow governments to interfere with the property markets*.

Do you really believe that this type of crash cannot happen to you just because your government says the worse is over? There is a very good description of the policies that governments and economists are taking, something that perfectly captures their lunacy, "kicking the can down the road". What this means is that a problem arises, whether its national debt or property values etc. and an action is taken to temporarily solve the crisis, more of a sticking plaster than a cure. The crisis does not go away, it is simply moved into the future and at some time that problem is going to rise up again, only it will be worse as problems that are not sorted always worsen and grow. All that's happened is the problem has been hidden and not corrected, it will sit waiting until we "catch up" with it again, this is what our governments and their economic advisors have been doing for years and is a major reason why we are in such a mess. Someone somewhere is going to have to face up to the fact that we have been hiding the truth and that all our policies have achieved so far is to "kick the can down the road". Problems do not go away if you move them or ignore them, problems are very patient, they lay in wait until they can hit us with added force.

There is something about problem's which is always overlooked and that is that a problem is a sign that we are on the wrong pathway and to change the problem into a positive requires a new direction – *not more of the same.*

I wish I had a dollar/pound/Euro for every misinformed fool who has said to me of the present recession "it will be over in a year or two, it always is", WRONG! we are not getting out of this until policies change and we stop borrowing and printing new money. Something that should have happened but didn't when the economies kept nose diving was that the value of gold and silver should have rocketed, this is always the expected reaction when money markets contract. Why didn't it happen? Because banks and governments colluded to force the prices down as too many people (countries – investments brokers – individuals) stopped buying government bonds in preference of the safer refuge of precious metals. Another dirty secret is that central banks are loading up on gold, building strong reserves and the forcing down of gold prices makes this a lot less cost when values are artificially forced down. A recent article that is wildly circulating the Internet is that the value of gold was deliberately forced down to allow banks to gain massive profits with their derivative betting as they bet against the value of gold rising, placing money on gold values falling sharply. More tricks to take more of our money, where will it all end?

Eventually we are all going to have to realise that we cannot save our national economies and there is one last action we can resort to that will stop the complete breakdown of society and just about everything else - and that is to **default on our debts**. This is one reason central banks are loading up on gold in preparation of defaults. We will be left with no other option than to do what all the people who had taken out mortgages they could not afford did and that is to walk away from the debt. Why do we keep propping up something that is falling apart and not savable? Why not let it collapse in an *orderly way* and start again from the ground up? The loans that are dragging down worldwide economies are mostly fake FAM to begin with and very little real money was loaned, by defaulting on the fake debt the fake money can be scrubbed out. Imagine what that will do for nations floundering and awash with debt repayments they cannot afford, what would that do for Greece, Ireland, The UK, Spain, Cyprus, Italy, The USA etc. etc. etc. Why will this move be repelled? Because the people who started the whole farce would not be getting their "pound of flesh" in the form of interest payments and repayment of loans of FAM – the banks. Think for a moment, the loans you have, the mortgages you have were are made up of FAM created by Fractional Reserve Banking and other "magic tricks" (you will learn about these later), which means your loans are as false as the national debt loans. What would slashing your loans and mortgage repayments do for your financial status? The banks will scream and shout that they will be ruined as their assets would be wiped out. As their assets are false and the only thing being wiped off of their books would be the fake money, FAM, If we all drop the fake FAM from the system at the same time, nobody owes too much, so the FAM will instantly dissolve, the only possible losers would be bank shareholders who are paid out dividends on the FAM, everybody else wins. Governments win as they do not have to repay nonexistent loans which means taxpayers would not need to be squeezed dry, mortgage and loan repayments would shrink and give people more money to spend in the open economy and boost the economy in the process. If mortgage repayments are slashed, this will offset the de-valuing of property prices that still has a long way to run to a point many experts think will be pre-boom property prices of around the year 2000 (has that shocked you?).

A growing economy would not require austerity measures or government spending cutbacks, and investment can go ahead in infrastructure, again benefitting the open economy. Win – win – win for all, almost! not for the banks and economists, the people who got us in the mess in the first place as they cannot charge us for the fake loans and mortgages anymore which will not matter if they are re-organised and their direction changed. Until we attack the real problems of our economies – there is only one possible outcome, complete collapse. Is this a "pipe dream" to believe that defaulting is the way out? only if we allow things to continue as they are and not come to our senses. We will only come to our senses if we start to accept truth and not practice ignorance of truth.

How does the idea of paying drastically less for loans and mortgages sound to you, or that we can leap from austerity, cut backs and recession to better times simply by taking matters into our own hands and wrestling control away from the banks? Does this sound too simple, too easy? *Is your old programming telling you this is too good to be true?* It is only going to happen if you ditch your old programming and dissolve your ignorance of truth – would that be so difficult a task with so much on offer? As I said in the opening of this book – mankind faces a choice, change and experience paradise as near as possible, or not change and probably perish. This is mankind's decision to make, it should be a "no-brainer" and maybe now you know more of the facts, it will be. Economists and economic commentators will deride and make fun of the principle of defaulting on debt, they will howl in protest and call the idea completely unsafe – naïve - insane with predictions of complete collapse – the worrying thing about this is they will fully believe this to be true. We should ask **them** why their policies are not working and to give us all a TRUE picture of the state of the world's economies before they deride the suggestion of default. Let's ask them about all the "fresh air money" and money printing, let's ask about the record levels of national debts and record levels of borrowing, let's ask them about how banks can legally get away with fractional reserve banking, let's ask how banks can play with fire by placing bets on derivatives with money that does not exist, let's ask about our loans and mortgages and how much real money we really borrowed, let's ask them how bankrupt governments can lend money to bankrupt banks or the other way around, let's ask them if any of these loans actually involved real money or is it FAM credit produced on paper only, let's ask them why bank's lending rates are between ten and forty times the official national interest rates, let's ask them why so many of the big name high street banks have been fined many billions of dollars for offences such as money laundering for rogue nations – mis-selling of investment products – laundering drug money – fixing derivative bets in their own favor – manipulating Libor rates and much more, let's ask them where the IMF gets its money from to loan out, let's ask them where all the numerous taxes we all pay end up, let's ask them what happens to the money that governments borrow and who receives it, let's ask them why they tell us they are borrowing to lend to banks so banks can lend to businesses and stimulate the economy and why this never happens. While we are at it, we can ask them for their ideas how we will all return to prosperity and not austerity. When they can answer all of these comments – **then** they can deride the idea of defaulting, which sounds a fair trade off to me and that should also prove very interesting and entertaining to watch as economists try to wriggle their way out of all this!

Let me add this to the theory of default: Would defaulting be good or bad for the world? I do not know, my point is that everything else that has been tried so far has made the situation far worse, so why not default? Also I am trying to suggest we all look at doing something other than the present insane attempts to stop the free-fall into financial oblivion. If default is as bad as present polices then let's find the right direction, just do something else other than what we are doing – before it is too late.

You have a choice, the world economies – stock markets – bond markets – currency markets – property values are going to collapse in some way <u>sometime soon</u> and only an elite few will benefit, the rest of the people will suffer like they have never suffered before. Don't you think it would be a better idea to let all our failing economies default and let property prices slide to a sensible level so we can start again from scratch? Shouldn't we shake out all the failing companies instead of propping them up and allow investment to be re-directed into new more successful companies? Yes it will be a painful few years as the transition takes place, this pain though would be nothing compared to the pain and suffering we will face should we let our leaders have their way. ***Don't you agree a slow controlled let down of failing economies would be better than an overnight crash where the people lose <u>everything</u> they have ever saved for overnight resulting in a loss of pensions, homes, savings etc.?***

There is no other choice than to take the world economies "by the scrap of the neck" and completely change everything! A total make-over is the only way to stop all world economies collapsing sometime soon (which we may never recover from). We cannot rely on governments, bankers, economists to do this as they are the cause of the mess we all find ourselves in and we would have to ask ourselves if these people want to change anything and are they satisfied with what they have produced? Also, we must ask ourselves if they really are "front men" for the NWO if we should allow them near our economies or lock them away?

The heavy influence on a nation's economy will have to be taken out of the hands of central banks as it is the central banks that have imposed all the failing strategies on us. Should you choose not to believe this last comment, think about this: Central banks have thrown

a massive ELEVEN TRILLION DOLLARS of stimulus (quantative easing) at the various troubled economies around the world since 2007 –
ALL fake FAM!! what has it achieved? Nothing! We are still in a mess,
unemployment continues to grow, debts are escalating and more
nations are getting out the begging bowls. The world economies are
still nose diving, only at increased speed - $11 trillion dollars has not
made a dent in the problem, which shows that the central banks do not
have a damn clue what they are doing. If you need further proof of the
Central banks running out of control, here it is. December 2012 and
the Federal Reserve Bank in the USA announces it is to over double
the FAM it is using to buy mortgage backed securities from $40 billion
a month to $85 billion a month for the foreseeable future!! This will
add a further trillion dollars of debt to the Feds bill in a year, taking
its total stimulus to $4 trillion. Throughout the world it is a serious
crime to produce counterfeit money, yet that **is** what the various central banks are doing, producing money from nothing and throwing it
at a wall where all it does is slide down and disappear into the gutter –
having no effect at all. There is one effect it has had, besides growing
into a debt mountain, and that is to keep interest rates low, which is
not good at all as one day those rates will have to climb. This latest Fed
decision was another nail in the coffin of the US economy. Why do we
place the most important national economic decisions with central
banks? They are after all private banks with shareholders and it is to
the shareholders that the central banks give priority, the shareholders invest in the banks and they demand return on their investments.
The Bank of England, the Federal Reserve in the USA, the European
Central Bank, all central banks are all privately owned banks and NOT
government run banks as many people believe, it is these banks that
tell our governments what to do and not the other way around. If this
is news to you, what do you think of that? private banks with their
obvious first priority to their own shareholders determining economic
policy for whole nations! that just cannot be right. This conflict of
interest must start to show you how much power and control the banks
wield, they can force a whole nation to dance, skip and jump to their
tune, does that sound right to you, especially as they are leading us on

a dance into ruin? Is there any wonder why were in the mess we are? How could our governments be so stupid to turn over the economic future of a nation to private organisations who have frequently proven they are untrustworthy and following their own failed agendas? the simple answer is that governments have no choice in the matter as the banks are the real rulers of the nation. Forget what you believe that it is Prime Ministers, Presidents and elected parliaments that are running your country, they are puppets dangling on a string, taking their orders from the true masters. Once again I state I know how hard that last sentence is to believe, the only trouble is that it IS true. Banks are corrupt – want proof of that comment? You only have to look at the multi billions of pounds in fines being imposed on major British banks for corrupt practices to see they cannot be trusted with their normal banking actions, which will be outlined.

- Here are details that should really drive home the total mess our central banks are in, that is naturally hidden from us. When Lehman Brothers famously went under in 2008 they were said to have insufficient capital, their assets were $691 billion but only had real money (equity) of $22 billion, which is roughly 3%. Lehman's assets collapsed more than the 3% which meant they were technically bankrupt. Looking at major central banks today is very eye opening, the US Federal Reserve has $54 billion in capital and $3.5 trillion in assets, which is about 1.53%, the European Central bank is at 3.69%, the Bank of Japan 1.92%, the Bank of England 0.843% (yes you read that right) and the Bank of Canada 0.532%. Therefore all these major banks with billions of people dependent upon them are sitting on a knife edge mostly worse than Lehman Brothers, should their equity get wiped out, they are history along with the savings of many under their influence. Governments would not be able to bailout the central banks as of course governments themselves are on the same knife edge – broke! If the US Federal Reserve assets lose more than 1.5% of their value, The Feds equity would be wiped out and anyone holding the

Feds "reserve notes" would lose, which basically means anyone holding dollars. As Simon Black, who is known as Sovereign Man says "This is one of the strongest indicators of all that the financial system as we know it is finished". Find Simon Blacks excellent "straight talking" at: sovereignman.com, I highly recommend this thorough no holds barred newsletter. Simon sums up so well the apathy we have with life with this comment "Over the past several decades, people around the world have become so brainwashed that few people really give much thought anymore to the safety of their currency".

<u>Here is a list of the major shareholders of Federal Reserve Bank of America:</u>

Rothschild Bank London, Warburg Bank Hamburg, Rothschild Bank Berlin, Lazard Brothers Paris, Kuan Loeb New York, Israel Moses Seif Bank Italy, Goldman Sachs New York, Warburg Bank Amsterdam. These banks are connected to the London Banking Houses which ultimately control The Fed. The Bank of England does not allow anyone to know who its shareholders are, do you think that is right, a bank that sets the rules and interest rates of the UK that does not let anyone know who owns it, it could be anyone from anywhere with desires to ruin the British economy? Do you still think the central banks are government banks? It looks much closer to the truth that governments are owned by the banks, otherwise they would not let foreign banks (as in the USA and possibly the UK) run the country's economy. This I assure you is just the tip of a very large iceberg.

Thomas Jefferson said "if the American people allow private banks to control the issuance of their currency, first by inflation and then by deflation, the banks and corporations that will grow up around them will deprive the people of all their property until their children will wake up homeless on the continent their fathers conquered". It is happening, repossessions are rife and US government figures tell us that there are 633,782 people living homeless on its streets!

<u>Look at the recent track record of national major banks</u>: All details supplied below are taken from national news reporting agencies and

not conspiracy theorists, they are not my figures. More and more banks are being taken to court for many different reasons, brief news reports are tucked away on news reporting internet sites that state which financial organisation is next in line for prosecution. As I am not sure of the technicalities of law concerning libel and slander, I will not give out the names of banks who have faced severe censure and massive fines for their wrongdoings. If you bank with a major high street name in The UK, your bank is likely to be one of these that follows. How do you feel about this, that your bank has had to pay out billions in fines for criminal acts? Was it your money being used to pay these fines? How would you know?

Four well known UK high street banks all reached agreement with The Financial Services Authority over the mis-selling of specialist insurance to thousands of small British firms, the estimated fines would be between £1.1bn to £1.4bn. Deliberate mis-selling by our trusted banks! the organisations we are supposed to trust with our hard earned money.

One major bank confessed to fraud as part of the Libor (London Interbank Offered Rate) rate rigging scandal that hit the news in 2011-12, a further 10-14 major international banks are expected to be dragged into this investigation. This bank faced a fine of around £290 million for its part in this scandal. Six more banks are under suspicion of colluding in similar attempted manipulation. Libor is the interest rate that banks lend money to each other, the major banks placed "bets" (known as derivatives) against the rate that would be set each day, then rigged the rates to win the bets over smaller banks. These derivative banking bets are frightening as at any given time they are worth between $500 -$800 TRILLION dollars. This figure will probably mean nothing to you as it is very hard to comprehend, if you added together all the goods and services produced by every country in the world during a year of trading, you would only achieve about 70 trillion dollars. What is even more worrying is that the money being staked does not exist, it is electronic FAM money only, it is being placed by a bank employee and yet there is no money to cover the bet, if the bank employee loses, the bank is indebted to the tune of the stake – even though it does not have money to cover the stake. The banks employees admitted to faking the interest rates to help the banks traders win the bets placed for day after day, year after year. The interest shaving Libor scam has skimmed an estimated $500-$800 billion per year from the losing banks and financial institutions. This discovery has been labeled "the greatest fraud in history", massive fines are being handed out to the guilty banks, it is though a lesser worry than when lawyers start going after banks with class action law suits, which is the real worry. This could cause the whole banking system to implode and trigger the next financial crash.

What do you think to that? deliberately cheating to rack up massive profits on what is basically a huge gambling scam and what is worse it could destroy the whole worldwide financial system over night.

Another UK high street bank used by "drug kingpins" says US Senate.This bank proved a conduit for ""drug kingpins and rogue nations" according to US Senate committee investigating money laundering claims at the bank. A Senate report said suspicious funds from Mexico and Syria had passed through the bank. The bank apologies for its wrong doing between 2006 and 2010. December 2012 saw the bank agree a world record "fine" of $1.9 billion for its "wrong doings". A bank deliberately laundering drug money! Whatever were they thinking of?

This next UK founded Asia-focused bank, was ordered to pay a multi-million dollar fine by a New York regulator for illegally hiding transactions with Iran allowing the country to break sanctions against it and sell its oil for dollars. It was stated that the bank laundered $250 billion over a period of a decade.

Another UK bank is also accused by the US Senate of failing to prevent money laundering. Its US business said it carried out 28,000 undisclosed sensitive transactions between 2001 – 2007, most of which involved Iran.

One of the UK government owned banks is also understood to be facing investigation into possible violation of US sanctions on Iran and Libor rate rigging. As this bank is a UK government "rescued" bank, will British taxpayers have to pay for its fines?

Yet another UK bank is being investigated over power trading in the west of the US during late 2006 through to the end of 2008.

This UK bank was fined $1.5 billion on 18th December 2012 for its part in manipulating libor rates.

An American bank and a Swiss bank between them settled a securities charge against them to the tune of $417 million after they misled investors in residential mortgage backed securities. Both banks settled without admitting or denying charges.

- there are many more such legal cases pending against banks worldwide! How do you view your lifelong trusted banks now?

You may be thinking "if the banks run governments, why are governments fining the banks?" When you dig deep you will find the banks are being very cunning and clever indeed, they know that the biggest hits they can take will come from being indicted on money laundering charges by criminal courts, by agreeing to settle with financial watchdogs, the criminal charges will not be raised. This was yet another trick up the sleeve of our "super trickster" banking magicians! They got off very lightly as usual for some very underhand activities they were caught doing, would ordinary people get off so lightly? This signals very clearly that banks can do what the hell they like.

The banks are playing with fire while placing their "derivative" bets (they know this) and who would be the losers on an unimaginable scale should the whole thing go wrong? the people, naturally. All the depositors who have entrusted their personal money to the banks, all would lose everything they have in their bank accounts OVER NIGHT. Do you think it cannot happen? Look no further than HRH the Queen of England who banked with The UK's oldest investment bank, Barings Bank when it went bust due to an employee losing £208 million while gambling on derivatives. One single employee lost the bank £208 million by the end of 1994, what if it had been several traders losing money and *hiding it*, which is possible when you see how derivatives are easily traded in sky high amounts with little tracking in place – until it's too late. In November of 2012 a Swiss bank was fined £29.7

million for failures that led to one of its traders losing the bank £1.4 billion while gambling on derivatives Exchange Trade Funds (ETF's). It was said he was two gambles away from ruining the biggest bank in Switzerland and was trading at one point $12 BILLION in deficit. How can these bets be placed if there are no funds to back them up? Answer, banks do what they like as they are tied to the real rulers of the world. For each winner there is a loser in this high stakes game, will it be your bank next? **The whole financial world, yes every country of the world, could be brought to its knees overnight by this dangerous game of derivative gambling if/when it goes wrong**. Should the NWO want to bring the world to its knees as many people claim, what easier way could there be than to collapse the derivatives gambling "game"? Isn't it time we learned what is really going on in the banking industry and the control relationship they have with governments? While on the subject of banks and governments, three thoughts:

- What I cannot get my head around is that governments are borrowing at record levels, who are they borrowing from? It cannot be the banks because governments had to re-capitalise them when they struggled post 2007 crisis.
- Which begs another question, how did governments who are up to their necks in debt manage to re-capitalise the banks if they themselves are borrowing at record levels?
- If it is the IMF (International Monetary Fund) that is lending all the governments the massive amounts, where does the IMF get its money from? (here's a hint – we breathe it in through our mouths all the time)

*** there is one very dark and dirty secret about some UK and European banks that even I cannot bring you as it WOULD collapse world economies overnight and I would not want that responsibility on my shoulders. Believe me, if this ever gets out we will see long lines of investors waiting outside banks to withdraw all their money and the knock on effect of this secret would destroy all world economies, no matter how strong they are. Also I can inform you that there are more exposures to come of dirty tricks from the banking sector which should surface in the second half of 2013, this will mainly focus on USA major banks and will most likely see massive fines imposed. We have not seen the end of all the fallout from the 2007-08 financial collapse yet, this lives on despite assurances it's all under control.

The IMF is likely the biggest trader of all in - FAM, fresh air money, money created out of thin air and it is all done by electronic means as nobody would have warehouses large enough to store the trillions of dollars and pounds being borrowed. Can you picture and imagine the phone call to the IMF fictional money storage warehouse, "Harry, dig out fifty containers of dollars, sixty containers of pounds and arrange shipping asap". No, what most likely happens is that a message is sent to say your loan of 50 billion is approved, and that is it. The money does not exist, it is credit only but the taxpayers of the borrowing country must suffer cuts to budgets, austerity measures, pension fund attacks, tax increases etc. to "repay" the loan of FAM to the IMF - plus interest, even though no money was actually exchanged. Many of the articles and books about the NWO state that the IMF is one of their specially created projects +under its complete control, so the above sounds logical, to supply FAM and demand it is repaid by real funds from the taxpayer which milks more money out of the pockets of the people. The whole process of nations borrowing and lending money to "bail out" banks or countries sounds like a farce when you break it down. Is Greece receiving any REAL funding, did Ireland receive any REAL money, or anyone else?

Nobel prize winning economist Friedrich Hayak said "With the exception only of the period of the gold standard, practically all governments of history have used their exclusive power to issue money to defraud and plunder the people". My favorite comment comes from US senator Ron Paul who is reported to have a sign on his desk that reads "Don't steal, the government hates competition".

Another thing that has me confused is that the EU set up a fund to bailout failing member countries and each member state had to contribute a large sum to this bailout fund – how

could the UK donate several billion euro's into this bailout pot if it is itself borrowing at record levels to stay afloat?

Was it yet another banking scam to cream away money from the taxpayer? Think about it, governments borrow as they have a funding shortage (not enough coming in to cover what is going out), the governments lend to the banks who are under-funded due to people walking away from loans and mortgages, how can an under-funded government loan to an under-funded bank and who is lending to the under-funded government, it cannot be the under-funded banks because – they are under-funded! The only obvious people left are well-funded governments or the IMF. If you were a "well-funded government" would you lend to an under-funded government if you stand a chance of losing your money and becoming under-funded yourself? Which only leaves the IMF fake money cash machine with its bottomless pockets of FAM. When the IMF lends out electronically "created" FAM, as soon as it is transferred by electronic means, it becomes real (even though it does not physically exist), "appearing" into existence even though it is not real as it is FAM. As soon as the electronic message arrives it is classed as an asset (yes even though it does not exist) But it is real in a way as governments can pay their bills with it (electronically of course) OR!! What governments really do is lend the FAM to the banks at 0.5% to buy the governments debts in the form of government bonds and the government will thank those banks for buying its bonds with the money the government borrowed by paying interest rates of 5% upwards back to the banks, which is a nice little scheme to pay your friends the banks. We the people are informed that our governments are borrowing to lend to banks so they can in turn lend to small businesses and help them grow – which as you just learned is a stretch of the truth, they are lending to their friends the banks to buy their bonds. Another well publicised detail is that the rising stock market gains are funded by quantitative easing and it is widely reported that quantitative easing is funded by money printing, which is another name for fresh air money – it does not exist. So if QE is false money and its being used to stoke up the fire under stock markets, the rising stock markets must also be fake and liable to a collapse at any time, a massive collapse at that. You have got to ask yourself this in light of all this skullduggery "what have our governments, bankers and economic advisors done with their insane actions?" Everything is swinging on the introduction of fresh air money which technically does not exist. And they call themselves experts.

Here is another fact to think upon, the Eurozone is not a member of the IMF, so cannot borrow money or be placed in its program – so where the hell is all the money coming from to bailout Greece, Ireland, Portugal, Spain, Cyprus etc.? Eurozone banks are basically undercapitalised, which is why they are not lending, if it is the banks bailing out the crushed countries it can only be financed with FAM, which means fake money is bailing out bankrupt nations, where do you think that one will end? There's hardly a country in the Eurozone that is well funded, so it's not from there, so where is all this money coming from that is flying around? Of course it's from the same source as that lent out by the IMF – from fresh air, money out of nothing! The European Central bank and other banks are using a magic wand and inventing money to lend to the failing economies. Does that sound sensible to you? To invent money to lend to a struggling countries, is this the way forward, tricks of illusion? Do you still believe that our leaders know what they are doing? Total money owed in The Eurozone is around 10.8 trillion euro's, which is hell of a lot of FAM.

Okay, I had a bit of fun in explaining this, the problem is that this is how it appears to work. The IMF and ECB loans fictional money via the banks, as soon as it is sent and received it becomes real (as real as it can get), an asset on the government account books. Governments then lend this new electronic only money to banks at 0.5% interest, in return the banks buy government debts in the form of bonds and the governments pay the banks a return interest rate of 5% or more on those debt bonds. The taxpayer has to pay the IMF back while the government uses the money from its selling of bonds and the banks make 5% interest or more without spending their own money (which of course they do not have, allegedly). The governments win the banks win – the IMF and ECB wins and (you know what I am going to say) the taxpayer LOSES as they foot the bill for the whole farce. Austerity measures, tax increases, budget slashing, mass borrowing, we should send them all back into the faces of the fraudsters.

Outgoing Bank of England governor Sir Mervyn King said in November 2012 that there will be no recovery until banks raise more capital to absorb potential losses on bad loans, adding the economy will remain weak until the capital needed is raised. How will banks raise more capital? They are not lending money, which means they will not accrue interest on loans. **All in all then, there will be no recovery unless debts are written off, there just cannot be a recovery under these circumstances.** Another very interesting announcement in this month was the announcement of the identity of the next governor of the bank of England to succeed Sir Mervyn King, it is a Canadian! The "Old lady of Thread Needle Street" (the Bank of England) is being put into the hands of the governor of the Central Bank of Canada, which keeps the bank nicely in the hands of a fellow central banker. Naturally the heavily influenced media welcomed the move as positive, just as we would expect. December 12th 2012 will be remembered as an important day for the NWO as it was the day that their pet project, the EU, passed laws giving the European Central Bank powers to rule over all banks within the EU. Another big step to taking total control of banks and national economies as European finance ministers reached a deal on rules for supervising Eurozone banks and around 200 of the biggest banks will come under direct oversight of the EU Central Bank, which will act as chief supervisor of Eurozone banks. "All in all it's just another brick in the wall" and it is the people who are being "bricked in" and imprisoned by their NWO captors. Closer and closer the net is being tightened on us all, little by little – brick by brick, so stealthy in its implementation so as not to raise the alarm of what is taking place and just like a mouse trap it will be sprung shut and it will be too late to get out of the way. This is an interesting fact – since the Federal Reserve was introduced in the USA, the value of the American dollar has reduced by 97%, what does that tell you?

* * *

This chapter of the book should have the bankers, economists and media broadcasters jumping out of the pockets of their NWO masters, rushing to shout down the suggestions outlined. I can see them now scrambling to dig out their charts and concoct statistics to discredit the ideas as laid out – **all petrified that the people could take back control of their own futures**, it will be amusing to watch them all scurrying around in panic. That's the trouble when truth is allowed to come through, the deceivers see an end of their reign of abuse and either panic or jump like rats off of the sinking ship.

Looking further into other areas of banking that you are sure to find disturbing. Do you know that any money you deposit into a bank is not in their vault? It's not in a vault at your banks headquarters either. Outside of a computer, your money does not exist. If a bank faced a "run on the bank", where depositors lined up to withdraw their money, only around the first 10-20% in the line would receive their cash. Most money is what I call Fresh Air Money as it does not exist. The system is called Fractional Reserve Banking. When a person deposits $1000 into a bank, the bank is legally allowed to loan out 90% or more of your money to other customers. One recent report stated that banks loan out as much as thirty times their cash reserves, what happens to this when interest rates go up and the borrowers walk away from their loans? Let's say someone borrows $900 for a second hand car, the old owner of the car then banks the $900, two people have deposited between them $1900 which came from the exact $1000 first deposited. This means $900 was FAM, created from nothing. The $900 paid in by the old owner of the car can now be loaned out again and again and again, making the original $1000 a considerable asset to the bank as it receives back the repayment of not only the FAM, but interest on top. The original $1000 will be lent and re-lent to a point that its loaned out value is around $10,000 of which $9000 is FAM, not a bad piece of business for the banks and they charge interest on top! This is what brought about the collapse of the housing markets across the world and caused the Global Financial Crisis in 2007-08 as people who could not afford their mortgages walked away en masse from their payments and their properties. As the money was FAM, by walking away from their debts, the money vanished from the system, something called a currency contraction. The money was borrowed into existence, even though it did not really exist, but it is regarded as an asset to the bank, which in turn meant the banks were under funded (also known as under-capitalised) as the FAM vanished. The money was on the bank files, but did not exist, meaning the banks were underfunded and for want of a better description - BANKRUPT. Central banks had no choice other than to start printing money (the infamous Quantitive Easing as it is known) to make up the shortfall (re-capitalising the banks) caused by the disappearance of FAM, which they lent to the banks at a cost to – you guessed it, us the people, the taxpayers, naturally. You, me and everyone, we picked up the tab for the gigantic bank fraud. The problem is though that money printing is not working (if it was ever meant to) and we are still spiraling down to financial oblivion, government debts have long exceeded record levels and are piling up more and more by the minute. Don't forget, the borrowing is being made at record low interest rates, when these rates rise, government interest repayments will also rise to a point they will not be able to afford repaying them and will effectively be bankrupt themselves. When this happens the central banks will send in their "experts" to sort out the resulting mess, effectively taking over the running of the banks, which is all part of the long term plan to take-over the complete running of national economies – which is the ultimate long term plan. Do you think this will not happen? Just wait and see.

We entered into this present trouble through insane lending and borrowing, caught a serious cold and our central banks reaction is to borrow more and more and more and so on....... Does this sound at all sensible to anyone? If a man digs himself into a deep hole, would you hand him a shovel to dig himself deeper or would you lower down a ladder to help him climb out? Then why the hell are we borrowing more and getting into worse trouble by the minute? Is it part of the NWO plan? It makes you wonder.

Something else for you to ponder on is this: If an action causes a serious problem, the first and most obvious thing to do would be to stop the action that caused the problem, as to keep taking the action must make the problem worse, yes? This is a common sense move, stop the cause before attempting to stop the reaction to the cause. The last thing anyone would do is to keep on performing the action that caused the problem. As we all know we do not add flame to a fire. Why then do we keep borrowing and lending more money if that action got us in to trouble in the first place? Why do we feed the flames of debt with more debt? That's two "burning " questions (pun intended) that our leaders and their advisors need to answer.

Something else for you to think over is that due to our economists and bankers lowering interest rates to next to nothing, people have been paying off their debts in record numbers. It's obvious that if you do not return anything worthwhile with your investments and you have spare cash, you want to do something positive with it, so paying off debt is the next best option and this is taking place on a large scale. There is a big drawback on this action for governments and banks as paying back debt takes money out of circulation, this is known as de-leveraging. With all these debts being fake money and people are not passing it around by purchasing things, it plays havoc with the national economies. National economies have to have money washing around to stimulate all manner of actions, paying back loans stops this. The UK has the highest private debt ratio in the world at seven trillion pounds, paying this back (even in part) will cripple The UK economy, so again we have to question our governments, bankers and economists and ask ourselves once more – "what have they done to us?" and "why do we go on trusting them?".

There are three possible conclusions as to why we are "sinking without trace"

- INEPTITUDE - our leaders and the central banks do not know what they are doing

- REALISATION – they know we cannot get out of the mess we are in, so they borrow money to put off the inevitable crash for as long as they can ("kicking the can down the road")
- DECEIT – there is no intention of saving our economies and the central banks are deliberately destroying our economies

My personal opinion is that it is a mixture of all three.

For whatever the reason, we are in a desperate financial state the world over, though unless you read anything but the daily newspapers and watch TV news, you would not know just **how deep we are.** Think on this, national debts are reaching or already at record levels, in response our leaders and central banks print more FAM, they borrow more and more which only can make the situation worse, economies are headed one way - down. Ask yourself this "if we are only borrowing more and more", getting ever further into trouble and not making any attempt to grow our way out of the mess were in, **how can we possibly get out of the situation**? The answer is we can't and there is only one conclusion, we will sink. Who is being hit the hardest? the middle and lower classes as they suffer the most and the rich, how are they doing? Make your own mind up with the help of these statistics:

- The only part of London where property prices continue to rise is the areas that bankers live
- Worldwide numbers of millionaires is soaring since the financial crisis of 2007-08, in 2010 alone the number leapt 8.3% to 10.9 million. Their total wealth grew 9.7% to a staggering $42.7 TRILLION IN ONE YEAR
- The total number of billionaires in the year 2011 broke to new records growing to 1210 worldwide
- Luxury goods are enjoying leaps in sales. As an example, sales of Porsche supercars rocketed in 2011 by 57% which was completely over shadowed by 2012 sales which hit a new record of 128,978 cars sold in eleven months, still one month to go to the end of the sales year. Demand from China and the US was up 70%, which shows only too well that the rich in the US are

getting richer and there are more of them. Sales of BMW's in 2012 reached record levels as are luxury Italian Maserati cars, Jaguar cars sales are up 32%.

Does this say anything to you?

A much used comment I have seen in the period from 2007-08 is that we are going through the biggest transfer of wealth and power in history (many mistakenly thought this was the transfer to places like China). The rich are becoming the "super rich" and the middle and lower classes class are becoming "the poor" as their wealth is drained from them. In fact the transfer is the action to steal money from the lower classes and re-direct more to the rich. That is a true recipe for change as the people who make up 99.9% of the population _will_ rebel, there is NO doubt about that and it is a matter of when, not if and a full reversal of fortunes is the most likely result. Before that rebellion, the people who are manipulating this situation have probably one last chance to put matters right and come clean with what they have been doing behind our backs, before matters are surely taken out of their hands "Arab Spring style". Those people who have led us to almost certain financial ruin will see their actions catch up with them, there is no other conclusion. Soldiers and police are unlikely to rush to protect those who have carried out the betrayal of the people when they realise that they would be **protecting traitors to their country and not patriotic leaders**. Politicians, bankers, religious leaders will fall and it will be as a result of going too far in their quest for power and absolute control. The honest politicians etc. will need to make it clear they are not in league with the secret rulers of the world. Martial law could be declared in many countries to remove corrupt governments, that could be any country.

According to a major report that was announced in July 2012 "there is a global super-rich elite that has $21 Trillion hidden in secret tax havens by the end of 2010. This figure is equivalent to the size of the US and Japanese economies combined. This figure of $21 trillion is considered conservative and could be as high as $32 Trillion (a trillion is 1000 Billion). The lost tax revenues is enough to make a big difference to the finances of many countries. So not only are they the "Super Rich", they do not intend anyone getting their hands on their money. How does that make you feel?

The financial mess the world finds itself in is one that certainly appears to have been created deliberately and from what I have read it is part of a 100 year plan that was initiated over 200 years ago, achieved step by step and softly, softly. Along the way various senior politicians and economists knowingly played their part, removing the gold standard was one move that seriously debased economies as it allowed the real value of money to drop dramatically and it made excessive borrowing simple. By creating The Federal Reserve Bank in the USA the future of world economics was sealed and many see this one move as the pinnacle to financial destruction across the world. The politicians all played their part as they plotted to steal more power and increase their control of their fellow countrymen, while sentencing their countrymen to a life of poverty (if that isn't treason, what is?).

Think on this: we should not be in the mess we find ourselves in, we are a modern society, the astronomical mistakes, negligent financial strategies and thorough bad planning cannot be as a result of poor decisions by our leaders – therefore it must be a deliberate plot to weaken world economies (it CANNOT be anything else). Nobody could make so many diabolical mistakes as those made by our leaders and their central bank advisors since the turn of the new millennium. Why has there been no condemnation from all areas of the media, it is too unthinkable – which very much proves the media are "in on this". This can only point to a plan that must be designed to destroy the wealth of the people which is being aided, abetted and covered up by the NWO controlled media. Can't you understand that? The errors and totally inept strategies being used to counter act the massive levels of national debt throughout the world are ridiculous, they have never worked and they never will – leaving one conclusion, they are not meant to.

Nothing can save the world economies and you had better understand that and prepare yourself for what follows the collapse (or you can help prevent the collapse), we are too deep in debt to get out of it by repayment. When the collapse unravels hundreds of small banks will disappear and be mopped up by the big banking cartels, hundreds of thousands of businesses will fold overnight, public services will be terminated or privatised which will make them much more expensive to the taxpayers and in the UK the National Health Service will be sold off to private owners and only accessible by paying private health insurance, while the state pension will be dissolved (do you think that won't happen?). There are big winners and big losers in the games that are being played out on the world stage, we the people are the biggest losers, though we are not supposed to find that out until the final moves are completed. By now you should realise who the winners are. How I wish I was standing with you right now, I would not move on to another subject until I saw the light of truth dawn in your eyes. Some people would need to be physically shaken and shouted at to wake them up to truth as their lifetime of programming (by the people carrying out the plan to steal our wealth) has them firmly in its grip. I would shout "people of the world, wake up now, you have a limited window of opportunity to change things before it is too late", we are just a few short steps away from a world that will resemble George Orwell's book 1984 and with a greatly reduced population.

Will you wake up from the illusion of a fake life that has been imposed on us all, or will you bury your nose under your bedclothes to shut out the truth?

Yes I am fully aware that many people will refuse to believe all this and will question my sanity, it is not my sanity that needs questioning, it is those who play out their power fantasies that require the summoning of the men in white coats. Could this be the greatest "I didn't see it coming", or "I didn't take any notice as it as it sounded so unbelievable" or "I rejected the idea as I don't like bad news" moment in history? As I keep reminding "you do not know the real world", we have all been brainwashed and programmed all of our lives to accept that which is spoon fed to us by our "trusted" newspapers, radio and TV stations. Everything has been subtly planned and smoothly put into place, with only a minority aware what is taking place outside of the people pulling off the sting. It helps nobody when people say they cannot read or listen to bad news, this is a time when bad news will rapidly change to hellish bad news if we ignore it and/or refuse to listen. A rejection of bad news is basically a rejection of the truth and it is truth most people are frightened of.

Would you have ever considered that many of our banks could behave in such an underhand way? making fools of us all as they pile up wealth (our wealth) while taking crazy risks in the derivatives sector that can only be described as insane. If we can't trust the banks or our leaders, who can we trust? And the answer to that question is easy, we can only trust ourselves.

If you fail to believe this chapter, then prepare to kiss what freedom you have left goodbye and wave farewell to your money, going – going – gone!

This is what I believe will unravel from the end of 2012, everything will start to fall apart (but be hidden as usual) and there just cannot be any other conclusion with the high number of threats to our various economies. If we only faced one or two threats we could get through the troubles, we though face many - many problems and that is why we will not be able to come through all this unscathed. By mid to late 2013 we will begin to see clear signs that the financial situation is worsening, I believe that stock markets will begin to falter from their high speed climbs with dips of ninety points one day and a small rise the next to be followed by a monumental collapse in 2014 (unless we change our ways now).The Eurozone will show signs of some really bad cracks opening up and this could well signal a beginning of the end with one country dropping out and setting a trend for others to follow. Property values will come under fierce attack and a further drop between 20% – 30% once the bubble bursts is something many could face by the end of 2014 and into 2015. Deflation could be the hazard up ahead and not inflation as lending dries up and investors run for cover from stocks – government bonds, commodities and precious metals. (The timing of catastrophic collapses is notoriously difficult to predict as nobody knows how much more fake money central banks will throw at the problems, my estimates could prove premature or be spot on, we shall have to wait and see.) This will not be at all obvious to anyone until it hits, I fully expect to see almost normal circumstances right up until the time this collapse starts to take place. Remember that everything looks normal until the train comes off the tracks, I would also expect that we will be bombarded with stories of recovery taking shape. Government figures will show that "the worst is behind us", politicians will welcome "the end of the recession" and stock markets could show signs of growing confidence with further record highs being registered. Yes, we could see the end of recession, but it may well be at the expense of a depression taking its place. The governments claims of recovery will of course be false and based on deception, as usual, hiding their failings, as usual. The people will not understand what is going on as we will have been misled, as usual. Whatever happens when the train does come off the tracks, the signs will be there that the nightmare situation is deepening. Government bonds could crash so hard that nobody will buy them, consumer spending will dry up to only cover that which is a necessity such as food, clothing and services like electric and gas. World economies face collapse like falling dominos and even the countries with strong economies will be hit hard as worldwide consumer spending is cut to the bone. Companies propped up by borrowing and with government help will fail overnight in record numbers. Investment will dry up to almost nil. As all this happens governments will have nothing up their sleeves to fight back with, they have been following insane strategies and are already borrowing to near or over their limits and deep in debt, the only actions left would be to severely further cut their budgets which will hit the people hard – very hard. Defaulting on national debt and devaluing currencies will be something else that there will be no other option to do. Government employees will be laid off en masse, military spending will be slashed and military personnel will be cut back heavily, projects such as HAARP will run out of funding (something positive at least) this must happen as there will be no money to pay for the military budgets, little money to pay government employees. There is a new phrase that has been coined to describe what the banks are doing with their actions, very appropriate it is too "The race to the bottom", describing the crash that is waiting to happen.

I sincerely hope that all the above is proven incorrect and I for one will welcome looking very foolish should this not occur as I know that the people of the world will be those who suffer the most should all this come true.

* * *

It is a well reported detail that China and Russia are fully aware of the plans of the Illuminati and the threat Illuminati plans bring to their economies, it is also well-known that China and Russia are united to defeat the Illuminati – could this be how they pull the rug out from under the Illuminati by destroying the economic base of the US and scupper the long term plans of the Illuminati? Have you wondered why Russia and China veto so many UN initiatives? Initiatives that "on paper" look reasonable. Russia and China purposely stand in the way of UN led moves as they come from leaders of The USA and these two countries see their veto's as a way of halting Illuminati moves. These two countries also take sides with countries that the US is threatening to attack or invade, again to stop Illuminati plans. Russia and China could be the only way that the Illuminati can be thwarted and may have already stopped the final push for total world domination – have you ever considered that? Personally I am sure we will know by 2015 what is planned, the importance of that year just keeps being "thrown at me" as more and more the year is brought to my attention. The world is changing rapidly, change is starting to really accelerate and the changes are forming a new chapter in man's history – yet the people are unaware of this due to the secretive actions of the controlled media.

All of this is inevitable, it cannot be avoided because the crazy people running our national and world economies have systematically destroyed our economies and taken away our economic foundations exposing us to unavoidable decline and default. Here today, it should be plainly obvious that all of this is unavoidable due to the insane actions taken since 2007 that have made the economic situation a hundred times worse. What the people who have made the situation decline may not have realised is that **"they have performed the world a great favour!!!"** Why? Because at last the people will wake up to the fact that we have been misled and cheated by these crazy people – we will recognise the chains binding us to a fake life. 2015 could and should be the most pivotal year in mankind's history as all the cheating, fraud, corruption and deceit is laid bare for all to see. 2015 will give us the opportunity to remove the despots, dictators, plotters, scheming bankers and fraudulent governments. 2015 could be the greatest year in our history so far, the year that positively changes the future of the world. Something good comes out of something bad, it always does. While this may appear like wishful thinking and more in hope than fact, think again as when the depths of despair are reached, the only way is up and we *are* heading into despair. To arrive at a better future will need us to pass through some very testing times and we should be prepared for this.

My strong belief is that from the end of 2012 we face ten years of serious change that could start with the decent into full blown collapse of our economies and signals the removal of those responsible for the collapse, the "coming together" of the people leading to a true "New World Order" run **"by the people, for the people"**. There will be no other choice, no other possibility when the people experience what is heading towards us, they will take matters into their own hands (maybe with a little help along the way from the Chinese and Russians!).

Many people will be sitting in stunned silence after reading this last information, unable to take it all in, fighting to make sense of it all and some will be, doubting – doubting – doubting! May I say that I under-stand this as if I had no previous knowledge of this type of information I would be experiencing some or all of the same emotions. This must feel as if you are being awoken from a very bad dream to discover that our lives resemble something more like the Twilight Zone than reality, life feels more like a storyline from a Hollywood disaster film than true life. You are advised to shake yourself as the details above are very real, we will "hit the buffers" HARD! It is up to us to pick ourselves up and start all over again. No matter how much doubt you have, you must prepare yourself (even those who refuse to believe this) do not panic - PREPARE. Governments – economists – banks, why do we continue to trust them, why do we let them loose on our financial futures after they have ruined our past and present? Do we believe they can redeem themselves, change their habits of a lifetime and begin to represent the people's interests? Well, pigs might fly!!

Recommended reading: Babylons Banksters by Joseph P. Farrell

The Secrets of the Federal Reserve by Eustace Mullins

Anything by Harry Dent junior

For the British readers, What Happens Next? By Vernon Coleman, yet another five star author in my view and an absolute must read

For all English speaking people I highly recommend looking at taking a subscription to Money Week magazine which has a UK and USA edition. I have Money Week mailed to me in Europe as I do not want to miss out on anything financial. Money Week is a good easy read and covers the financial topics that we need to concentrate on. An on-line service is also available and you will receive daily updates into your mail box, this service is called Money Morning. Also check out The Daily Reckoning on line, which is another free to subscribe to daily message delivery service from among others Bill Bonner the owner of Money Week.

Also I advise taking a free subscription to another excellent on-line service called "The Schiff Report" from Peter Schiff. This is a no nonsense "tell it like it is" commentary on the economic and financial markets. Look up any of the books that Peter Schiff has written for hardnosed truth of what is *really* happening in the world.

Again I wish to be proven wrong in all of my comments and for someone to stand up and explain in detail that all of this is wrong, again from a major leader and not a political or economic presenter from television or newspapers. I will welcome being proven wrong, so someone please come and do this and tell us all we do have a strong financial future ahead. The gauntlet has been thrown down, will anyone pick it up or will we have to rely on our own intuition and accept this chapter is as near to truth as we are ever likely to get?

We are being fooled each and every day by our governments – economists – bankers, to me there is not a scrap of doubt about this. Until we re-plan how our countries are run and placed on a fair, honest and positive pathway we the people can only suffer at the hands of the leaders we mistakenly trust. Our leaders are too busy trying to carve their names into the history books and following personal selfish agenda's to willingly agree to change that will benefit the people who elected them, which is why it is vitally important to expose their trickery into the open. Only by publicising the dirty secrets of our leaders will change take place, while these dark secrets remain hidden nothing will change. It is the responsibility of the people to make sure that all dirty secrets of our leaders are uncovered, made public and that is an important role each of us must agree to do, to become part of a "Peoples Peaceful Revolution" and make sure everyone knows what has been going on and which continues to thrive under cover of secrecy. When these secrets are exposed we will face times of disturbance as old systems are replaced with more efficient methods, that is the price which will have to be paid. The disturbance we face by not taking actions will be total as government systems completely buckle under the strain of debt.

WHY? You may ask must we change? Here are a few reminders: National economies cannot be saved as too many governments have reached record borrowing levels and continue hour by hour to borrow more on a massive scale. While debts only grow, a recovery is impossible and interest repayments multiply hourly. Even now as the debt levels deepen, our leaders continue to inform us that a recovery is imminent, which by now we should all realise is hype with no foundation in truth. With the largest debts and the highest levels of borrowing in history weighing us down and our leaders only response is to lie to us and "kick the can further down the road", isn't it time we changed the whole sorry and sordid arrangement from top to bottom? How can we trust our leaders when they try to pull the wool over our eyes almost daily?

We are informed by our leaders that they will cut unemployment levels drastically, which is another impossibility and they should face up to the fact that the future carries with it high unemployment. In the USA to keep up with population growth, 150,000 jobs need to be added each and every month. Also in the USA, since 2009 the labour force has increased new job numbers by 847,000 BUT! those who are no longer included in the labour force, those who gave up looking for a job in this same period was a staggering 8,208,000, there are 88,000,000 (88 million) Americans who could work that are not working. Mechanisation in industry is reducing manning levels, office staffing levels are falling massively as more and more computerisation and on-line services replaces staff. With less money being earned at company level due to recession, staffing levels are the first place that cost cutting hits, this is the "downsizing" syndrome we hear so much about. With banks refusing to loan money out to companies, expansion is curtailed and more staff will not be hired. Population levels are rising, which can only point to more people without employment, add in the extended retirement age where people hold onto their job longer and you can see the future for employment. Along with several other reasons it is clear that employment levels only face a downward route, high unemployment is here to stay.

Our leaders have a fixation with a growing property market and will do whatever it takes to push up property values as they know that this produces the "feel good factor", when property owners see themselves as better off than they really are and spend more money they do not have. This "feel good factor" is vital to governments as it will make people content with the government and more likely to re-elect it and that is all its about, conning the people to get re-elected. By kick starting property prices a government is playing with fire and it is the property owners who eventually get burnt when rising prices hits the point that a price crash is unavoidable, which it always does. Property values should be allowed to run with market forces and not forced markets by our leaders who seek to look good as elections approach.

Banks must be completely re-focused back to being banks and not wildcat predators stalking its customers and stopped from being irresponsible speculators taking ever more dangerous moves to accrue profits. Fractional reserve banking practices and the production line of "fresh air money printing" has to stop as while this is allowed to continue bank customers are in serious danger of losing all their savings should banks collapse overnight under this fraud. The fraudulent derivatives sector has to be taken down, it is all fake yet it carries such a serious threat to all our livelihoods. Britain has 2,436 bankers who are paid more than £860,000 per year, all other EU countries between them only muster 739 paid this much, what does that tell you?

As governments finances crash due to insane "over" borrowing and huge debt build up, it will not only be public services that are destroyed, health services will be heavily impacted as will pension payments. This will strike into the hearts of the people and cause them so much added misery, it will worry them more than many other problems. If our government officials were to be honest with us, they would inform us that at the moment pension payments are staring into a black hole of insufficient funding to pay its pensioners and with a greatly increasing number of pensioners as more people live longer. Health services are a massive drain on national economies and should a government hit the financial brick wall, health services, pensions and public services are the places that the axe will fall first.

Stock markets around the world are smashing through record barriers as more and more money pours into stocks, the problem with this is that the money behind these record levels is mostly coming from central banks money printing. As you know by now, that money is fresh air money, so stock markets are over inflated by fresh air nonexistent funding. Hmmm I wonder how that can end?

If we leave all of the above to our leaders to tinker with – nothing will change and we the people will be the only losers. Leaders have got to change or we need to change the leaders (peacefully of course). It is 100% certain that I will be accused of spreading doom and gloom with the words above, these accusations will come from people who still do not get what is happening – we are being lied to, we are being kept in the dark, the truth is being withheld from us, government finances are in a stage of collapse and until the truth is announced, we can only drop into a deeper mess. If the truth is considered to be gloom and doom, then we are in a worse situation than I believed as we are obviously not prepared to do anything about our situation and prefer to attack the whistle blowers and not get on with sorting out the problems. We have got to "clear the decks" and get ready for a fight, a fight to put our national economies back on firm ground and get away from all the fraud.

Consider this, no matter how difficult you find the text of this book to believe, just for a few minutes accept the messages and think this over: If World War Three broke out tomorrow and your country was attacked with bombing, invasion etc. or your government declared your country bankrupt with no services available to you such as policing – fire service – waste disposal – street repairs etc., or your own bank went into liquidation leaving you penniless. If a complete takeover of the world was achieved by a secret organisation and your every move from that point was monitored and controlled. What would you do, what could you do? The simple answer is not much. As we all know "shutting the gate after the horse has bolted" leads you nowhere and that is the situation we would all face, acting when it's too late. Whether you believe all the text of this book or not, your only sensible path is to make sure none of the above happens. Will you let your disbelief (ignorance of the truth) stop you from taking action, will you bury your head in the sand and hope it's all a bad dream or will you laugh it all off and dismiss it all as crazy ranting's of deluded whistle blowers? Perhaps you will take your anger at learning the truth out on this book, accusing the text of trouble making, just think that one through, the book is uncovering deceit and not creating it. Remember, hundreds of millions of people do believe the threats above are 100% real, tens of millions of articles are published on search engines warning of the threats above and there are tens of thousands of book titles stating very clearly that the threats are based in reality and there's hardly a person who refutes all the accusations. Who are the fools, those that believe the threats or those who don't? Is risking the future of the world worth taking a chance that the threats are not real? **Shouldn't we find out who is right?**

Let's finish this chapter with something to think about. If a company runs out of money in the bank and could not meet its obligations to pay bills, wages etc. it is declared bankrupt. If a nation finds itself in the same position where there is no money in the bank and it cannot meet its obligations – it borrows and increases its debts. The borrowed money is made up of fresh air money, quantative easing, money printing and does not exist in physical terms. The "bailout" is very shaky as the money is basically fake "funny money", do you think this is a stable sustainable way to solve problems? Do you think that a recovery can take place when the foundations of a nations finances are fraudulent? Can a recovery take place when all we do is increase debt hourly without paying any debt off? Do you believe a recovery can take place when our leaders obviously have not learned a thing from the last assault on our economies? Can a recovery take place with so much deceit and fraud wrapped around our economies? **"don't believe the hype".** NO, no chance and until the economies are removed from politicians, banker and economists there is only one potential outcome.

Do you understand what happens when a nation goes bust? There would be no refuse collections, no policing, no fire service, hospitals and doctors services would be privatised, national pension schemes would not pay out, banks would be closed and so much more. Now are you wondering "what the hell have our leaders done to the world?"

As this lengthy chapter draws to a close you should have a better understanding of the hidden deceit that is taking place, let me ask you for your opinion when considering these facts: Don't you agree that an enormous collapse in world economies is very close when Quantitative Easing floods our economies with fake money – governments have racked up record debt and add to it every second of every day – stock markets are being pushed up by QE fake money that has no real substance – fractional reserve banking loans out fresh air money without any equity to back it up – governments are growing the property market bubble with insane stimulus incentives that will soon crash the whole system – the media and governments are picking up on anything to assure us there is a recovery taking place and "gloss over" the fact they are bankrupt – the price of gold has been "pushed down" by banks and government action. When will the collapse happen? We will not have to wait too long to find out.

My final comment here is "please God let all this be wrong, let it all be a bad dream and nothing more, please prove me wrong". I hope I am wrong and would like to be proved wrong, but I don't think I am.

What if? What if many of our banks are deliberately destabilising national economies and creaming off tax payers money, will you believe this of what are national institutions? What if some banks equate to what must be the biggest criminal organisations in history with the vast deceitful schemes they have "pulled off", how will you now see them knowing this and will you agree that they need to completely change their practices? What if national economies are too bankrupt to save, shouldn't we try something else other than failed schemes we know do not work AND to allow our economies to default? What if we all find ourselves penniless tomorrow due to the fraud and deceit, will we try to "close the gate after the horse has bolted?"

Let our leaders stand before their nation and publicly state the truth and answer all the accusations leveled against them, placing their right hand on a bible and swear under oath before they give us the truth – will any dare?

It is time to change

ten

Final Score, Growth 0 Stability 1

* * *

This will be one of the briefest of chapters, short, sharp and to the point, yet it has as much importance as any of the longer more serious chapters. This chapter I have added directly after the chapter dealing with financial and economic affairs to highlight the importance of the area covered, it is also financial based but rightly deserves its own separate section. Should people be able to grasp the message of this chapter, I am sure they will see that in the past we have had some very misplaced goals and beliefs lead us down the wrong pathway where financial and economics is concerned. Of course these misleading goals and beliefs have as usual been programmed into us by those who shape our lives from the outside and yes as usual this programming benefits the outside influences more than ourselves. By now I am sure you will be recognising how much we are influenced from outside and how our lives are shaped for us without our input, what follows in this chapter will confirm this principle.

When economists talk about growth we mostly all have an understanding that has been programmed into us that growth is a necessity of government and without strong growth a national economy is in trouble. We are informed we must invest to stimulate growth, we are told that strong growth is the way out of recession as we need to see national growth to show we are balancing the national books. The news media holds nations with strong growth figures up as a shining example of what we should be aspiring towards. What if all this rhetoric is wrong? What if it's all government and economists gibberish, hype and a part of the never ending mis-programming of the people who know no different? Look at China, they have been held up like a shining star due to their meteoric rise to a super power measured by their impressive growth record, growth in industrial output, house building, GDP growth, growth in this and growth in that. As soon as China suffered a hiccup and growth slowed due not to Chinese problems but the problems of the Western World, people started to shout that China is collapsing. Growth in China has fallen around 1% and that is considered an indication of a fallout, this fallout is equal to a reduction from annual growth of around 8% to 7%, which of the struggling nations would not want this problem, to have a fallout from 8% to 7%? (what a luxury). The UK is struggling to achieve 1% growth in total, China drops 1% and it's a sign of collapse, something is hopelessly wrong in this equation. Personally I believe The UK's 1% growth is preferable to China's rocketing 8% because in my opinion, GROWTH IS NOT SUSTAINABLE.

To explain this, look at government actions to help people quit smoking cigarettes, they increase (grow) the price of cigarettes as they know that people will cut down or give up smoking when the price experiences strong growth, strong growth therefore equals an unwelcome situation. The growth of the price of cigarettes is purposely designed to wipeout smoking or to cut back the desire to smoke. If it works on cigarette smoking then the same principle must work on everything, if excessive growth is encouraged there is a price to pay, growth therefore does not mean safety or expansion, strong growth can have the opposite effect, never forget the saying "the higher you are the further there is to fall", or "the bigger you are the greater the fall". Chase too much growth and the harder it hurts when it does not happen or it happens and then collapses.

It is a well-known fact that when governments hike tax bands up, they accrue less tax as the tax payer will use any means possible to avoid paying the tax. This is a clear case of more being less, the more tax growth, the less the revenue collected.

Keep property prices growing and the supply of buyers dries up, killing the property values dead, a case of excessive growth equaling shrinkage (more being less).

- Keep growing the prices of oil and people cut back on consumption
- Keep growing the price of domestic gas, electricity, water and people cut back
- Keep excessively growing the price of food and people seek out lower cost food and cut back
- Keep wages and salaries growing too fast and employers cut back on staff levels or impose wage restrictions (as is happening right now)

The worst thing we can keep growing is world population, which is another prime example of the downside of growth. We cannot feed the world's population at seven billion, which is proven by the millions who die of starvation each year, yet we continue on a path of population growth. How will we feed eight million – nine million – ten million – and more if we cannot feed seven million now? How will we house, find employment, look after medically, educate billions of extra population? Important, how will we find enough water for billions extra if we are struggling now to deliver a clean safe supply of water to large areas of the world?

Continuous excessive growth is a myth, it is impossible and at some point the law of commonsense says "you must hit a peak, a brick wall where growth has to stop, slow down, or even recede". Growth is not never ending, there has to be a limit which is why we suffer regular corrections in the form of recession, property price collapse, it is a natural cycle coming around again, this has always been labeled "boom and bust". It is not excessive growth we should aim towards, it is stability. Stabilise property values, food prices, the cost of gas – water – electricity – oil etc. Should we do this and not keep "shooting for the moon", we may just stop "boom and bust" situations arising. Stability at something like a 1% p.a. increase appears to me to be a sensible goal compared to the excessive target of between 5% - 8% which again to me is just not sustainable. Everyone will benefit from stability as prices do not escalate out of reach for many.

If our national economies had been targeted towards stability and steady sensible growth instead of strong growth – we would not be in such an economic mess we are now. If we had not allowed greed to run riot in the property markets, we would not be in the mess we are now with a badly unstable property market fueled by false growth, there would have been no crash, no repossessions and we would all have more money in our pockets to spend if we were not handing it over in such large amounts for our inflated mortgages and rents. If we had stabilised food prices we would not be buying lower quality budget foods that are low on nutrition. If we had stabilised oil prices we would not have exorbitant petrol/diesel prices which hurt everyone when high costs of transportation are passed on to consumers one way or another. But of course this does not happen, shareholders want their dividend profits and they want them to continue to grow, they will not invest in a company with low or no growth. Placing too much emphasis on growth can only increase prices or lead to a reduction in investment, which means the end user loses out to protect shareholders. If a company gets their sums wrong and the company loses its customers – the company folds and shareholders lose everything, another downside to the chase for growth. Again, should companies aim at stability against unsustainable growth, there would be a better long term base to work from and far less pressure to achieve the unachievable if we choose stability.

To concentrate on continuous strong growth therefore is a formula for disaster. China is discovering this as are many of the "emerging nations" who are all suffering reversals at one level or another. Had they settled at targeting a realistic longer term sensible growth, they would most likely not be looking at finding solutions to "halt their decline", The financial meltdown of 2007-08 was caused by governments seeking too much growth by encouraging lenders to over-extend their lending with criminal mortgage loans that backfired seriously.

Everyone suffered and many are still suffering and bear the scars of this chasing of unrealistic growth figures, we have not recovered from this and yet governments still attempt to stimulate the property markets, clearly they have not learned anything from the pain suffered by so many just a few short years ago.

Do the people seek unsustainable strong growth? No. Would the people prefer stability and not face rocketing prices, austerity and collapsing markets? Yes.

Strong growth 0 Stability 1

eleven

Poor Health And Deadly Diet

* * *

Each day another extra 200,000 mouths are added
to the world's population to be fed.

When I learned of this statistic above I was deeply shocked for here
we are with millions of lives being lost each year through famine and
malnutrition and the problem is being compounded day by day with
many more mouths to feed. "Experts" say that the world population
will eventually find its natural level and does not need any help in
doing it, what figure do they expect to reach before that "natural level"
is found? nine billion, ten, more? How are we going to feed that many
people if we are struggling to feed seven billion now? Does this worry
you?, well, hold onto your hats as this chapter of the book is not about
population explosion, it has an equally worrying subject matter than
the diet of the people we *may* need to feed, **it is about the diet and
health of those** *already here.*

Whenever I return to England, my home country, I am amazed at
the ever increasing number of seriously overweight and obese people.
Government statistics tell us that in the UK during 2009 obese and
overweight people reached 61.3% of the population, while in the
USA 64.1% women and 72.3% men were overweight in 2012. Is that a
shock? not really when you understand why and yes not surprisingly it
is something else carefully planned. Just think about this for a moment

"overweight people don't fight" that should read they "don't fight back", which is exactly what our leaders want, a docile public. Our quality of food is being deliberately lowered, it is being deliberately filled with potentially harmful chemicals and it is being over loaded with sugar and other "waist increasing" substances such as carbohydrates. This will sound ridiculous to many I know, but our leaders want people to be overweight as they perform a number of desired functions in that condition. As mentioned, overweight people do not fight back as they are unfit, they are generally suffering ill health due to their weight which means they need medication that pharmaceutical companies provide at exorbitant cost to the taxpayer and lastly they die because they are overweight and strain their hearts etc. which helps meet the target of population reduction. You can jump up and down, scream and shout, laugh at the suggestion with derision, it does though, IF you think about it, make sense. If it is not a deliberate plan to make food calorie laden, why is food calorie laden? Why spike food with sugar, corn syrup, artificial additives, excess salt, flavor enhancers such as monosodium glutamate, preservatives etc.? Can you think of a suitable and good reason for poisoning our food in this way, does it make any sense at all, why does this happen – any suggestions? Our food is made to taste better than it is to make us eat more and it is full of ingredients that are very bad for our health, clogging up our arteries, piling on the kilos, causing heart problems, liver and kidney failure, diabetes and much more. The manufacturers know this, the government knows this – so why does it happen? We are bingeing on carbohydrates – bread, white flour products such as cakes and pasties, pasta, rice, potatoes, all high in carbohydrates and very inclined to add body fat. Supermarkets sell low priced cakes and doughnuts, cheap pastas with the almost nil rated goodness content and as we are in recessionary times we spend our meager money on this type of cheap unhealthy food. For me this situation we find ourselves in was put into perspective by the sight of a young very overweight mother standing on a British seafront promenade, it was 10.30 in the morning and she had a container of potato chips in one hand and a hamburger in the other, was this breakfast or lunch, or was it a mid-morning snack! What example was she setting for her young daughter to follow? Have you noticed the very overweight people just seem to have a cake, chocolate bar or an item of fast food in their hands? They are addicted to the unhealthy diet by the flavor enhancers and additives, they cannot stop themselves eating in the same way smokers cannot stop smoking.

We have lost touch with basic good eating habits and the food that is available is mostly "spiked" with excessive sugar, salt, carbohydrates and any number of added extras. How did this happen, where did we go wrong? It is like so much else described in this book, we have been led astray by the leaders we thought we could trust and we are being exploited via programming and brainwashing. Be honest, who would willingly allow themselves to double their normal weight having to drag around all those extra sagging kilos, suffer terrible health problems, meet an early exit into the grave and be an embarrassment to themselves (apologies to those people who are really ill and cannot keep off their weight)? Food becomes like an addictive drug when life is falling apart, it is the comfort food we hear so much about, we eat to feel better, we gorge on food to forget the misery of life. When that comfort food is loaded with calories and artificial ingredients, it is no comfort - it is a killer, but we cannot see that because we are already low in morale with the way life is heading down. This is a very vicious circle, the more we eat - the more we want and the worse we feel, so the worse we feel - the more we eat and so on.

There is another vicious circle linked to carbohydrates, after eating carbs a wicked side effect kicks in as we start to feel hungry again within half an hour or so and our stomachs urge us to eat more of the same, piling on more body fat. Carbs serve another useful purpose for governments as they tend to make us feel sleepy, which is why we suffer mid-morning and mid-afternoon energy "dips" after eating bread for breakfast and or lunch. After eating the carbs our brain starts to close down and we become tired and sleepy with our heads "nodding" and our eyelids become heavier. Sleepy, tired and dozy people are not the sort of conditioned people who make revolutionary moves against government as along with the sleepiness they are docile. As I said "overweight people do not fight" especially if they have been filling up on carbs, while you may think this is too much to believe, check out the facts about the effects of carbs on our bodies. I will say at this point that I am aware that there are good carbs, we just do not eat them enough and I accept that we do need to eat an amount of carbs in our diet, but not binge on them.

One "flavor enhancer" guaranteed to cause controversy is monosodium glutamate, we find MSG in so much of our food and sauces. The food manufacturers claim it is safe while independent researchers say it is very dangerous with many accepted health issues. MSG is in so much of our food, it is very important you learn about it, some researchers claim it is a cancer causing substance. If you look at on-line search engines you will be confused by what is offered, websites that look like independent websites are not what they seem, so beware. I suggest you log on to www.truthinlabelling.org who claim this of their information "The truth, the whole truth and nothing but the truth about MSG". If MSG is cancer causing – why is it in our food?

Let's look at what I call the "trilogy of contempt" that is a big money earner for the secretive organisations operating in our world. Food manufacturing is being controlled on a large scale, allowing the people to be filled and pumped full with harmful additives and fattening them up like farm animals. Manufacturers therefore accrue money from the sale of the unhealthy food on an increasing level as we eat more and more. Pharmaceutical companies who make exorbitant profits from the sale of prescription drugs that are needed when people fall ill from eating poor quality chemical laden and fattening foodstuffs are also under control, which is a win-win situation. Poor food equals poor health which equals increased numbers of deaths, meeting another one of the much publicised goals – population reduction, a win – win – win situation. You have been informed that the planning is subtle, perhaps you can see this now as the money is made from us from at every point in the "trilogy of contempt". It's the same as when the support is given to all sides in a war by supplying weapons and ammunition to everyone, its win-win and profit all around. If you cannot believe that food is spiked with unhealthy additives, buy one of the small booklets that are sold which tell you what all the labeled E number. ingredients are which are put into your food and what potential harm they can do to us (this is scary when you learn the truth of this). When you understand the terrible truth of the chemical cocktails found in your daily food, ask yourself why would a manufacturer put these ingredients into your food as they are obviously not good for your health? Excessive levels of sugar and salt added to your food is not good for your health either, so why is it added in such levels?

Aspartame is a sugar substitute that sparks considerable amounts of hot debates, it is regarded as poisonous to health by many and should never be included in food and drinks (when you see food and drink labeling that states "low in sugar" or "diet", it usually contains aspartame). The aspartame manufactures and those who add it to food and drink are the ones who say it is safe while everyone else who investigates it say it is unsafe and carcinogenic (can cause cancer). Why would anyone put a cancer causing substance into food?

Moving on to the next question, why would manufacturers put a known carcinogenic cancer causing ingredient into many of our household cleaners, personal grooming products (shampoos, soaps, toothpaste, shower gels etc.)? Sodium Lauryl Sulphate, or SLS as it is known, is included in the majority of the products mentioned. SLS was originally used as an engine degreaser and to clean up oily garage floors, it is carcinogenic and when transported by road it is legally bound to carry one of the warning signs on the back of the transport vehicle if that vehicle is involved in an accident and it spills. This warning sign advises any emergency service that SLS is toxic and to use breathing apparatus and full body suits to avoid contact on the skin with the SLS. What do you think of that little statistic? What the hell is SLS doing in the majority of our home and personal cleaning products – IT IS DANGEROUS TO HEALTH? Think on this, if you take a bath or shower, the hot water will open up the pores of your skin and allow SLS in your shower gel, bath gel, soap, hair shampoo and even the cleaner you use on your bath and shower to penetrate your skin faster. Here is another very good question, why is SLS included in baby care products, even the accepted "safe" brand named products? The manufactures say that the levels of SLS in their products are at a safe level – do you believe that? Why put this terrible chemical in the products at all? Some people say that the reason for including SLS is that it is cheap, so obviously profit margins matter more than customer health and safety or could it be that topping everyone's SLS levels up is aimed at increasing the ever growing number of people suffering cancer? Statistics freely tell us that before aged 80 one in every two people will suffer some form of cancer, does that surprise anyone when you learn that we are smothering ourselves each day in SLS and eating all sorts of e–number chemicals in our food? SLS is in our kitchen worktop cleaners – kitchen unit cleaners – our floor and carpet cleaners – our bathroom cleaners – our furniture sprays – it is in our washing up liquids and dishwasher tablets – it is in our clothes washing powders/liquids/tablets. Are you getting the picture yet? A harmful chemical that has strict safety instructions when transported is being mixed into our everyday much used products. Again consider this, where are we informed to place a pill in the mouth if it needs to be absorbed fast? Answer, under the tongue. Toothpastes with SLS in them must get under the tongue while brushing, which means SLS is rapidly ingested into the body. Some toothpastes carry printed warnings like those printed on cigarette boxes which is so frightening as it advises adults to supervise children's brushing so they do not ingest (swallow) the toothpaste, IF they do swallow the toothpaste **the child should be taken immediately to a toxicologist, (poison expert)**. What do you think to that? Do you know that manufacturers advise everyone not to swallow toothpaste? Have you ever been unlucky enough to flick some toothpaste into your eye? I had this misfortune once and believe me it was hellishly painful, like a pin stabbing me in the eye which shows how strong the toothpaste is. We all trust the brand name manufacturers of our cleaning and personal products because (once again) we have been programmed to trust them all of our lives and we have never had reason not to trust them because we have never been given the truth, until now. For those wondering what role SLS achieves in the cleaning product, it is responsible when mixed with salt for making the soap lather, the soap suds we associate with soaps and cleaners. Look up SLS on the Internet and read for yourself about this carcinogen, you will find webpages that play down the risks, guess who placed those on the web? Be aware that manufacturers try to hide SLS under other names, look on the list of ingredients of a product for similar named ingredients. Get wise to SLS and its dangers.

Are you shocked by this? Do you think this sort of thing is isolated? WRONG! It would need another book to go over everything, as a brief example, ladies make-up contains some very nasty ingredients, if you take a lipstick and put a stripe on the back of your hand and then rub it with a gold ring – if the lipstick turns black – your lipstick contains LEAD! you read it right ladies. What is lead doing in a product that gets spread over your mouth? Try reading the warnings printed on a container of garden weed-killer – you will not want to use that weed-killer again and you will understand why it is recommended to dispose of unused weed-killer at one of the special containers at your council rubbish tips. For you and your families health, find out why we need to open windows in a room for several days after a new carpet or new furniture is fitted and NOT sleep or sit in those rooms for several days? What is the base carrier liquid in sun oils? Would you believe it is an ingredient we put in our car engines to stop the water freezing? Ladies you will be shocked when you learn all about those highly expensive facial deep cleansers and moisturizers you use that actually have the opposite effect to what you buy them for. Find out as soon as you can how fresh air sprays and plug in's work! So many harmful products around us and we do not have a clue - and that's how it is meant to be.

I have not bought shop supplied hair shampoo – conditioner – toothpaste – deodorant – household cleaners – washing up liquid and much more for over twelve years, I buy my products direct from a huge range of safe products supplied by a company called Neways International. Neways is a network marketing company, but with a difference as people can choose to be preferred customers and buy at much reduced cost, they can be just customers and buy at normal prices or they can become independent distributors and own their own business while receiving good reductions in product costs. Products are not tested on animals, they are though superb.

We trust government health services and would not think about questioning health department practices, I am not joking when I say that our trust is putting our health at risk. This is not a condemnation of hospital doctors and nursing staff, who are dedicated and marvelous. The problem is that the practices our doctors and nursing staff are made (should read - forced) to adhere to can be dubious to say the least. We know that one in two people suffer cancer and that cancer patients on the whole live longer than they used to, if a school report was issued on hospital cancer treatment it would be marked "could do better". Alternative cancer treatments are available across the world with exceptional results, they are not though the treatments used in normal hospitals that rely on chemotherapy, radiation and surgery (known as cut and burn treatment). With so many people likely to need treatment, why do we use such out dated and failing treatments? (failing in comparison to other treatments). Answer - because the treatments used in hospital are not very effective but they do move huge amounts of health funding across to the pharmaceutical companies, it's a massive business for them. The last thing the pharmaceutical companies want is treatments with a lot less profit and that work much better than "cut and burn" treatments. Pharmaceutical companies do not produce cures (yes some do I know), they produce treatments to "manage a condition", there is little profit in a cure but huge profit in having a system that manages your condition – for the rest of your life. You probably do not believe me that something so callous could exist, so let me direct you to several sources of information to prove the point.

1. Go to the website of Doctor Joseph Mercola, Mercola.com This person is another hero to me as he stands up to all the many scams going on in the medical world. Search his website for all sorts of answers, look at the articles on breast cancer for starters and be ready for shocks. Look at articles about fluoridation of water, amalgam tooth fillings (**very scary indeed**), genetically modified food (you will most likely get very angry). If you or a loved one suffer with a medical condition, look it up on

the Mercola website for different advice you would normally not receive. The website is crammed full with controversial information that governments and the pharmaceutical companies would rather you did not see. Sign up for his free daily newsletter. Dr. Mercola is another who is subjected to attempts to blacken his name for daring to challenge the crooked work of many.

2. Go to the "Cancer defeated" website to learn of the many alternative treatments available.

3. Go to the What Dead Doctors Don't Tell You website, a brilliant website that covers all kinds of health issues.

4. Read KNOCKOUT by Suzanne Somers, this is a New York Times number one best seller. The subtitle of the book is "interviews with doctors who are curing cancer and how to prevent getting it in the first place". A brilliant five star book that will open your eyes to alternative medical treatment of cancer.

5. Read Outsmart your Cancer by Tanya Harter Pierce M.A., MFCC, a book again about alternative and complementary medicine for those suffering cancer. Another five star book.

6. Read Anti Cancer, a new way of life by Doctor David Servan-Schreiber. Highly recommended.

7. Read Foods that Fight Cancer by Professor Richard Beliveau and Doctor Denis Gingras. Great book advising essential foods to help prevent cancer. * A must buy if you want to improve your chances of avoiding cancer.

8. AN ABSOLUTE MUST is to look up all the work, books, videos of Hungry for Change and Food Matters. Want to know about food, how important the quality of food is, which foods are good for us and which are not? What you need to know about eating healthy you will find on these web pages. Read all you can and direct others to the sites. Another five start rating from me.

9. Look up the books and website of Doctor Mark Hyman who is another person who fights for the rights of the people against the many unscrupulous organisations of the world.

10. Do you want to know more about the link between autism and other illness and modern day vaccines?? Go to www.childhoodshots.com You will not like this, in fact you will feel very let down by your government health department.
11. Take a look at greenmedinfo.com for good healthy tips.

The quality of our food influences so much of the quality of our health, eat a poor diet – suffer poor health, eat fattening foods – become overweight and unhealthy. Trust the wrong people to supply your food and pay the consequences. If you want to lose weight and eat a better diet to boost your health and immune system, you need to get the right information. With diabetes hitting so many people it is so important to choose a healthy diet as diet is considered by many to be mostly at the heart of the diabetes epidemic. With sickness and disease so widespread, we need to look after ourselves as we cannot take care of others if we ourselves are falling apart. I think the right question to ask now is "what would you prefer, a life of bed bound sickness and suffering or a healthy life of happiness? Your diet and your choice of cleaning and personal grooming products could make the difference between the two.

"I would rather have an ounce of prevention than a pound of cure"

The above is a very old saying, one which I take very seriously as it is common sense advice. In more modern terms it would probably read "I would rather have a gram of prevention than a kilo of cure". As I have said a few times in this book, we do not give enough thought to the consequences of our actions, we act when it is too late or we say "I did not realise it was dangerous". We fall ill and suffer, then regret doing what we know caused our illness, being overweight, not keeping fit and exercising, smoking, eating and drinking the wrong things, not taking enough rest and sleep. That's the thing about hindsight, it is painful as we know it is usually our own fault we are suffering. We know only too well that if we eat barbecued food that may not be fully cooked and drink too much alcohol as we eat the undercooked food that we stand a good chance of being ill – but we still do it! I have to admit to doing that one in the past, but not now as I learned from the hindsight of days lost to stomach upset and alcohol induced headaches. While this is a good example of prevention over cure (I could have easily prevented those days of sickness) it is the less obvious preventions that need to be discovered and heeded, such as:

- cutting out excessive indulgence of carbohydrates
- cutting out heavily "spiked" food and drinks full of sugar, salt and MSG
- completely removing products with aspartame in them
- reducing our exposure to dangerous (it is the right word and not unhealthy) E numbers and additives
- cut down the amount of sugar we knowingly consume
- cut out carbonated (fizzy) drinks completely
- remove potentially dangerous cleaning products

These are common sense pieces of advice and people should start to see and feel the benefits of doing them very quickly as their body fat levels start to drop and they have increased energy. You will notice I have only dealt with the health side of food and drink, the weight loss diet plans cannot be offered wholesale as we are all different and a diet plan should be much more personalised. From experience I can say that recently I lost five kilos in five weeks without "going on a diet", I almost completely cut out carbs and changed my exercise regime, but I did not "go on a diet". By taking rice – pasta – potatoes out of my diet and changing from normal bread to gluten free bread, my body fat began to drop off me without reducing the amount of food I ate. My gym routine was also changed to doing INTERVAL TRAINING, look this up as it will help most people, this allows much more body fat to be burnt off. Go to the Doctor Mercola website and look up "peak eight training", his advice is free and you can watch videos of Dr. M doing the exercises. For anyone who attends a gym and spends more than ten minutes on rowing machines – cross trainers – running machines, you really need to find out about interval training as you could be wasting most of your time on these apparatus if you do not use interval training (and yes I know that doing this even the wrong way is better than doing nothing).

I am going to stay away from conspiracies, though I would recommend you look up on the Internet "Big Pharma conspiracies", of which there are thousands of pages. One comment I want to make here though is that we should all be campaigning for the removal of restrictions on natural health remedies. Governments around the world "fixed" for their friends in the pharmaceutical industries the threat to "Big Pharma's" profits from natural health suppliers when they brought in laws to heavily restrict the use of natural remedies. The death of one person who had a reaction to a Chinese herbal cure was used to outlaw worldwide the use of some natural cures and to weaken the contents of others. This when you can find figures all over the Internet that tell you people are dying in their thousands each week from direct reactions to prescription drugs. This is a clear case of crooked politicians enforcing legislation that favours their friends and pays them handsomely with backhand payments and gifts. This is yet another example of the fraud that goes on which hits the people hardest.

This that follows will shock you. In the USA there are 15 million people diagnosed with depression, the UK rate is one in ten people and according to the World Health Organisation there are 121 million people worldwide suffering depression of some kind. One set of research I read was dedicated to the insidious profits drug companies make from selling their pills, bearing in mind the numbers of depression sufferers listed above, let's look at the profit margins on one of the bestselling anti-depressant drugs. These details that follow can be found in full in Jim Marrs excellent book "The Trillion Dollar Conspiracy" along with many more covering many named drugs. Prozac is reported to be marketed at around $247 per 100 pills, the cost of its active ingredients (not the base filler) are about $0.11 each, which returns a very healthy mark up of over **220,000%**, you read it right! Think on the number of people listed above that take anti depression medication and think on the astronomical profits being made. Next consider all the other illnesses that hit people, cancer – diabetes – heart problems etc. etc. now is it any wonder that government health services are draining so much of the various nations budgets away? The conspiracy theorists will tell you how the drug companies pay very handsome back handers to GP's to prescribe their drugs and that most government ministers and senators have had their hands filled with cash and other rewards to allow the drug companies to fleece the tax payers. What do you think after seeing what they get away with when charging such massive amounts for drugs and the governments pay without quibble? Does it sound right to you? Just think of the better uses this huge amount of money could be put to as government budgets are being slashed and austerity measures are hitting the people hard while pharmaceutical companies pile up the cash. Are you annoyed? Do you feel let down? Are you getting the picture yet that we are being made total fools of by our leadership? Do you find it hard to believe that politicians could accept "backhanders", secret payments for looking after the pharmaceutical companies? Just think back to the major scandal that hit British politics when it was found that parliamentary politicians and members of the House of Lords had been caught faking expense claims. How can we trust them after that?

Think further on this report. Doctor Mark Hyman, a well-known name in the world of free thinkers, has said on his website blog that "anti-depressants do not work", which would sum things up nicely wouldn't it – <u>overpriced drugs that do not help the patient</u>. Find Dr Hyman on Huffpost Healthy Living which is a free site and free newsletter delivering excellent medical advice (yes, alternative advice).

I feel quite sorry for those reading details like this for the first time, it must be a big shock to the system, it is of course so very typical of the deceptions we face in all areas of life and not an isolated incident. The world of medical drugs and their efficiency (do they work or not) is as big a secret as the workings of the NWO itself and the punishment that the pharmaceutical companies dish out to those who challenge it is often fatal (they meet sudden unexplained endings), which puts them in the same league as organised crime. I fully expect many skeletons to come out of the pharmaceutical companies closets when they are exposed, doctors – researchers – alternative health practitioners who have all been subjected to threats of harm and having funding removed if they announce their findings of corruption against the pharmaceutical companies. You will be very shocked once these stories are made public.

Tip. For one week try to cut out completely all gluten products, carbohydrates and sugar. For the first few days you may have an energy dip and feel a little low, after that you may receive a pleasant surprise as you begin to feel lighter in yourself and your body, your mind will brighten and your energy levels will gradually pick up and the heavy dozy feeling should become less and less. Try adding some exercise, even just a an evening brisk walk or some cycling. Do all this rigorously and see how you feel after a week. New evidence points to the cutting down of gluten products, carbs and sugar can seriously remove the threat of Alzheimer's disease as well as boosting your immune system and energy. Consult your doctor before you undertake exercise (that is the usual disclaimer). Give it a try and do not cheat!!

What if? It all sounds so hard to believe that companies could promote and produce drugs merely to milk away tax payers money and not make drugs to cure illness, what if it's true? What if companies are knowingly including cancer causing chemicals in our everyday essentials, shouldn't we be closing them down? What if people are being exposed to terrible diets that manufacturers know are making its customers ill and overweight, shouldn't we be changing their recipes and fining them? What if it's all true?

Summary

You could be the richest person in the world, but if your health is poor or ruined, that money cannot buy good health. We have to prevent illness as much as we can by learning what harms us and by accepting a healthy living diet into our lives. By making sure our health is a priority we can save huge amounts of money for ourselves and our governments as public health spending would be cut AND we would greatly benefit from feeling good about ourselves.

You MUST find out about health issues, they are bankrupting national health services and if we get it right we can save large numbers of lives and stop suffering.

twelve

Amen

* * *

I had no intention to add a chapter about religion as it is an area I firmly believe to be very personal subject to people and they should have the right to decide for themselves which religion to follow and how often they want to attend a religious service. Due to the section on leadership earlier in the book I have decided to add this extra short chapter at the end of the book. Where I use the description God, please be aware that is for ease of my preparation and that those of a faith that use another name for their God should substitute the name God for their own beliefs description.

Never before have we needed good religion (whichever faith and God you follow) than we do now, the people always seek out religion when life turns sour, life is certainly sour at the moment.

**With our world in desperate turmoil, the message is
very clear – we need religion - honest religion.**

As mentioned earlier in the book, I would like to see every church – chapel – mosque – synagogue – cathedral and place of worship full for every service as I believe religion and church services play such an important part of life for the people, more so than ever in times of trouble. Something else I feel important is that each faith should offer two types of service, traditional and modern as the young are turned off from attending services steeped in historical procedures, rituals and pomp, which to them is not attractive or inviting. Preachers who spout fire and brimstone services do not appeal to younger church members either. At a time when attendances are dropping across nearly all faiths, more attention should be taken of the young and their needs if religion is to have a future. A recent vote within the Anglican Church in the UK shows just how out of touch religion has become when once again the idea of appointing females as bishops was defeated, this does the church no favours when it is being seen as sexist. Double standards cannot be good for anyone, with churches closing due to falling attendances, all religions need to look at themselves very closely. Religion is important and can do so much good, with the world in so much absolute turmoil at present, religion is needed now more than ever.

This brings us to leadership within religion that is the very, very obvious problem surrounding religion just as in all areas of life. The church leaders are forcing/enforcing their personal views on the church members, they forget they are there to listen to the views of the members and not the other way around. The leaders should lead it is true, this should be after listening to their members, the members should be the ones who dictate policy as if this does not happen there will be more churches close and attendances will continue to fall. But just as discussed in earlier chapters, church leaders are no different to political leaders as they lose their senses when power corrupts them. A case in point is the idea that is given out from the pulpit that God is an angry deity who will "smite us down if we do not do this, this, this and this". If God was an angry deity it would be some the church preachers and leaders he would punish for taking God's name in vain. We are told by most religions that theirs is the only true religion and that their God is the only real God, also that other religions must be opposed, why? The only reason is that the church leaders fear losing their own members to other religions and weaken their personal power, it is all personal to the leader and not the religion they represent. For all the religious battles and wars that have taken place, few occurred because a religion was under attack, what was under attack was the actions of the religions leaders who were probably encroaching onto the attacking religions grounds. No ordinary member of a religion instructs their leaders to fight wars on their behalf, it is the other way around. We are informed by church leaders that God has commanded them to slay members of other religions for having alternate beliefs. Well if God made the world and God is all powerful, couldn't God take care of non-believers himself as he is so powerful, why would God demand others do his work for him? In truth God does not tell us to murder anyone, it is as usual church leaders making these decisions to protect their own interests. God will not strike down anyone as God is not the angry "father in heaven" we are lead to believe (by our leaders).

Isn't it time that church elders and leaders listened to their members before more churches disappear, isn't it time to bring religion out of the dark ages, isn't it time to give the people what they want instead of what church leaders think they should have?

In August 2012 Roman Catholic Cardinal Carlo Martini died at age 85, in his last interview he said of the Catholic Church "that it is tired….. our prayer rooms are empty". He urged the Church to recognise its errors and to embark on a radical path of change, beginning with the Pope. He said the Church is 200 years behind times. He was also quoted as saying "Catholics lacked confidence in the Church, our culture has grown old, our churches are big and empty and the bureaucracy rises up, our religious rites and the vestments we wear are pompous". His recommendations to, "conquer the tiredness of the Church" was a "radical transformation, beginning with the Pope and his bishops".

Let's forget he was talking about the Catholic Church, for we can submit just about all religions and say the exact same thing – they are 200 years behind times. The world needs religion and it needs religion to come of age, to modernise itself before religion is lost.

It is said that man's greatest sin is to "place God outside of himself", which is a comment I did not understand until it was explained. Religion teaches us to praise "God on the high", to "look towards heaven for God", modern teachings state that God is everywhere and to look within ourselves for God, for God is both within and without. It is claimed that by preaching that God is outside of us we are in fact denying God and that God is being rejected, so why do churches say this? – how does that fit into your religious teachings? Shouldn't this be something to learn about in church instead of the same tired old readings and scriptures spouted week in week out? Religion like so much in our world has lost track of its original purpose and has taken to the path of grabbing power and influence over a path of service to its followers. Just like so many other areas of modern life that is failing, religion must return to its original calling and take to its original pathway or face decimation.

Many of the books, online videos, Internet pages state clearly that most of our major problems can be cured by "returning to God". What does this mean? We need to turn to God and not reject God by placing God outside of ourselves, which our religions teach us is so. "The God on high, The God in heaven etc." is what we have thrown at us from religion, we have to accept in place of that the principle that God is within us and everything and everywhere. Would we commit many of the sad actions of today if we accept God within? By realising that we are all connected to God at all times, we would be much less likely to behave in some of our more barbaric ways or commit heinous crimes. We are informed time and time again that the secret world rulers are atheists and satanic devil worshippers, this would certainly add up if you consider the above ideas wouldn't it? How hard would it be to accept this principle of a "return to God"? especially when so many sources state that this **is** our route to salvation. Many say that a return to God is the way to defeat the secret world leaders as they are atheists. You do not have to be a devout religious person to accept the principle of God within, to accept that God is within and without is enough, this will stop what is described as "the rejection of God". This should be a very good starting place and people could watch and see how their lives improve should they take this on board. You will never see or hear me spouting lines from a bible, attending church services in their present form, but accepting God within, yes that's for me, how about you?

Throughout my searching and researching I gradually became immune to the shocking discoveries contained in this book, though the ideas on religion where we have to return to God and that God is within cropped up so many times and in so many diverse places continued to surprise me. Obviously we need to consider these principles very deeply, whether you are a regular church attendee or not as these principles are repeated often. How hard would it be for you to accept these ideas? Wouldn't you like to know more, use your Internet search engine.

Summary

The world needs religion, the people of the world need religion, we also need that religion joins the modern world before it is lost altogether as a punishment for not changing. We also need religious leaders who are dedicated to their followers and not the other way around, it is religion that people follow, not leaders.

thirteen

Crucial Final Summary And Message –

Which Pathway Do You Take?

* * *

Congratulations on making it through to the end of the book, I'm sure it's been a rollercoaster ride for you. By now you should have realised that what I said in the opening part of the book when I referred to our world being a mirror image of Alice's Wonderland to be very close to the truth. Our world is as unreal as Wonderland and many of our leaders are as misleading as the characters in the story lines of Alice in Wonderland. Hopefully you have followed my line of intent to first try and demonstrate what is wrong with our world and then to explain there is a very simple way to create a greatly improved new way of life. Truth and accepting truth, mixed with the action of taking change on board are the greatest ways to cut away the chains of deceit that binds us to a fake life. Taking action is another key to changing the world for the better, without action – everything stays the same, is that what you want? **Which pathway do you choose now you know you have a choice?**

The book contains many logical conclusions and no matter how much you may have laughed at some text or got angry, fearful, there can only remain the logical conclusions. Economies can only collapse as they are full of growing debt with nothing being done to repay the debts. Social unrest is escalating as the people of the world grow weary of the misery being heaped on them by our governments. Substantial evidence points conclusively to a worldwide secret organisation that runs our world and aims to not only control everything, It will do so after eliminating 90% of the world population. The countries who are the driving forces of world financial systems The USA – The UK – Japan – Europe have been the main targets for financial destruction which will take place in the not too distant future, aided and abetted by banks and leaders. The fateful condition of economies in those countries cannot be anything other than a deliberate plan as it would be impossible to create such massive debt levels by error or poor decision making alone – it has to be purposely created. All news reporting services are firmly under direct control of the secret world rulers, which is why we do not know they exist and why we do not know how bad world economies are. Our food and home products are full of highly dangerous chemicals which should not be included in those foods and home products, they are included which indicates they have a designated secret purpose, if that is not true – why put them in? None of these subjects above could be accidental as they are too outrageous, they can only be part of a grand master plan.

Whoever the Illuminati are, whether they are religious leaders, bankers, Nazi's, fascists, communists, it is not their religion – beliefs – position in politics etc. that is the problem. Being the head of a nation, religion, banking organisation is not the reason for the outrageous deceit, fraud, warmongering and genocide. Nobody should place any blame for all the many sick actions of these people on the nations, religions, banks they represent. It is all down to what I term "Power Insanity", the corruption of a person due to power being rested on their shoulders. "Power corrupts, absolute power corrupts absolutely", how very true those famous words are. Our leaders are possessed by power and will kill – steal – go to war – commit fraud - slay their own people, cause the mass deaths of innocent children to protect and grow their power as Power Insanity eats into them. Do not blame religion, do not blame the people of a nation for their leaders actions, do not hate banks, it is the leaders who make the decisions and lead all astray. Just 0.01% rules the lives of 99.9% and that 0.01% are effected at some level by Power Insanity, THAT is why we have to change the system of distributing power and decision making. Politicians, religious leaders, military chiefs, bank heads, industry heads must change to a system of power sharing, not power hoarding to stop the destruction of our world. From the information that has started to be loaded onto the Internet I would say we have months and not years to make the changes we need before it is too late.

In one paragraph I will show you the simple way to not only stop all the deceit that is taking placed and planned, but to go forward and create a truly magnificent life for everyone. The actions that are slowly destroying our world, that are tightening the stranglehold grip on our lives using stealth and secrecy, the very last thing the plotters want is that the people of the world discover their plans and intentions. **Which is how they will be defeated, by "blowing their cover", exposing their plans.** You the reader have an important part to play, because the simplest way to alert everyone to what they need to know is to either buy or lend them a copy of this book or to recommend they buy it themselves. The Daily Press and TV news will not make any of this information public - so we have to. Let me assure you this is not a way to boost sales of this book and earn me a fortune, I will publish my accounts online to prove this. It is so very simple – we have to make sure EVERYONE finds out what is going on under the cover of secrecy. By exposing the secret plans of those who have taken control over our world, we should be able to stop all those plans in their tracks. The only thing the plotters have ever feared was being found out before they can execute their final moves, which makes now the time to do exactly that – expose them. Inform everyone, make sure that every single person fully understands what has been planned for us all and what has already taken place.

We must replace the corrupted news reporting agencies with honest services that are not controlled by outside influences. There will be no need for violence – street protests – riots – revolution – rebellion – disorder of any kind, we have to make everything being planned known and public. The alternative to taking back our freedom is just too unthinkable to consider. The change to the new positive world should be gradual as too fast a process can have the opposite effect that is desired with runs on banks and people venting their anger on the wrong people. To change the future is simple, but it must happen in such a way that minimises the problems associated with a transfer of power. Nobody should be chased by a "lynch mob" out for revenge, that is the action of barbarians and something we all need to move away from. Never forget this old much used saying "Today is the first day of the rest of your life", let us all make sure that the rest of our lives and that of our children can be lived in freedom love and joy. Before us is something like ten or twenty years of complete change, we must be in charge of that change and planning it every step of the way, not to change will have un-imaginary bad consequences that none of us desire.

A quote from Charles Darwin, taken from The Origin of Species:

"It is not the strongest of the species,
nor the most intelligent one that survives.
It is the one that is most adaptable to change."

There is no other choice than to change the way we live our lives at the moment, our present accepted way of life is letting us down badly and with potentially much worse to follow. If we are to survive we must recognise and see the error of our ways and admit we have got just about everything wrong. The world and our world systems will not continue to exist without a top to toe makeover and the chance we all have to experience a great new life will be lost forever. If the world descends into serious decline it will be all of us who are at fault and caused the decent to oblivion if we fail to take the necessary actions to save our world. Throwing our hands in the air and saying "what can I do about it?", not taking action out of fear or rejecting the idea we have a problem will not save our world and that is ultimately what we are looking at – saving our world. No matter how dramatic that last comment appears, it is the only possible conclusion that can be drawn from the mountains of evidence that is laid before us all. We can go on ignoring the details and believe we are here forever and that threats will amount to nothing, what though if we are wrong? What if this time the threats to all our lives are real and the only way to stop them is to take action? What would be a suitable epitaph for mankind when our race is wiped out? It would not be "we didn't see it coming" as we have been warned, it would most likely be "we just didn't believe it possible".

Which pathway do we choose. The pathway to a great new life that requires us to take action if we are to experience it, or stay on our present pathway that leads to hell by taking no action? It's your move, which way will you go?

* * *

*** This paragraph is an add on, added the 17th December 2012. I have just returned from sitting with 120 schoolchildren for an early morning Christmas celebration, a celebration that had 120 pairs of sparkling happy eyes, 120 fresh faces all thoroughly enjoying themselves. To see such happiness, such innocence, such joy is overwhelming and made me realise that we must all fight with everything we have to stop the evil intentions of the sick secret organisations planning to destroy us all. As I sat with these children I realised that the NWO not only want to imprison these children with their chains of complete control – they want to slaughter 110 out of 120 of those children. Can we allow that to happen, can we dismiss this from our minds and say "I don't believe a word of this rubbish!", can we turn our backs on this young innocence that is due to be crushed? Or can we create a world that is as innocent and as joyous as the mind of a child? *This will depend on the actions you take now you have come to the end of this book.*

* * *

None of us can do everything, all of us can do something.

US President Theodore Roosevelt said: "in any situation the best thing you can do is the right thing, the next best thing you can do is the wrong thing, **the worst thing you can do is nothing"**

We have before us potentially the greatest and most peaceful times in the history of mankind, a time of great joy and abundance for all, a time of unlimited freedom and equality, a chance to live in total happiness free of fear – the only thing that can stop this happening is if we fail to take action to grasp this wondrous future – *it is there, it is ours for the taking, the only people who can stop us are ourselves by not taking action.*

Our lives, whatever we achieve during our time on Earth, will count for nothing if we do not leave the world a fit place for our children to grow up in and this is something we can all now do!.

Final what if? What if everything in the book is as close to truth as we can ever get? What are YOU going to do about it?

Take just six minutes to watch an on-line video filmed in 1992, search for "the girl who silenced the world for 6 minutes" briiliant!

Will you choose pathway one and take action or pathway two and do nothing, is it to be heaven or hell?

* * *